THE GREATEST STORIES
NEVER TOLD:
SPECIAL OPS

LAURENCE J. YADON

LYONS
PRESS

Guilford, Connecticut

An imprint of The Rowman & Littlefield Publishing Group, Inc.
4501 Forbes Blvd., Ste. 200
Lanham, MD 20706
www.rowman.com

Distributed by NATIONAL BOOK NETWORK

British Library Cataloguing in Publication Information available

Library of Congress Cataloging-in-Publication Data

Names: Yadon, Laurence J., 1948- author.
Title: The greatest stories never told : special ops / Laurence J. Yadon.
Description: Guilford, Connecticut : Lyons Press, [2019] | Includes
   bibliographical references.
Identifiers: LCCN 2019021975 (print) | LCCN 2019022401 (ebook) | ISBN
   9781493042135 (pbk. : alk. paper) | ISBN 9781493042142 (e-book)
Subjects: LCSH: Special operations (Military science)—History. | Guerrilla
   warfare—History. | United States—History, Military—Anecdotes.
Classification: LCC U262 .Y33 2019 (print) | LCC U262 (ebook) | DDC
   356/.160973—dc23
LC record available at https://lccn.loc.gov/2019021975
LC ebook record available at https://lccn.loc.gov/2019022401

For my family

Contents

Introduction

Close combat, man to man, is plainly to be regarded as the real basis of combat.

—Carl von Clausewitz

David was a fugitive from justice at worst or a soldier of fortune at best—a man that relied on guerrilla tactics to stay one step ahead of the authorities. His lieutenant, a man named Gad, led David's band of fugitives through the countryside, ever on the lookout for the army that might surround and kill them all. David hoped to find support among his own people, even as his archenemy Saul recruited more and more men to help him on the manhunt. Saul ordered the death of one follower—a reputed holy man—even as David raided and captured a walled and gated town called Keilah. He asked Gad whether they should stay, only to be told that it would be best to move on, since the good townspeople of Keilah would turn them over to Saul if they got the chance.

And so, David, Gad, and the rest of their merry crew simply faded back into the countryside. David considered his options, and from a hiding place nearby, sent ten men to muscle a rich rancher named Nabal with hints of what might happen to his three thousand sheep if Nabal didn't invite the entire army over for dinner and supplies.

The prophet Samuel so described some of the early guerrilla warfare conducted in about 1000 BCE by the young man who eventually became King David of Israel, in one of the earliest, yet little-known, series of special operations.

Some 753 years later, during the First Punic War between Carthage and Rome, an obscure figure named Hamilcar Barca took command of what was left of the Carthaginian Army in Sicily. Little is known of Barca, whose name is thought to be derived from the Punic word for lightning. His new command was a thankless task, since the Romans had driven the Carthaginians from nearly every nook and cranny in Sicily, the 9,900-square-mile island that was then the principal battleground between these two ancient powerhouses. Rome controlled the entire island that comprised Sicily except Lilybaeum (present-day Marsala) and Drepanum, the site of present-day Trapani.

Barca began his offensive with a coastal raid near Bruttium, present-day Calabria at the toe of the Italian peninsula. Historians have speculated that Barca initiated this attack in a search for booty with which to pay off his small yet effective band of mercenaries. We don't know whether Barca found the plunder he was looking for, but his next target was an obscure place called Heircte, near present-day Palermo. Here, the Carthaginian general established a mountain base from which to conduct guerrilla attacks against the Roman rearguard.

Barca's guerrilla forces broke through a formidable Roman blockade almost at will, eventually setting the stage for his comparatively small band of twenty thousand men to capture an ancient mountain city in western Sicily then known as Eryx, at the site of modern-day Erice. Despite ever-increasing Roman pressure, Barca now initiated a series of guerrilla attacks on Italy itself, surprising Roman forces as far north as Cumae, an ancient city some twelve miles west of present-day Naples.

Despite Barca's best efforts on land, a major Roman defeat of the Carthaginian Navy in 241 BCE in which fifty ships were lost and some ten thousand forces were reportedly taken prisoner ended the First Punic War. Barca's better-known son Hannibal is considered one of the best military strategists in the ancient Western world, if not the best.

Guerrilla warfare typically involves a relatively small group of combatants using ambushes, sabotage, raids, petty warfare, hit-and-run tactics, and mobility to fight a larger and less-mobile traditional military evolved through the centuries.

There is no better example of this during the medieval period than the tactics used by the sixteen-year-old "Leper King" Baldwin IV of Jerusalem against the Islamic leader Saladin on Friday, November 18, 1177, at a ravine called Montgisard, southeast of Jerusalem. Some versions of events claim that Baldwin commanded only five hundred Knights Templar that day, although it is more likely that the Templars were supported by many more archers and other troops.

Whatever their number, the Baldwin forces were outnumbered by all accounts. Despite this, the forces led by the Knights Templar swooped down on Saladin's men when they were fully occupied with crossing the Montgisard ravine, taking them entirely by surprise. Some accounts relate that a significant number of Saladin's generals were slaughtered. Whatever the truth of this, there seems little dispute that a second Templar charge forced Saladin to take refuge among his elite guard, which consisted of some one thousand Mameluk warriors. That charge was so effective that Saladin avoided capture only by fleeing the battlefield for refuge in Egypt.

Exploration of the New World meant new challenges, which in turn required new strategies and tactics, none better exemplified than those developed by British officer Robert Rogers (1731–1795) during the French and Indian War (1754–1763), employing strategies and tactics learned from Native Americans to capture enemy prisoners, scout enemy positions, and conduct successful raids.

Indicted for counterfeiting the very year the French and Indian War began, but never convicted, Rogers was born in Methuen, Massachusetts, to parents of Irish heritage, and moved with them at age eight to New Hampshire. There his parents founded Dunbarton, now a town of some two thousand near Concord. In 1746 at the advanced age of thirteen, Rogers joined the New Hampshire militia during King George's War (1744–1748). Ten years later, British colonel John Winslow authorized twenty-three-year-old Rogers to raise and command a company of irregulars to conduct raids on French towns and military bases, using makeshift snowshoes, sleds, and sometimes even ice skates to cross frozen rivers. Eventually they came to be known as Rogers's Rangers, and grew to a complement of six hundred men.

The US Army Rangers, as well as the Queen's York Rangers of the Canadian Army and several other military units, claim Rogers as their founder. In 1757, Rogers wrote a manual for guerrilla warfare as conducted by his Rangers, still in use today. Considered revolutionary at the time, Rogers's rules blended Native American tactics he had observed with his own innovations. He combined these rules with extensive training and live-fire exercises designed to enable Rangers to maximize mobility, as well as preparing them to be capable of living off the land for long periods of time, skills almost entirely unknown to conventional soldiers of that period.

A plainspoken, folksy version of these rules created by novelist Kenneth Roberts for his 1937 portrayal of Rogers in his book, *Northwest Passage*, counsels Rangers: "Don't forget nothing," be ready to move at a minute's warning, sneak up on an enemy as if he's a deer, don't take unnecessary chances, march single file with enough space between men so that one shot won't go through two men, take different routes going out and coming back from missions, post scouts twenty yards ahead and on each flank of a raiding party, get up before dawn (when the French typically attacked), kneel, lie down, or hide behind a tree when the enemy attacks, circle back and attack an enemy force that is following you, and finally, "Let the enemy come till he's almost close enough to touch, then let him have it and jump out and finish him up with a hatchet."

A version of this manual is used to this day at the US Army Ranger School. During an October 1759 advance on Quebec, Rogers's Rangers conducted an attack against the British-allied Abenaki tribe at Saint Francis, a village that had been used as a staging area for Indian raids into New England, killing some thirty women and children, almost bringing Abenaki raids against the British frontier to an end.

Although Robert Rogers remained loyal to Britain his entire life, the guerrilla strategies and tactics he pioneered during the French and Indian War helped to ensure American victory in the War of Independence. And no one was more successful at using those tactics than Francis Marion, known in the Carolinas as the Swamp Fox.

CHAPTER 1

Extinguish the Rebellion

During his lifetime, only one man rivaled George Washington's stature as a hero of the American Revolution. Yet Francis Marion is largely unknown today, even though numerous towns and counties across the country are named for him, and he was the true-life character behind Mel Gibson's epic film *The Patriot* (2000).

Tuesday, July 25, 1780, found Marion leading some twenty men, including a smattering of blacks and Catawba Indians, toward a farm owned by the Hollingsworth family near the Buffalo Ford of the Deep River in North Carolina. Marion was only five-foot-two, at a time when most American men were half a foot taller. His stern face was rendered all the more serious by black, flashing eyes, a large hook nose, and a permanent frown. Worse yet, he walked with a pronounced limp exacerbated by *Genu valgum*, a childhood medical condition described then and now as "knock-knee." One observer that day also noted that the blue Continental uniform on his back, reflecting his appointment by the Continental Congress, was more rumpled than it should have been.

This was hardly a joyous occasion. Scarcely two months earlier, Charleston (originally named "Charles Town"), the critical South Carolina port loyal to the American cause, fell into British hands at the end of a six-week siege. The British promptly capitalized on this victory by establishing a line of outposts and forts from the Atlantic Ocean to the far mountains of the South Carolina interior, some 260 miles to the west.

Francis Marion should have been with the rest of the Patriot garrison at Charleston on Friday, May 12, but avoided capture because he had left town to nurse a sore ankle. Although the real reason he had a sore ankle has been lost to history, a Charleston urban legend tells us that shortly before the siege, Marion was at a drinking party at 106 Tradd Street, on the corner of Orange and Tradd in downtown Charlestown. The party was hosted by his adjutant, Alexander McQueen, and attended by several other officers. Following a seemingly inexplicable custom of the time, McQueen locked all the doors so that no one could leave until the party was over. Despite this, Marion found his way to the second floor of the house, which still stands, opened a window, and jumped out, causing his own injury—or so the story goes.

Later learning that the British occupied Charleston, Marion spent most of May and June hiding among friends along the Santee River in the "Low Country," comprised today mostly of southern counties along the Atlantic Coast of South Carolina.

Early July found Marion and his twenty-man crew (at largest) offering their services to Johann Kalb, a German self-proclaimed baron then serving as interim commander of some 1,400 men, which made up the Southern division of the American Continental Army. Kalb's force, resting near present-day Ramseur, North Carolina, at Cox's Mill, needed food and water and intelligence about British troop locations. That mission accomplished, Marion led his men back to the Hollingsworth Farm just in time to see the arrival of General Horatio Gates, who was there to lead the Southern Continentals in an attack against British forces at Camden, South Carolina, commanded by Lieutenant General Charles, Earl of Cornwallis.

Gates, an English-born former major in the British Army, was less than impressed by Marion and his ragtag crew. That said, as a gesture of congeniality, Gates tasked Marion and his men to serve as Gates's personal bodyguards during those first few days of the Camden expedition. Yet another opportunity soon presented itself when a self-described militia based in the Williamsburg Township northeast of the Santee River asked Gates for a commander. Gates obliged, instructing Marion to use his new command to scout for enemy troops and destroy any British boats they found. The larger goal was defeating British troops at Camden, thereby preventing them from escaping to Charleston.

Marion arrived at the largely Scots-Irish Presbyterian Williamsburg settlement around August 17, but didn't initially make much of an impression. One fifteen-year-old recalled later that Marion was "rather below the middle stature of men, lean and swarthy. His body was well set, but his knees and ankles were badly formed and he limped on one leg." The teenager immediately noticed the eagle beak nose, jutting chin, "and a large, high forehead." The teenager, whose name was William Dobein James, recalled forty-one years later that Marion had a wiry frame "capable of enduring fatigue and every privation necessary for a partisan." Perhaps it was so.

The volunteer militia Marion met that day didn't know that he had ditched the blue uniform that identified him as a Continental Army officer. Some among them might have even been impressed by the leather helmet of the 2nd South Carolina Regiment, featuring a silver crescent above the forehead inscribed with the single word "liberty," the sole remnant of his uniform.

One thing is certain: Most of them knew that they could come and go as they pleased, since they were not enrolled in a formal military organization. Had it not been for the urgings of the teenage scribe's father, Irish Presbyterian John James—who served with Marion when both answered to General William Moultrie, seconded by Hugh and Peter Hory, brothers of French Huguenot stock like Marion—Francis might have lost his second command right then and there. Instead, Captain Henry Mouzon, Marion's first cousin, who had a score to settle with a British cavalry officer named Banastre Carlton, sealed the deal by kissing Marion on both cheeks—French Huguenot style.

Within days Marion had cobbled together an entire brigade composed of several familial and regional factions, including Scots-Irish Presbyterians, South Carolina "Low Country" Huguenots, and assorted small farmers. His first objective was to strike any and all British forces operating on or near the upper Santee River by destroying any British boats they could find, after dispatching part of his brigade to the lower Santee to do the same.

Only then did Marion learn to his great consternation that just a day after sending him on this very mission, British troops led by Cornwallis had routed General Gates and his combined Virginia and North Carolina militias, some 2,500 of whom, when confronted by British troops with fixed bayonets, simply threw down their own weapons and ran for their lives. Latter-day excuse makers mentioned that Gates had placed his least-experienced men, many of whom were dealing with diarrhea supposedly brought on by bad food, against the highly experienced British right wing.

Baron de Kalb, the very officer who gave Marion his first mission, had been mortally wounded at Camden and died three days later. Horatio Gates, whose military career was no doubt ended by this debacle, envied Kalb for his honorable end.

General Banastre Tarleton and his force of only 160 struck a second blow for the King two days after the August 16 Camden disaster, this time at a place called Fishing Creek, only four miles above Camden on the Wateree River, routing Thomas Sumter's 800-member Patriot militia.

Despite this bad news, Marion now initiated the irregular warfare tactics that made him famous in his own lifetime. Generally, these "partisan" tactics consisted largely of attacking larger, regular forces, often identified by American spies, from hidden places the British didn't see or weren't looking for, before quickly blending back into the woods or South Carolina swamps, often thanks to superior horsemanship.

However famously the Revolution began in the North with shots fired at Lexington and Concord, by 1779 the British occupied New York City even as the French Navy dawdled some 1,300 miles away in the West Indies. George Washington camped only thirty miles away from the Big Apple in Morristown, New Jersey. Gripped by deadlock, only six months earlier Washington and Nathanael Greene had fought their foremost rivals, Clinton and Cornwallis, to a draw at a then-obscure corner of New Jersey called Monmouth Courthouse. The stalemate irritated the war-weary British Parliament, already bogged down in equally serious (and expensive) continental conflicts with France and Spain. The British prime minister, Frederick North, 2nd Earl of Guilford (known as Lord North), signaled an end to the conflict, if one final initiative in the American South could not produce victory.

This Southern strategy (not to be confused with the somewhat mythical yet identically named Republican initiative to reclaim the American White House in the 1970s) was premised in part on the relatively modest enthusiasm for independence that the British perceived south of Pennsylvania. The Southern strategy proponents based such claims mostly on the large number of British Loyalists who lived there and might well have been expected to do much of the fighting. Some British strategists even speculated that in a worst-case scenario, several of the Southern colonies might remain with the Crown even if the Northeast was entirely lost.

The new strategy found its first success in the December 1778 conquest of Savannah, which in turn provided a base of operations for British general Clinton's second initiative to occupy Charleston, which had escaped his grasp in 1776. Clinton did better (or was luckier) in mid-May 1780. The Holy City, so called for the vast number of church steeples that crowded its skyline, had become complacent; its population was far more concerned with a social calendar crowded with concerts and theater events than hard-core military drills and the preparation of defensive works. Enter General Clinton, who, after a respectful interval, stared at a wordy and lengthy written address thanking him for restoring the most important settlement in South Carolina to the Royal Crown. Off went the traitors to prison in Florida, even as Loyalists trudged in from the hinterlands to sign loyalty oaths and join the British forces. Several former American patriots, notably including Charles Pinckney, first president of the South Carolina (colonial) Senate, and even a former president of the Continental Congress, duly accepted British protection and, by implication, British sovereignty.

Many complacent Patriots wallowed in this British protection, if only until Clinton miscalculated the strength of his position and attempted to tighten the generous terms of his initial parole policy into something more stringent. When he first arrived in South Carolina, Clinton granted the Whigs (former rebels) full pardons, with the understanding that the parolees were expected to live quietly in the homes the British general allowed them to keep. This was entirely satisfactory until South Carolina Tories began complaining that the former rebels had been treated far too generously.

Saturday, June 3, 1780, brought the public announcement that all of these generous initial paroles were now null and void. Whigs (paroled American Patriots) who chose to stay in the King's good graces had to leave the neutrality of their peaceful homes and actively assist their Tory brethren in defense of the Crown. Those willing to accept the new terms had to do so by June 20, or be considered once again in wrongful rebellion. Clinton justified reneging on his first terms by assuring himself that this change would rid him of any rebel agitators strutting around under the King's protection.

Although far from his original intention, the Clinton policy change, combined with rumors—some true, some not—of British atrocities drove more and more South Carolinians into the Patriot camp. Indeed one of Clinton's most trusted officers told the general that by his estimation, nine out of every ten nominally neutral state citizens had joined the Revolutionary cause.

John Oller, whose recent biography *The Swamp Fox: How Francis Marion Saved the American Revolution* has largely been relied upon in chapters one through three, observed that "As a result, South Carolina became the setting for a bona fide civil war—a conflict *within* the state far less 'civil' than the one *between* the [American] states eighty years later. It involved not merely a clash of professional armies, as was typical of European conflicts at the time, but also an insurgency and counterinsurgency that engaged much of the civilian population, more characteristic of the conflagrations of centuries to come."

What most distinguished the war in South Carolina was its vicious and personal nature. This conflict pitted not only neighbor against neighbor and brother against brother, but father against son. Unspeakable atrocities were committed, as men in their homes, sick with smallpox, were roused from their beds and executed; soldiers waving the white flag were mercilessly cut down with the sword; and captured enemies were summarily hanged for past crimes, real and imagined. And most of the brutality was not visited by British upon Americans or Americans upon British, but by Americans upon Americans. Rhode Island's general Nathanael Greene, a battle-hardened officer who came south to replace Horatio Gates as the commander of the Southern Continental Army, had never seen anything like it. "The whole country is in danger of being laid waste by the Whigs and the Tories [Patriots and Loyalists] who pursue each other with as much relentless fury and beasts of prey."

Unlike many civil wars, this one was not based on geographic boundaries or even mainly on differences of political philosophy. South Carolina Whigs (Patriots) were not necessarily motivated by the lofty ideas expressed by Thomas, nor were Tories (British Loyalists) inevitably inspired by devotion to King George. Instead, the decision whether to take up arms, and for which side, was frequently driven by private grievances and desires for revenge. A man's horse was once stolen by a Whig; he became a Tory. Another man, feeling slighted because the Tories had passed him over for promotion, might join forces with the Whigs. So indifferent were some to ideological issues that they switched sides during the war as many as three times, or even more, depending on who was winning.

These tendencies originated in the Carolina backcountry during the 1760s, when vigilantes who called themselves Regulators hunted down and sometimes executed bandit gangs, a practice that drew resistance from counter-vigilantes, who came to be known as Moderators. Eighty years later these terms were employed once again during the Texas Regulator–Moderator War in Harrison and Shelby Counties from 1839–1844. No less than Billy the Kid served as a Regulator during the 1878 Lincoln County War in New Mexico.

Yet now, in the South Carolina of 1778, Francis Marion somehow avoided many of the more-negative tactics of partisan warfare, even as he wreaked havoc on the British and their Loyalist allies. Time and time again, and most often in circumstances where he might have obtained revenge against British soldier and Loyalist alike, Marion declined to seek personal vengeance and prevented his own troops from practicing cruelty, stopping torture, hanging, pillaging, and house burnings wherever and whenever he encountered such practices. Indeed, Marion strongly encouraged his officers and men to reconcile with defeated Tories as soon as possible.

The grandson of a Huguenot (French Protestant) who immigrated to South Carolina sometime before 1700, and born on a small Berkeley

County, South Carolina, plantation, Francis Marion began a life of intermittent adventure at the age of fifteen. For reasons that remain unclear—perhaps driven by the fact that he was practically penniless and without any other obvious prospects in 1756—Marion became a sailor on a Georgetown, South Carolina–based ship bound for the West Indies with a crew of six. Although the details have never been fully documented, his vessel filled with water and sank. The entire crew clambered about a lifeboat, but two of them died before the rest drifted to land.

Now animated by an intense desire to fit in, Marion threw off whatever French Huguenot vestiges remained in his habits and concentrated on fishing and hunting for days at a time. In time he returned from Georgetown to St. John's Parish, near a town called Moncks (not Monks) Corner.

Soon Francis also became a rice farmer in St. Stephen's Parish, near present-day Pineville, South Carolina. His acreage, now known as Hampton Hill, adjoined the Belle Isle plantation, which his brother, Gabriel, and Gabriel's wife, Catherine Taylor Marion, had received from her father as a wedding present. All too soon this pastoral tranquility was interrupted by events in western South Carolina.

On January 31, 1756, Marion began his first military service at age twenty-four as a member of St. John's militia, which every able-bodied man in the Parish was expected to periodically serve, bringing their own ammunition and weapons. Most of the training drills were conducted just outside the St. John's Parish church right after Sunday services.

All that drilling served a purpose three years later when British royal governor William Lyttelton—later, Lord Lyttelton, only seven years older than Marion—mounted an expedition against Cherokees then conducting raids in the western reaches of the state. The British conflict with the Cherokees in South Carolina had complex beginnings.

During the Seven Years War against France (1756–1763), the Cherokees were loyal British allies, but became angry when the British failed to replace the horses the Cherokees lost in the conflict, as had been promised. While returning from the Ohio Valley, the Cherokees stole horses along the Virginia frontier, prompting the Virginians to kill and scalp a number of Cherokees. Rather than attacking the Virginians directly responsible for these massacres, the Cherokees retaliated against western Carolina settlers who had nothing to do with the conflict.

In October 1759, Governor Lyttelton refused a symbolic deerskin laid before him by the legendary Cherokee warrior Oconostota as a peace offering, to preempt an expedition Lyttelton was planning. Instead, Lyttelton took the entire Cherokee peace delegation hostage and planned a punitive expedition.

Francis Marion pledged his service to the governor along with his brother Gabriel and several South Carolinians who later became prominent in the Revolution. After signing up for the expedition on October 31, 1759, Francis Marion became a captain in a cavalry unit his brother Gabriel commanded.

Governor Lyttelton immediately led the expedition to Fort Prince George in the northwest corner of South Carolina near several Cherokee settlements ("Lower Towns"). Lyttelton offered the Cherokees a deal in which his peace delegation hostages would be exchanged for twenty-four other Cherokees who Lyttelton would execute. Marion Francis couldn't help but notice Lyttelton's arrogance, and how quickly large numbers of militiamen deserted the expedition in the midst of a smallpox outbreak without so much as a fare-thee-well. These developments left the royal governor with little choice but to sign a face-saving meaningless treaty that laid the foundation for his new governorship in Jamaica.

No sooner had the expedition survivors returned to Charleston than Cherokee war parties provoked by the French began attacking settlements on the South Carolina frontier, scalping and killing women and children, not to mention men of military age.

The British deployed Colonel Archibald Montgomery, commander of the 77th Highland Scots Regiment from Canada, whose 1,700-man force burned several Cherokee villages near Fort Prince George, but was ambushed in a narrow pass some eight miles south of Etchoe (near present-day Otto) in North Carolina. The Cherokees, as Francis Marion undoubtedly learned later, fired long rifles down upon the British expedition in the pass, armed only with shorter-range and therefore ineffective muskets. The Montgomery expedition retreated even as the Cherokees captured Fort Loudoun near present-day Vonore, Tennessee, but massacred twenty-nine captives, including three women, before forcing the fort commander to dance until he died after being scalped alive.

This prompted the British to organize yet another expedition, composed of some 2,800 men, half of whom were South Carolina provincials and specially trained rangers, as well as some 57 Mohawk, Catawba, Stockbridge, and Chickasaw Indians and 80 slaves. This time Francis Marion served under Captain William Moultrie. Lieutenant Colonel James Grant, a Highland Scot, led the expedition.

Early June 1761 found the Native American contingent and some four dozen South Carolinians dressed Indian style leading this motley crew into Cherokee country, only to be ambushed less than a mile from where Montgomery's Expedition had been ambushed the year before. Oconostota himself led the six-hundred-warrior contingent, which fought several hours and then retreated after running out of ammunition. One source claimed later that Colonel Grant had ordered that anybody captured be executed. Pushing on to some fifteen settlements clustered around Etchoe, the British burned them all, destroying every crop they could find, and driving five thousand or so Cherokee men, women, and children who lived in the area into the mountains. This forced the Cherokees to sue for peace and establish relations with the British, which endured throughout the American Revolution.

Francis Marion's responsibilities and experience in this expedition are largely uncertain to this day. Parson Weems, the biographer who fictionalized Washington chopping down a cherry tree, wrote that Lieutenant Colonel Grant chose Francis Marion to open the narrow Etchoe Pass for the rest of the expedition. Although this mission was accomplished, in the ultra-heroic Parson Weems account, only nine of the thirty-man advance team survived.

No doubt the Weems account is exaggerated, but it does have some basis in fact. In the opinion of John Oller, Marion's most recent biographer, Francis Marion likely was placed in charge of a platoon of light infantry under the command of William Moultrie, sent as an advance party across a ford to cover the rest of the expedition as it crossed.

That said, Oller's in-depth research revealed that "to call it a suicide mission would be an exaggeration." According to contemporaneous army accounts, the light infantry who were in front were fired at from a great distance and suffered only one slightly wounded private. Out of Grant's entire army of 2,800 that day, only 11 soldiers were killed (and only one of them a Carolina provincial)—barely half the number of dead that Weems ascribed to Marion's unit alone. Moultrie, whose 1802 memoirs preceded Weems's book by seven years, merely described Marion as "an active, brave and hardy soldier" during Grant's campaign. William Dobein James, another early Marion biographer, wrote that Marion "distinguished himself . . . in a severe conflict between Colonel Grant and the Indians, near Etchoee [*sic*]," admitting that the specifics were simply unknown.

Embittered British journalists writing for *The Guardian* after the 2000 release of *The Patriot* opined in an article entitled "Mel Gibson's Latest Hero" that Marion was "a rapist who hunted Indians for fun," despite the lack of evidence that Marion participated in any atrocities against the Cherokee except when ordered.

In a letter Weems quoted, however creatively, Marion complained to a friend: "We arrived at the Indian towns in the month of July," continuing, "The next morning we proceeded by order of Colonel Grant [Marion didn't object] to burn down the Indians' cabins. Some of our men seemed to enjoy this cruel work, laughing very heartily at the curling flames, as they mounted loud crackling [*sic*] over the tops of the huts. But to me it appeared a shocking sight. Poor Creatures."

In any event, fully documented statements Marion made some twenty years later demonstrate that his sadness about atrocities against Cherokee noncombatants was matched only by the enthusiasm with which he later embraced the Cherokee ambush and hit-and-run tactics in actions against the British and their Tory allies.

A 1761 treaty with the Cherokees freed Francis Marion to add 450 acres of swampland amenable to rice and indigo to the 350 acres adjacent to land owned by his brother, Job. By 1773 Francis was prosperous enough to buy a small 200-acre plantation with a house on the west bank of the Santee River, called Pond Bluff, which he eventually expanded to over 1,400 acres.

Marion was nearly forty-three when British soldiers fired at an American Patriot militia at Lexington, Massachusetts, on Wednesday,

April 19, 1775. His initial reaction to these events is lost to history, but his conciliatory nature and presumed allegiance to the British, who had provided asylum to his French Huguenot ancestors, land to his grandfather, and the local Anglican church he attended weekly, suggest that ordinarily, his decision might not have been easy.

That said, his brothers Job and Gabriel were fully integrated into the local community, as lay church leaders, military officers, and even justices of the peace. Of equal or even greater importance, the Allston family of Georgetown, whose intermarriages with the Marion family are too numerous to describe here, brought Francis and the rest of the family into the Patriot fold.

Only four months before Lexington, in December, eligible voters of St. John's Parish elected Job and Francis Marion to serve in South Carolina's First Provincial Congress, an extralegal legislature. Their brother Gabriel joined them in early January, just before that South Carolina body endorsed the Continental Association, a component of the First Continental Congress.

Ironically enough, on April 21, 1775—two days before Lexington, and long before the South Carolinians learned of that history-changing battle—American Patriots in Charleston raided British armories and powder magazines, taking away everything they could carry.

Marion participated in several operations over the next fourteen months, notably including one in which he retrieved cannon ammunition at great personal risk during the late-June 1776 British siege of Fort Sullivan. Despite claims by Weems to the contrary, Marion did not personally fire the cannonball that sank the British flagship man-of-war, the HMS *Bristol*.

Five months later, Marion was appointed lieutenant colonel of the 2nd Regiment of the Continental Line and became the commander shortly thereafter. Whatever joy this brought was no doubt drowned out by the sorrow of losing three of his four brothers over the next two years, bringing Francis new parenting and guardianship duties.

September 1779 found Marion leading his regiment toward Savannah, Georgia, 108 miles southwest of Charleston, as part of a 3,000-man expedition that joined forces with some 4,000 French, including the future designer of Washington, DC, Pierre L'Enfant, and some 500 free Haitian blacks. Attacks on the morning of October 9 against the place later called the "Hostess of the South" proved unsuccessful, choking a ditch directly in front of the city with 250 dead South Carolinians. This mortality rate of 62 percent was largely attributable to South Carolina Loyalists led by Thomas Brown, a British native of Whitby, Yorkshire, living in Georgia. American Patriots had tarred and feathered Brown in his own front yard four years earlier. French casualties (dead and wounded) were even worse. The assault cost the life of Polish count Casimir Pulaski, considered the father of the American cavalry.

Worse yet for the South Carolinians, the British forces marched into Charleston on Friday, May 12, 1780, while Marion was still recovering from his injury with relatives at a plantation on the Santee River. He recovered in time to join Gates's Continental Army in August.

August 23 found Marion and his men conducting operations against British forces at Murray's Ferry, and later, Nelson's Ferry, then the major crossing point on the Santee River, between Charleston and Camden. On the evening of August 24 yet another unique opportunity presented itself when a Tory deserter walked into Marion's camp with some critical intelligence.

Fearful that Continental soldiers of the Maryland and Virginia line recently captured when he seized Camden, South Carolina, were carrying smallpox—or worse yet, malaria—British commander General Cornwallis marched the American prisoners in groups of 150 toward prison ships waiting for them in Charleston. In fact, some 150 of these men were held that very evening at the abandoned plantation house of American Patriot Thomas Sumter on the Great Savannah River, guarded by a force of only sixty men composed of British regulars and Loyalist provincials of the Prince of Wales Regiment.

Marion had only seventy men, since most of his command was busy that evening burning British boats on the lower Santee. He resolved to conduct an attack in the darkness just before daylight. Upon arrival near the Sumter plantation house, he sent his relative, Colonel Hugh Horry, with fifteen men to seize the high ground above a creek that paralleled the Santee River. This would block possible British reinforcements that might otherwise arrive from nearby Nelson's Ferry. Marion and his remaining fifty-three men circled behind Sumter's house, then standing on high ground above a swamp.

Horry's element of the attack was promptly discovered by a British guard who fired at the Americans, alerting the rest of the British defenders. Seizing the initiative, Horry led a mounted charge toward the front door, discovering that luck was with him after all. Nearly every British musket at the house was stacked next to the front door.

Bursting into the house, Horry's forces killed two British and took twenty prisoners, five of whom were wounded in the surprise attack, as the remaining thirty-five or so English soldiers ran for their lives.

Yet the surprises were not over that day. Only three of the liberated men volunteered to join Marion. Some eighty-five of the New Jersey Patriots Horry and Marion liberated were so demoralized and battle-fatigued that they traveled on to Charleston to become prisoners on British ships. Another sixty declined to join Marion, but departed for North Carolina, supposedly to rejoin their old units. Later research suggested that most of these sixty simply deserted.

Yet this incident, proudly reported later to the Continental Congress by General Gates as the "Battle of Nelson's Ferry," and sensationalized in numerous Patriot newspapers, was the beginning of the Swamp Fox legend.

British general Cornwallis was infuriated by the Great Savannah incident, combined as it was with continuing partisan operations conducted by Marion, which blockaded British supplies that otherwise would have flowed from Charleston to Camden. Impatient to be done with South Carolina and move his forces north, on August 25 Cornwallis directed Major James Wemyss (pronounced "Weems") to conduct a sweep between the Santee and Pee Dee Rivers to disarm anyone that, in Wemyss's opinion, could not be depended upon, destroying any and all plantations on which concealed weapons and ammunition were discovered.

Cornwallis later wrote to his other outpost commanders that "I have ordered in the most positive manner that every militia man who had borne arms with us and afterwards joined the enemy *should be immediately hanged*. I . . . desire that you will take the most rigorous measures to *extinguish the rebellion in the district* [emphasis in original] in which you command and that you will obey in the strictest manner the directions I have given in this letter relative to the treatment of this country."

CHAPTER 2

Behind Every Tree

Nominally an officer in the Continental Army, Marion was, in reality, on his own, making up partisan warfare tactics against the British as he went along, hoping very much to stay alive, if only for a while.

In early September, nine days after his victory at Nelson's Ferry, Marion received intelligence reports informing him that the next day, some 250 Tories would attack Marion from the north. Curiously enough, the Tory commanding officer, Major Micajah Ganey, had served in Marion's 2nd Regiment, at least until an unknown Patriot had stolen his horse. Captain Jesse Barfield, second-in-command to Ganey, had also once served with Marion, but now both men would be trouble to Marion for many months to come.

Worst of all, Marion only had 53 men (with horses) to face the Tory 250. Counterintuitive it might have been, but Marion decided his best option was to attack. And so, on the morning of September 4 he led his small contingent north to find the Tories. And surprise them the Patriots did, killing all but 15 of a 45-man Tory foraging party. Riding on another three miles they stumbled into the other 200 men on their way to a swampy ditch with blue water and blue mud, nicknamed "the Blue Savannah."

Outnumbered four to one, Marion won the battle, but exactly how remains something of a mystery. Marion later said that he conducted a direct attack, driving the Tory two hundred into a nearby swamp. That said, one of the Patriot participants told his son that Marion had feigned a retreat into the same swamp and then ambushed the Tories, most of whom had fled, leaving thirty British Loyalists dead on the ground.

Even as the British command reportedly dispatched six death squads to find him, Marion built a small earthen fort fortified with two ancient artillery places at a Pee Dee River crossing called Port's Ferry. Fortified by larger numbers drawn to his successes on Thursday, September 7, Marion crossed the Pee Dee–bound for Williamsburg to confront some 150 Tories reportedly burning the homes of Marion's men.

Stopping briefly at a Patriot haven called Indiantown, he learned from a Tory prisoner that some four hundred British regulars and Tories assembled in Kingstree, about twenty miles away, were coming after him. Another two hundred British regulars were now at Georgetown on the South Carolina coast, two days' march away. Much to the consternation of his men from Williamsburg, Marion had little choice but to hide out at Britton's Neck, a narrow strip of land at the junction of the Great Pee Dee River and a black-water tributary called the Little Pee Dee, near his makeshift fort at Port's Ferry.

And there, matters went from bad to worse, as British forces led by Wemyss gathered to his west, a Tory militia from Georgetown gathered to his south, and his old comrade, the turncoat Ganey, moved toward him from the east. Marion's only slim chance was an escape to the north.

His battle strength depleted by releasing many of his men to check on their farms and families, Marion set out at sunset on Friday, September 8, for North Carolina with some sixty men and two war-weary cannon that he eventually dumped in a swamp along the way. One week later he camped in the Great White Marsh in Eastern North Carolina, not to be confused with an identically named locale in Maryland, even as his British nemesis of the moment gave up on chasing Marion and conducted a week of depredation. Wemyss, himself a Presbyterian, burned down a Presbyterian church in Indiantown and hanged a local ferryman in front of his wife and children, for refusing to carry British officers across a creek—or, in another version of events, for shooting at a slave owned by Tory captain John Brockinton. A local doctor who tried to intercede watched his own house burn down as a consequence.

Forty-four years later, in the biography he co-authored with Brigadier General Peter Horry, Reverend Mason Locke Weems (better known as Parson Weems) described Wemyss as "by birth a Scotsman, but in principle and practice a Mohawk." John Oller, Marion's most recent biographer, elaborated that Wemyss

> [i]n reality was to emulate the malevolent Cherokee campaign of British colonel James Grant. On his march north for Kingstree to the town of Cheraw, Wemyss cut a path of destruction seventy miles long and five miles wide on both sides of the Pee Dee River, burning fifty houses and plantations along the way. He [Wemyss] claimed that these "mostly" belonged to people who had broken their paroles or oaths of allegiance and were now in arms against the British. (He offered no justification for burning the others.) Wemyss also ordered his men to destroy blacksmith shops, looms, and mills and to shoot or bayonet any milk cows and sheep not taken by the British for themselves. The residents thus lost not only their shelter but their means of livelihood, food and clothing. Wemyss's scorched earth policy would have echoes in Sherman's famous march through the South in the Civil War.

Wemyss rightly considered himself less successful in his pursuit of Marion and Colonel Hugh Giles, writing to General Cornwallis on September 20 that "I never could come up with them." Wemyss continued his complaint, describing his Tory allies as dispirited: "It is impossible for me to give your Lordship an idea of the disaffection of this country." This missive somehow neglected to mention the pillaging and burning that Wemyss himself conducted, accusing Marion and Giles of "burning houses and distressing the well affected in a most severe manner."

Wemyss accurately reported these burnings but misidentified the perpetrators. One Maurice Murphy, a captain in Marion's brigade, had in fact committed some atrocities. Marion wrote General Gates about these events: "I am sorry to acquaint you [sic] that [Captain] Murphy's party has burnt a great number of houses on Little Pee Dee and intends to go on in that abominable work—which I am apprehensive, may be laid to me. But I assure you there is not one house burnt by my orders, or by any of my people. It is what I detest to distress women and children."

Soon, another Marion subordinate, Colonel John Ervin, also began burning houses. When Marion expressly forbade him from burning any more, Ervin left Marion's brigade for a brief period, returned, and served the rest of the war without committing additional atrocities, eventually attaining the rank of colonel.

Marion's most recent biographer contrasts Marion's situation with that of Cornwallis:

> *That two of Marion's officers committed what, today, would be considered war crimes goes to show that few commanders could claim a spotless record for their soldiers' atrocities conducted during South Carolina's civil [Revolutionary] war. No officer could completely control his men in that setting; the question is how hard one tried. Marion disclosed his men's transgressions to his superior, Horatio Gates, when it would have been easy to stay quiet about them. Lacking any [actual] legal authority over his volunteers, he nonetheless was anguished by their behavior, did what he could to change it, and for the most part succeeded.*
>
> *By contrast, Cornwallis said not a discouraging word when Wemyss boasted of having laid waste to fifty houses and plantations; indeed, Wemyss had acted completely in accordance with Cornwallis's wishes. Cornwallis defended any brutalities committed on his watch as justified retaliation for rebel cruelties or punishment of parole breakers. "I have always endeavored to soften the horrors of war," his Lordship insisted just a few months after ordering the "total demolition" of private plantations and the immediate hanging of rebels formerly in British arms.*

Two weeks at the Great White Marsh brought the Patriots boredom, mosquitoes, and, for some, the symptoms of malaria, which forced them to go home. Marion invited one of the youngest in the camp, fifteen-year-old William Dobein James, to share unsalted beef and sweet potatoes one evening. Young James recalled years later how somber the entire company looked.

Within a day or two, William's father, Major John James, returned to camp with news about all the destruction at Indiantown and elsewhere back in South Carolina, including the burning of Major James's own house, prompting Francis Marion to do exactly what he'd been thinking about during his two-week exile at the Great White Marsh.

Marion and his remaining sixty men left their hideout on the afternoon of September 26, covering fifty miles in two days before swimming or riding their horses across to the east side of Little Pee Dee River the next day. They crossed the Great Pee Dee River itself the next day and camped at Port's Ferry, knowing that the British were on the west side of that river.

They crossed back over the Great Pee Dee on September 28, and learned upon arriving at Lynches Creek that some Tories were camped some fifteen miles away. They decided to attack them that very evening.

The British Loyalists targeted were not strangers. In fact, Marion knew most of them, notably their commander, the Tory colonel John Coming Ball, to whom Marion was related by marriage. Marion later described these adversaries as "good men" he might have hoped to make into Patriots.

Marion decided at twilight to give his men a few hours' sleep before the attack, awakening the company at about midnight. The target was the Red Tavern Inn, which Patrick Dollard built on the banks of Black Mingo Creek near Sheppard's Ferry, when Dollard arrived from Ireland in about 1770.

A single musket shot from the Tory camp on the far side of Black Mingo Creek told Marion as he crossed the Willtown Bridge that the ever-important element of surprise was lost. He immediately improvised a three-pronged attack on the front door and sides of the Red Tavern. Marion couldn't know that the Tories were not in the Red Tavern. Instead, the instant he was warned of the assault, Ball had led his men to a field to the southwest where he had lined them up in a formation to face the Patriots coming from the west.

Approaching the front door of the Red Tavern and the Tories Marion hoped against hope were still inside, he couldn't know on this moonless night that, in reality, most of Ball's men were to the right of the tavern, waiting to ambush them from the darkness. Even when the Tories first spotted Marion's infantry approaching, led by Hugh Horry, the Tories held their fire until the Patriots were only thirty yards away. Horry's Patriots were totally surprised, since they thought the Tories were still in the tavern. They initially retreated, but Captain John James stopped and ordered them to charge in the direction of the Tory muzzle flashes, just as Captain Thomas Waties attacked Loyalist Ball's right flank. After fifteen minutes of this, the Tories retreated into Black Mingo Swamp.

Despite the small numbers (seventy Patriots against forty-seven Tories), the engagement was significant, given the guns, ammunition, and horses Marion and his men acquired, not to mention the significant number of Tories that became Patriots then and there. Peter Gaillard, the Tory second-in-command, soon inquired whether he too might join them. Marion himself interviewed Gaillard and personally escorted the new recruit into camp, so as to mitigate any Patriot grudges. In his recent Francis Marion biography, John Oller took the broad view of this small battle, noting that

> [t]he victory at Black Mingo—Marion's third straight in a month—
> also brought Tory activity in the South Carolina Low Country to a
> virtual standstill. Ball, who managed to escape after the battle, refused
> to take the field again until late in the war. John Peyre and his brother
> Charles, both captured in the fighting and unrepentant, were sent off
> to prison in Philadelphia. With such prominent local men put out of
> commission, the Tories in the Santee region were in no mood to fight.
> As Marion explained in a letter to Gates in North Carolina a week
> after the engagement, "[T]he Tories are so affrighted with my little
> excursions that many are moving off to Georgia."

Oller further observed that "Marion's victory reinforced the growing British belief that the Loyalist militia was close to useless, at least without support from the regular British Army. 'I have found the militia to fail . . . totally when put to the trial in this province.' Cornwallis wrote to Clinton a few days before Black Mingo. Indeed, before learning the outcome of that action, Cornwallis predicted that Ball's militia 'would meet with some disaster.' Two days later one of Cornwallis's subordinate commanders wrote to him to say, 'Depend upon it, [Tory] militia will never do any good without regular troops.'"

Oller continued,

Cornwallis and other British officers were probably overstating the deficiencies of the Tory militia; Marion, for one, never underestimated their ability to rebound and cause him trouble. But overall the Whig partisans did deliver greater value to the revolutionary cause than the Tory militia provided to the Loyalist side. It may be that the loyalists were simply too few in number or too uncommitted in their support of the Crown to constitute an effective counter to the patriot militia. An estimated one-fifth to one-third of the free population in South Carolina became loyalists during the Revolution, but those percentages are much lower than what the British had been led to believe—or had convinced themselves to believe—when they embarked on their southern strategy.

Oller pointed out yet another little-known factor in the significance of Revolutionary War partisan efforts, which today we would describe as special operations:

Another factor may be even more important. With few exceptions the loyalist militia lacked the same high quality of leadership that partisan commanders such as Marion, Pickens, Sumter, and Elijah Clarke brought to the patriot side. When colonial militia elected their officers, they usually chose men of property and standing in the community, and, as the British were discovering, "all the leading men of property have been on the rebel [Patriot] side." Most of the Americans who had distinguished themselves in the Cherokee War also became patriots, creating a talent pool the Tories could not match. Many leading Tories had left or had been banished from the province early in the Revolution, and Cornwallis found those who remained to be "dastardly and pusillanimous"—so weak-willed and incompetent in combating the patriots that he lost all sympathy for them.

A Tory militia commander named Robert Gray considered Marion and Sumter the two leading partisan commanders on the Patriot side, describing them as possessing a "decided superiority" over Tory opponents, even though he perceived two different styles, considering Sumter "bold and rash," while Marion, in Gray's view was "timid and cautious and would risk nothing."

Marion biographer John Oller recently took exception to the Gray opinion, noting that "Marion was anything but timid—[British commander] Cornwallis called him 'cautious and vigilant'—and he often took risks, though they were always calculated ones. He would not jeopardize his men's lives by sending them into battle hopelessly outnumbered." He further sought to minimize the perils of war through a combination of intelligence operations, careful planning, and shrewd tactics. Among the latter were his attacks on lightly defended targets, ambush and surprise (often at night), the use of rivers and creeks as a buffer against the enemy, and strategic retreat.

In the 238 years since Marion narrowly avoided a disaster at Black Mingo, military historians have speculated about how exactly Ball and his Tories discovered that Marion was about to launch a surprise attack. Parson Weems explained this by stating that loudly rattling horse hooves crossing the creek bridge just above the Red Tavern Inn alerted the Tories that an attack was imminent. This particular Weems fabrication was discredited by at least four Revolutionary War pension applications submitted under oath. Those veterans swore independent of each other that before crossing the Willtown Bridge, Marion's men spread blankets across the bridge surface in order to prevent the Tories from hearing the approaching attackers.

That said, Marion explained in a letter sent to Gates a week after Black Mingo that the element of surprise that day was lost because "They [the Tories] had intelligence of our coming." This makes sense to contemporaneous historians, since it is now clear that numerous Tories living near the Red Tavern would have enthusiastically ratted Marion out to the British.

Yet Marion had intelligence reports of his own, which indicated that notorious turncoat and Loyalist John Wigfall was now headquartered at the Salem Black River Presbyterian Church, within easy reach of Marion's Patriots. However, Marion reported to Gates that he could not pursue Wigfall, since most of his company wanted to see their wives and families.

Although Marion saw no action during that first week of October, British leadership had hardly forgotten him. Wednesday, October 4, found General Cornwallis at Charlotte, North Carolina, planning a two-week expedition into the northern reaches of that state. Yet he took the time three days later to order Wemyss to the Williamsburg, South Carolina, region, "to prevent the enemy being thoroughly masters of the country you just left."

Although he probably didn't know it, Cornwallis had much bigger problems that day some forty-one miles to the west, at King's Mountain, South Carolina. There on Saturday, October 7, 1780, so-called "over mountain" men from present-day Tennessee, as well as militias from Virginia, Georgia, and South Carolina, surrounded a Tory army and attacked uphill, killing some three hundred and taking twice that many captive.

Shot dead by some six rifle balls while on horseback, British commander Patrick Ferguson was stripped naked, even as the rebels slaughtered surrendering Tories until their officers forced them to stop. Worse yet from the British perspective, King's mountain exposed the Cornwallis left flank to a gathering storm of backcountry rebel militia, even as the Cornwallis right flank lay exposed to Marion, who, according to Cornwallis, had so affected the population between the Santee and the Pee Dee that "there was scarce [sic] an inhabitant that was not in arms" against the British. According to Oller, "Cornwallis had planned to reinforce Ferguson's militia with Wemyss's 63rd Foot, and Wemyss would have been available to do so had he not been off chasing Marion."

These conditions in effect forced Cornwallis to abandon his planned invasion of North Carolina. Instead, he retreated back to Winnsboro, South Carolina, some sixty-six miles to the south, where he fought a feverish cold so severe that he was forced to relinquish his command. Young Francis Rawdon, twenty-five-year-old commander of the

Volunteers of Ireland Loyalist provincial regiment, received a temporary transfer of the Cornwallis command, even as replacements for Wemyss and his regiment were raised.

After returning to Port's Ferry on October 24, Marion learned of a new opportunity some fifty miles to the west at a field near the ominously named Tearcoat Swamp. A large number of Tory militia camped there under the command of a turncoat who had started the war on the Patriot side. According to the scouting report Marion listened to with great interest, thirty-something Virginian Samuel Tynes, now a colonel who Cornwallis considered "weak" but "well-intentioned," was sitting on a massive store of equipment, ammunition, and weapons that Marion could put to far better use. Since the "large force" consisted of more than 200 men, Marion was fortunate that his own force rose to 150 as they marched toward Tearcoat on October 25.

Scouting reports Marion received that evening confirmed that the Tory outpost guards were careless and that most of the camp was asleep. Those few still awake were playing cards. Marion quickly arranged the same type of three-pronged attack he had mounted at Black Mingo, positioning them around the camp for a quick nap. Marion started the attack at midnight by firing his pistol—the prearranged signal to rush in shrieking and squawking like Cherokees.

This tactic worked, sending the entire Tory force, including Tynes himself, running for the swamp, leaving their weapons and everything else behind. Amos Gaskens, a Tory reputed to have conducted numerous house burnings, died with an ace, deuce, and jack in his hand, shot by Marion himself—or so the story goes.

More certainly, the Tory boodle captured that day included eighty fully equipped horses. Once again, as at Black Mingo, several chastened Tories straggled into the camp and joined the Patriots. Despite all of this, Marion was unsatisfied, since Tynes himself had escaped—but not for long. Marion dispatched an expedition led by Tory-phobic William Clay Snipes to go after Tynes. About a week later, Snipes brought back Tynes, several unknown Tory militia officers, and even two justices of the peace. Once again, a small-scale initiative led by Marion had yielded disproportionate strategic problems to the British leadership.

According to Oller,

Marion's victory at Tearcoat Swamp left the British high command in a state of panic. With no effective enemy force in the field, Marion now had the ability to strike at will throughout the entire area of South Carolina, east of the Wateree River and north of the Santee. As a result, it had become almost impossible for the British to safely send supplies or communications from the coast to Cornwallis's army. The Santee, the major navigable river flowing through the heart of the state, did not connect directly to either Georgetown or Charleston. Therefore, to move supplies from the coast to Camden and Winnsboro, it was necessary to use both roads and waterways. Typically, the British traveled either overland or by boat to Nelson's Ferry, where they crossed the Santee, then by wagon to Camden. But because of the threat Marion posed, the British were afraid to cross at Nelson's and began taking a longer, more circuitous route to the northwest over more difficult roads to Friday's Ferry on the Congaree River. From there they crossed the Congaree and traveled overland to Camden and Winnsboro.

However arcane this dilemma might appear to the modern eye, Cornwallis was desperate to resolve this state of affairs, along with the dominance of Marion's small force between the Santee and Pee Dee Rivers. In fact, the British commander at Charleston was concerned that this situation would, in effect, end the consistency and reliability of British communications with Cornwallis's army.

When confronted with this problem, Berwickshire, Scotland, native and professional soldier George Turnbull turned once again to dashing Banastre Tarleton for a solution.

Tarleton's father back in Liverpool had made his fortune in slave trading. His son Banastre used a portion of those ill-gotten gains to attend Oxford, and later, London's Middle Temple, studying law, if only long enough to decide on a military career, as had his close friend Francis Rawdon, whose remote ancestors lived scarcely a mile from Yeadon, in West Yorkshire.

Tarleton, the more colorful of the pair, purchased a commission and participated in the first British attack on Charleston. During the subsequent occupation of Philadelphia, he spent his time gambling his wages away, nearly got himself into a duel by flirting with a friend's mistress, and even joined a theatrical group with a Benedict Arnold associate, later hanged.

Despite these odd, colorful beginnings, Tarleton soon distinguished himself in South Carolina leading New York–born Tories scattering American Patriots on April 14, 1780, at Moncks Corner and Lenud's Ferry in the prelude to the occupation of Charleston. After that, in a Herculean chase after South Carolina governor John Rutledge and 350 Virginia Continentals commanded by Colonel Abraham Buford, covering 150 miles in fifty-four hours, Tarleton caught up with Buford at a place on the South Carolina–North Carolina border named for a local Indian tribe called the Waxhaw, and almost captured Governor Rutledge as well. There is little dispute that in the battle between the Continentals and the Tories that followed, the Americans sustained a 70 percent casualty rate, consisting of 113 killed, 150 wounded or captured, as against 19 British casualties, only 5 of whom died.

Contemporary Patriot stories claimed that many of the American Patriots were killed after surrendering; thereafter any British refusals to accept Patriot surrenders were called Tarleton's Quarter, meaning no prisoners would be taken. In later years, Tarleton in effect admitted that atrocities had occurred, but claimed that they were caused by false rumors in his ranks that Tarleton had been killed.

Now known to the American Patriots as "Bloody Ban," Tarleton's perfect battle record brought him a choice assignment on November 1, 1780. The new target was Francis Marion, who, according to Tarleton's commanding officer, George Turnbull, "by his zeal and abilities, showed himself capable of the trust committed to his charge." The race was on.

Joined by the "South Carolina Rangers," a hundred-man Loyalist unit commanded by Tory Major John Harrison, the combined Tarleton–Harrison force became one of several groups known to history as the Tory "banditti." The Tory Duo left Camden on November 5 in search of Marion, hunting for him in the High Hills of Santee before following the trail south some thirty miles to Nelson's Ferry, where a wary-eyed Marion had already been alerted and was laying plans.

First Marion tried to ambush the banditti at Nelson's Ferry. When that didn't work, he nearly launched a surprise night attack against Tarleton near Richardson's Plantation, still occupied by the widow of the late Patriot, General Richard Richardson. Just before Marion began the attack, Richardson's son appeared and cautioned him that Tarleton had set a trap.

November 7 found Tarleton wondering why Marion hadn't attacked—at least until a British prisoner escaped from Marion's camp in time to report that Marion knew about the planned trap near Richardson's Plantation.

After a seven-hour hunt on the night of Wednesday, November 8, 1780, Tarleton called it quits, due to Marion's head start and the difficult terrain around the Ox Swamp outside present-day Manning, South Carolina. He supposedly called out to his banditti, "Come on, boys! Let us go back, and we will soon find the Gamecock." This meant Thomas Sumter, complaining, almost as an afterthought. "But as for this damned old Fox," meaning Marion, "the Devil himself could not catch him," or so the story goes.

Tarleton unilaterally decided to give up the chase, but falsely claimed years later that he did so upon direct orders from General Cornwallis. While the general did issue such an order, Tarleton did not receive that direction until after he had given up the chase.

Marion was not described as "the Swamp Fox" in positive terms until many years after the Revolution. The Parson Weems 1804 biography of Marion quoted two young women keeping company with British officers during the Revolution as calling Marion "a vile swamp fox"—hardly a compliment in a place and time when "swamps were dark, dank places fit only for lowly creatures." The first use of "Swamp Fox" in a positive context came in an 1829 poem quoted in an 1844 biography.

Above all, Tarleton had failed Cornwallis. Marion's most recent biographer stated, "Tarleton's frustration was evident from his actions immediately afterward. As he told Cornwallis, he [Tarleton] 'laid . . . waste' to all the houses and plantations of the Rebels around Richardson's

Plantation." So far as is known, Cornwallis did nothing about these self-reported Tarleton war crimes. More specifically, Marion's most recent biographer reported that

> *Tarleton paid a visit back to the widow Richardson's home and, as Marion reported to Gates, "beat" her to "make her tell where I was." Doing what he had earlier pretended to do in order to lure Marion to battle, Tarleton then burned Mrs. Richardson's home and some of her cattle, destroyed all her corn, and left her without so much as a change of clothes. From Nelson's Ferry to Camden, he destroyed the homes and grain of thirty plantation owners. Worst of all, Marion reported, Tarleton had "behaved to the poor women he distressed with great barbarity . . . It is beyond measure distressing to see the women and children sitting in the open air around a fire without a blanket, or any clothing but what they had on, and women of family, and that had ample fortunes; for he [Tarleton] spares neither Whig nor Tory."*

In spite of these circumstances, Tarleton trumpeted a false claim of triumph in a November 11 proclamation from Singleton's Mills, claiming, "It is not the wish of Britons to be cruel or destroy, but it is now obvious to all Carolina that treachery, perfidy and perjury will be punished with instant fire and sword." Tarleton boasted to Cornwallis that "The country seems now convinced of the error of insurrection."

Cornwallis somehow saw positive results despite the fact that Tarleton never found Marion on this expedition, since Marion had been forced into the swamps. Beyond this, Cornwallis opined that Tarleton had convinced the Tory population that "there was a power superior to Marion" that had "so far checked the insurrection." In fact, Cornwallis opined to Clinton, Tarleton had been so effective "that the greatest part of them have not dared openly to appear in arms against us since his expedition."

Despite these public boastings Cornwallis clearly understood that Marion was still a problem. In fact, he soon wrote Lieutenant Colonel (later Major General) Nisbet Balfour, admitting, "I do not think that Tarleton flattered himself that he had done more than stopping his immediate progress and preventing the militia from joining him." Beyond this, bolstered by the false report that two Patriot leaders had been killed, Cornwallis wrote Balfour that "We have lost two great plagues in Sumter and [Elijah] Clarke," adding that "I wish your friend Marion was as quiet." In reality, not only were Sumter and Clarke still alive, but Marion was gathering new forces. This time, the target was Georgetown.

While Tarleton was distracted by Marion, Thomas Sumter, newly commissioned as a brigadier general, moved within thirty miles of the Cornwallis winter headquarters before Major James Wemyss discovered that Sumter was very much alive. Cornwallis approved a Wemyss attack on Sumter featuring a five-man hit team to kill "the Gamecock." Marion's most recent biographer eloquently describes what happened next:

> *James Wemyss was good at burning plantations and hanging rebels when no enemy was around to stop him. But he was no battlefield tactician. Finding that Sumter had moved to Fish Dam Ford five miles downstream from where he was thought to be, Wemyss ordered an ill-advised post-midnight cavalry assault. In his eagerness, he had ignored Cornwallis's orders not to attack at night. The Americans repulsed the British and Tory horsemen and shot Wemyss through the arm and knee, unsaddling him from his horse and maiming him for life. Taken prisoner, Wemyss was paroled, then exchanged, but he never took the field again. He would be remembered in history mainly as the man who set fire to Presbyterian Church "sedition shops."*

Sumter had barely escaped the Tarleton assassination squad by running half-dressed out of his tent and into the woods, where he hid for the night. After the American victory at Fish Dam Ford, Sumter added another seven hundred men to his force of three hundred or so, he claimed. Whatever the size of his force, when Sumter encountered Tarleton on Monday, November 20, at Blackstock's Plantation, some seventy miles from present-day Winnsboro, Tarleton's estimated force of three to four hundred sustained 60 percent casualties, but at a cost: Sumter was wounded seriously enough that he was out of action for three months, leaving Francis Marion to cover all of South Carolina by himself.

In the meantime, Marion had experienced a significant personal tragedy. During yet another expedition testing British fortifications at Georgetown, then a Tory stronghold, his nephew Gabriel Marion, who had just turned twenty-one, was captured on November 13, and later executed when his identity was discovered. One day later, without his knowledge or permission, one of Marion's men killed a British prisoner suspected—without evidence—of killing young Gabriel. Marion quickly reprimanded the officer leading the prisoner guards for allowing this to happen.

Adding to these concerns, despite their accomplishments in partisan warfare, Marion's militia was losing heart, as he wrote Gates on November 21: "Many of my people [militia] have left me and gone over to the enemy, for they think that we have no army coming on, and have been deceived." He continued, "As we hear nothing from you in a great while, I hope to have a line from you [suggesting] in what manner to act, and some assurance to the people [Marion's militia] of support." Marion complained to Gates the very next day, saying, "I seldom have the same [militia] a fortnight, and until the Grand [Continental] Army is on the banks of the Santee, it will be the same."

Marion went on to alert Gates that some two hundred Hessians and Tory militia led by Scottish major Robert McLeroth would soon be joined by more Tory provincials bent on killing Patriot livestock and destroying provisions, in the manner of Wemyss and Tarleton.

Given this state of affairs, Marion and the militia who remained with him stayed in hiding near Britton's Ferry until circumstances he discovered in early December forced his hand. Samuel Tynes, the Tory colonel captured during the Tearcoat Swamp fighting, had escaped and was back in the area, raising Tory forces to join British regulars in yet another initiative against Marion himself. Thus challenged, Marion recruited a large number of new volunteers from around that region who had heard that Tynes was back; the volunteers now had time on their hands, since the harvest season was over.

Yet another series of rumors, these reporting that Harrington's Patriot army was marching down from North Carolina, prompted many Tories to desert their posts. Tynes, in turn, fled to Rawdon's side, complained that he could do nothing with the Tory militia, and resigned there and then, inadvertently providing Marion with another opportunity.

His brigade swelled to over three hundred souls, Marion learned that the Scot McLeroth and his 64th Regiment of Foot now marched from Nelson's Ferry toward Camden with some two hundred fresh recruits designated to eventually join Cornwallis in Winnsboro. This was far too tempting a target to resist. A locale called the Halfway Swamp, some twenty miles north of Nelson's Ferry, near Richardson Plantation, provided a seemingly perfect venue for the Patriot attack on December 13. First, Marion's riflemen fired upon the British pickets, driving them into a run back to the main English column. Marion followed this with frontal and flanking attacks, prompting McLeroth to order his forces toward the meager protection of a picket fence adjoining an open field. Once there, McLeroth raised a flag of truce, whined about his pickets being shot, and dared Marion to an open field engagement.

Marion no doubt smirked before making one of the most unusual counterproposals in the history of modern warfare—but with precedents dating back to biblical times—perhaps the source of Marion's idea. Marion refused to engage in general combat, but proposed that each side pick twenty "duelists" who would meet on open ground and decide the battle, one way or another. Whatever reasons Marion had for making this proposal, bordering on team sport, and what exactly McLeroth thought to himself about this strange proposal are lost to history, but McLeroth accepted.

The William Dobein James account of what happened has been ably summarized in the recent biography of Marion. The men were picked and each side formed a line facing one another more than a hundred yards apart. Marion appointed Major John Vanderhorst to take command of the Patriot team, and Vanderhorst asked Captain Gavin Witherspoon what distance he would choose for firing the opening round of buckshot. Witherspoon replied, "Fifty yards," and Vanderhorst, explaining that he was not a good judge of distances, told Witherspoon to tap him on the shoulder once they were fifty yards from the enemy. The two opposing lines then marched forward, but when the British advanced to within a hundred yards, they shouldered their muskets and retreated back toward the main body. Marion's men let out a cheer, claiming a moral victory. Without a shot having been fired, both sides retired for the evening to plan the next day's operations.

In his typically cursory report on the encounter with McLeroth, Marion omitted any mention of an unorthodox duel, saying only that he had "skirmaged" with the enemy. Perhaps he was reluctant to admit that he had gone along with such a gimmick. Or maybe the whole story was made up. The source of it—not Weems, for once, but William Dobein James—appears to have gotten it years later from Gavin Witherspoon, who claimed to be the first man picked for the Patriots' team. Witherspoon could have spun a tale for James that the author (James) regarded as too good not to use.

From a modern perspective, it seems clear that McLeroth was stalling for time, since his campfires were kept burning all night, even as his forces prepared for a quick march before dawn toward relative safety at Singleton's Mill, some fifteen miles to the north.

The "Swamp Fox" had been skunked, but he quickly recovered. Accurately guessing McLeroth's destination, he sent a detachment led by Major John James racing ahead to take possession of those houses at Singleton atop a hill. This was not as easy to do as Marion might have imagined.

> James reached the buildings just as the British infantry arrived at the foot of the hill. But there he [James] found a new enemy more dreaded than the British and Tories; the Singleton family had just come down with smallpox. James's men got off a single volley and killed a captain before fleeing the infected premises. McLeroth was reinforced there by 130 infantry . . . under loyalist Captain John Coffin and Marion elected not to pursue them.
>
> This episode effectively ended the career of Major Robert McLeroth, whose resignation Rawdon quickly accepted, while criticizing his lack of aggressiveness. The McLeroth debacle did not go unnoticed. On December 17 General Cornwallis wrote Rawdon, directing that Marion be disposed of.

Marion could not know that in the meantime, Cornwallis, the general who had only answered one of his ten letters, had turned his command over to a new commander on December 3, three days before Marion's last letter.

Nathanael Greene, a Quaker and a pacifist by heritage and birth, had no formal military training at all, but learned the basics and more in his personal 250-volume library. He had organized his own militia in Rhode Island in 1774, and rose from private directly to Rhode Island state army general the following year. By June of 1775, he was a thirty-two-year-old brigadier in the Continental Army. After serving with Washington at Germantown, Pennsylvania, he helped Washington avoid losing yet another battle at Monmouth Courthouse by holding off a vigorous attack led by British generals Clinton and Cornwallis.

General Washington appointed Greene the fifth commander of the Continental Southern Army in mid-October 1780. Arriving at Gates's headquarters about forty-five days later, he wrote to Thomas Jefferson and George Washington, among others, reporting the deplorable condition of the 2,300 men he found at Charlotte, only 1,500 of whom he considered fit for immediate duty. Greene shared none of this with Francis Marion, who received Greene's December 4 letter eighteen days later at Benbow's Ferry, which read:

> I have not the honor of your acquaintance, but am no stranger to your character and merit. Your services in the lower part of South Carolina in aiding the forces and preventing the enemy from extending their limits have been very important, and it is my earnest desire that you continue where you are until further advice from me. I like your plan of frequently shifting your ground. It frequently prevents a surprise and perhaps a total loss of your party. Until a more permanent army can be collected than is in the field at present, we must endeavor to keep up a partisan war and preserve the tide of sentiment among the people as much as possible in our favor.

These things said, Greene was far more interested in victory through set piece battles, noting, "The goal of the war in the south was not to capture little outposts but to win the contest for states," expressing the opinion that the British would not give up in South Carolina until they saw a greater obstacle than volunteer militias. He shared none of this with Marion. Instead, Greene dutifully responded to the requests that Cornwallis had now answered, even promising to provide a surgeon if one could be found, before making one request to Marion for immediate help.

"Spies are the eyes of the army and without them a general is always groping in the dark or annoying his enemy," Greene complained, before asking him to "fix some plan for procuring such information and for conveying it to me with all possible dispatch. The spy should be taught to be particular in his inquiries and to get the names of the corps, strength and commanding officer's name, place from whence they came and where they are going." Marion responded on December 22, explaining that procuring such spies would require cold, hard cash, before repeating his earlier request to Gates for one hundred Continentals.

And with that, Marion went into winter camp on Snow Island.

Greene decided in early January 1781 to send Marion the Continentals he had asked for, and then some. A mixed cavalry and infantry legion commanded by Princeton graduate and Middle Temple–trained lawyer Lieutenant Colonel "Light-Horse Harry" Lee arrived in early January to conduct operations with Marion under what Greene considered to be a joint command. Lee, then half Marion's age, dressed and acted as a Virginia gentleman whose outsized ego contrasted sharply with Marion's modesty. The unlikely pair somehow overcame these differences to begin planning their first initiative against the British on January 22. The target was Georgetown, which Lee's infantry surprised at dawn three days later, taking the garrison commander and two other officers captive on the edge of Georgetown before immediately paroling all three. In the meantime, the rest of the British garrison barricaded themselves within the sturdy, unassailable fort that had been built there.

Following this moderate success at Georgetown, Marion and Lee learned that on January 17 Daniel Morgan, yet another partisan commander, successfully executed a difficult-to-attain double-pincer attack on both of Tarleton's flanks in northwestern South Carolina at a place called Cowpens. This battle is often compared with Hannibal's victory over the Romans in 216 BC at the Battle of Cannae. The Cowpens affair cost Tarleton 85 percent of his 1,050-man force, 600 of whom were captured, along with 2 cannon, 800 muskets, and 100 horses.

Eight days after the combined Marion and Lee attack on Georgetown, Greene recalled Lee from South Carolina for help in the "race to the Dan" River on the North Carolina–Virginia border, with British troops in close pursuit. This left Marion in South Carolina with few reinforcements and, worse still, new correspondence from Greene telling him that for the present, he would be reporting to General Thomas Sumter.

Early March took Sumter to other battles outside South Carolina, leaving Marion to face the redundantly named Lieutenant Colonel John Watson Tadwell-Watson (Watson), who had received direct orders from Marion's old adversary Rawdon to take Marion out. Watson confronted Marion on Wednesday, March 7, 1781, with a bayonet charge from across a causeway (a roadway supported mostly by earth or stone) at Wyboo (Wiboo) Swamp, which sent Marion's men running in retreat, if only to fight on another day. Marion fared no better in a similar confrontation on March 9 at Mount Hope Swamp Bridge two days later.

In an effort to divert Watson from occupying Williamsburg and Snow Island, locales populated by large numbers of pro-independence Patriots, Marion moved toward Georgetown. Initially, Watson followed, but on March 12 Watson reversed course and marched toward Kingstree, on the road to Williamsburg, South Carolina.

Once Marion learned this, he quickly took action, ordering seventy men commanded by Major John James astride the swiftest horses available to reach a place called Lower Bridge on the Black River, the gateway to Kingstree. Since many of the men on this expedition were from the Kingstree area, they knew the shortcuts that placed them at Lower Bridge in time to dismantle part of the structure and set it on fire. Having done that, James and his detachment waited on the east side of the Black for Watson and the Tories to approach from the west.

Marion and the rest of Marion's command joined them in time to dodge the cannon fire Watson's artillery now rained down upon them, in a repeat of tactics that had brought Watson victory a few days earlier at both Wyboo and Mount Hope Swamps. But this time geography and random chance worked against Watson. The cannons were initially positioned so high on the hill above the Black River that they could not effectively be aimed low enough to strike Marion's men, who watched Watson's grapeshot harmlessly strike the tall pines above them. And when the British and Tory artillerists tried to move their cannons lower into the valley, Marion's sharpshooters—armed with long rifles commanded by William McCottry—drove them away.

Still determined to cross the Black, Watson sent an advance element led by an officer carrying a sword to cross the stream. The officer was shot in the chest, and four men sent to the rescue died with him in the water. After retrieving the dead and wounded, Watson retreated to a nearby Witherspoon plantation. Witherspoon's daughter, herself engaged to one of Marion's officers, heard Watson complain that he'd never before seen such shooting.

The next day, Marion sent McCottry and his men to harass Watson's pickets and guards on the outskirts of the plantation. According to one version of events, a Patriot sniper shot one of the British officers in the knee from a distance of three hundred yards. Watson retreated to yet another plantation, this one surrounded by open fields rather than the tall trees that had been so convenient for Marion's snipers.

Watson occupied himself the next three days by sending letter after letter to Marion, complaining about alleged Patriot atrocities against Loyalists. Marion stopped responding just about the time Watson tried to retreat on March 18 toward Georgetown, South Carolina (and desperately needed supplies), down the Santee River road on which he had chased Marion just a few days earlier.

Now that Watson the pursuer had become the pursued, Marion split his forces for simultaneous frontal and flank attacks. Thus encumbered, Watson moved ever so slowly toward the Sampit River Bridge, nine miles from all the supplies Watson thought awaited him at Georgetown. The British and their Tory allies discovered on March 20 that the rebels had destroyed that bridge too, but out of desperation, jumped into the river. Watson successfully led the crossing, but at the cost of twenty dead soldiers and the horse Watson was riding on. Marion declined to follow Watson into British-occupied Georgetown.

Oller, Marion's most recent biographer, astutely assessed the so-called Bridges campaign this way:

> *It had showcased Marion at his most brilliant, first in evading and then in demoralizing an enemy blessed with superior numbers and fire power. Watson's casualties in the campaign were in the dozens, while Marion's were minimal. On March 21, while camped at Trapier's Plantation, just outside Georgetown, Watson complained about Marion's style of warfare. "They will not sleep and fight like gentlemen," Watson told the plantation owner, "but like savages are eternally firing and whooping around us by night, and by day waylaying and popping at us from behind every tree."*

Had he heard this indictment, Marion might have taken it as a compliment.

CHAPTER 3

Without Fear, Without Reproach

THERE WAS MORE TROUBLE TO COME FOR THE BRITISH—MUCH MORE. Marion's targets included Irish-born Colonel John Doyle, whose New York Volunteers found and destroyed Marion's Snow Island retreat. Marion found Doyle on March 30 in present-day Lynchburg, South Carolina, but let him escape due to lack of adequate manpower for a conventional attack.

Despite that frustration, early April 1781 brought Marion news of significant developments. Two weeks earlier, Nathanael Greene had lost a battle with Cornwallis in North Carolina, but in that defeat inflicted such heavy British losses that the Battle of Guilford Courthouse was a strategic victory for the Americans. And Light-Horse Harry Lee was on his way back to South Carolina.

Freshly inspired by these developments, General Greene decided upon a "war of posts" in which the American forces would focus on assaulting the largest British garrisons in South Carolina. He assigned Fort Granby to Sumter, and smaller forts on the Georgia border near Augusta to Pickens. The attack orders for the two newest British strongholds, Forts Watson and Motte, went to the Marion–Lee partnership.

Earlier, after Sumter had failed to take Fort Watson, Marion found the place defended by 250 men and declined to attack it. Now reinforced by his new subordinate, Lee, and his 350-man legion, Greene insisted that Marion try again. Arriving on Sunday, April 15, Marion and Lee demanded that Fort Watson surrender. Lieutenant James McKay, the acting British commander in Watson's absence, suggested that the rebels "come and take it."

Fort Watson was hardly the size of a European castle, with only a twenty-yard-by-twenty-yard diameter. Yet it was an inherently strong position atop a twenty-three-foot-high ancient Indian temple mound. Three rows of abatis (branches of trees laid in a row, with the sharpened tops directed outward) surrounded the area just outside the fort, from which all outside trees and shrubs in shooting range had been cleared.

Lee and Marion's first tactic was posting snipers to shoot the British leaving the fort to reach their water supply at nearby Scott's Lake. McKay responded by digging a well just outside the fort walls that could be accessed at night using a covered passage. During the next few days, Marion began receiving correspondence forwarding British claims that Marion's men had murdered at least three prisoners. His aggravation at this, and official approval of "Sumter's Law"—permitting Patriot recruits to be paid in horses, equipment, and even slaves taken from Loyalists— only deepened Marion's frustration with the stalemate.

Soon, Lieutenant Colonel Hezekiah Maham pitched an idea dating from ancient times. He proposed to construct a wooden tower over thirty feet tall from which Patriot riflemen could fire over the seven-foot stockade wall atop the twenty-seven-foot Indian mound down into the British in Fort Watson. The tower, complete with portholes at the very top, was constructed by April 21 and moved into place next to the fort the night of April 22. Maryland Continentals posted in front of the tower behind a breastwork of logs protected the contraption from frontal British assaults.

American sharpshooters at the top of the contraption began raining fire into Fort Watson at dawn even as patriots moved close enough to the fort to dismantle the abatis and start axing the stockade walls, as Marion sent McKay a second surrender request. This time McKay raised the white flag, marking the first time since the fall of Charleston to the British one year earlier that Americans anywhere in the thirteen colonies had captured an entire British garrison.

Exactly two weeks later, on Sunday, May 6, Marion and his expedition were standing in front of what turned out to be their last significant combat assignment of the Revolution—"Fort Motte," a five-acre fortification surrounding a three-story house at the Mount Joseph Plantation owned by the widow Rebecca Motte. The British had confiscated the plantation the prior year and constructed a substantial fortification. "Although small by traditional fort standards, the enclosure was at least double the size of Fort Watson, with about forty yards on each side. The plantation house sat atop a 245-foot hill. The protective wall, just outside the plantation house, was made of thick wooden stakes, almost ten feet high, buttressed by an earthen rampart. The ditch was seven and a half feet wide and six feet deep. At the corners of the fort were two blockhouses with apertures for guns."

Lee and Marion developed a specific plan of attack, as Oller recounted in his work, *The Swamp Fox*:

> *Marion's 150 partisans spread themselves around the perimeter of the fort while Lee and his 250-man Legion camped on a hillside about a quarter-mile north. This time, the Americans had the six-pounder Greene had sent them at Fort Watson . . . Their plan was to dig zigzagging trenches ever closer to the wall and then pound it with cannon fire. Marion's riflemen would provide cover for the excavators and Lee's infantry would then storm the fort with bayonets. Lee figured that because the defenders were without artillery themselves, their defense would fail unless they were reinforced by Rawdon.*

During the early days of the siege, Marion became aggravated with the most recent in a series of requests from Nathanael Greene, for sixty to eighty dragoon horses, taken, or so Greene had heard, from British Loyalists. He now wrote Greene that he would resign his militia command as soon as Fort Motte was either taken or abandoned by the Patriots. Marion sent a single horse off to Greene, just before learning that his old adversary Rawdon was coming after him.

The danger was obvious enough. On the evening of May 11, everyone at Fort Motte, Patriot and Tory alike, could see the campfires of the British Army burning in the distance. Even before that dismal reminder, Lee and Marion knew instinctively that they didn't have much time before the

British arrived. They resolved to take Fort Motte the next day, or abandon the effort.

The roof of the Motte mansion at the center of the fort, now within range of the Patriot trenches, offered one enticing possibility. Either Lee, Marion, or both of them directly asked the widow Motte for permission to launch a flaming projectile onto the mansion roof. All accounts agree that the widow freely gave her permission, but differ on how exactly the deed was accomplished. Once the roof was on fire that Saturday, May 12, the British inside quickly surrendered and the mansion was saved. The only casualties that day were three notorious Tories who Henry Lee had hanged before Marion kept him from hanging a fourth.

Marion met with Nathanael Greene, reconciled most of their differences, and continued on for three months, leading South Carolina militia in both conventional battles and irregular warfare, including a debacle on July 17 caused by the rash impatience of Thomas Sumter. Early that morning, newly arrived British lieutenant James Coates burned a church as Patriots led by Sumter, Light-Horse Harry Lee, Wade Hampton, and Francis Marion slept nearby. The Americans chased Coates across Quinby Bridge over a creek of the same name near present-day Huger, South Carolina. Coates thoughtfully made the American crossing all the more difficult by having his men tear up some of the bridge planks after crossing the structure themselves. Despite this, the first American wave successfully crossed and captured some one hundred British foot soldiers. The second wave of Americans crossing Quinby Bridge destroyed even more bridge planks in the process, leaving most of Lee's forces on the far side of the creek without a practical means of following.

Yet somehow they did. By midafternoon Marion and Lee were assessing a newly devised redcoat defensive position at Shubrick's Plantation nearby. The redcoats occupied the two-story mansion house on elevated ground surrounded by excellent makeshift defensive structures, including barns, rail fences, and slave quarters. Marion and Lee arrived on the scene before Sumter could see that Shubrick was now far too formidable a defensive position to attack directly, since a cavalry charge was of little use. Also, the infantry would have to attack without bayonets or supporting artillery across a large, wide-open field.

When Sumter arrived at 3:00 p.m., he swept aside the reservations expressed by Marion and Lee, even refusing to wait for the artillery to come up. Sumter moved his own men to relative safety behind the slave quarters, after ordering Marion to conduct a direct attack across the open field, at least until Marion's men had to rescue militiamen led by Colonel Thomas Taylor from a Tory bayonet attack.

Forty-five minutes later Sumter called off the attack, too late to save Marion and Taylor's men from sustaining significant losses. Taylor refused to serve under Sumter again; Marion wrote Nathanael Greene, and, according to Marion's recent biographer, strongly implied that Sumter "had ordered him to assault an impregnable enemy position without a field piece or adequate ammunition while Sumter himself remained distant from the action." That evening, all but one hundred of Marion's men left, after complaining that they had been sacrificed while Sumter's men safely watched. Soon thereafter, Sumter resigned his commission and disbanded his brigade.

Yet Marion's greatest accomplishment as a partisan fighter awaited him at Parker's Ferry, some twenty-eight miles west of Charleston on the Edisto River in late August. There, following the August 4, 1781, British hanging of popular South Carolina Low Country Patriot Isaac Haynes, Marion, now commanding some 400 men, looked to get some payback. Marion attacked some 540 enemies led by Hessian lieutenant colonel Ferdinand Ludwig von Benning, then loading boats with food and forage destined for British troops at Charleston. Despite having no artillery available to answer two von Benning cannons, Marion turned to one of his specialties: ambush.

On the evening of August 27, Marion sent an advance guard to interdict von Benning and his diverse crew of Hessians, redcoats, Tories, and provincial dragoons on a causeway at Godfrey's Savannah, best described as a grassy swamp west of the Ashepoo River. Instead of challenging von Benning, Marion's advance party, seeing how greatly outnumbered they were, simply allowed the British to pass them by.

Marion tried again three days later, placing his men along both sides of a narrow, barely elevated causeway crossing an extremely thick swamp just southwest of Parker's Ferry, where the British would have to cross the Edisto River along the way to Charleston, some twenty-eight miles to the east. Spies told the Americans that some one hundred Tories—commanded by Brigadier General Robert Cunningham, the highest-ranking Tory in South Carolina—waited for von Benning and his men on the east side of Edisto. John Oller, Marion's most recent biographer, ably describes the battle:

> *Moving swiftly to get ahead of the British, Marion found a good spot for an ambush a mile southwest of Parker's Ferry along the road leading directly to it. . . . He formed his men in three groups. The main body of dismounted musket- and riflemen, commanded by Marion, concealed themselves behind felled trees in the swamp, parallel to the causeway and within forty yards of it. The Second group, the eighty men commanded by General Harden, were ordered to retire a hundred yards from the line and to charge forward once the shooting began. A third group of sixty mounted swordsmen, under Major George Cooper . . . stayed back of Marion's line with orders to fall in the rear of the enemy once the firing became general, and to "follow them whenever they moved, and to keep in [the fight] at all hazards."*

It was near sunset on Thursday, August 30, when some of Cunningham's men began crossing over onto the west bank of the Edisto, apparently looking for von Benning and his men. "The Tories passed in front of Marion's line as the rebels waited in ambush. Marion intended to let the small group go by unmolested, and they had all but gotten past when they spotted one of Marion's men." Supposedly seeking a white feather in his cap, "The Tories called out to him, and when he failed to answer they started shooting." Marion could restrain his men no longer, and when the Patriots returned the fire, "[Cunningham's] Tories scampered in fright back toward the ferry, in the same direction from which they had come. Marion sent a few horsemen . . . who chased them back across the river."

Von Benning, not far away, apparently thought that Cunningham had run into a few Patriot militiamen. "Marching up front with the infantry and artillery, von Benning ordered [Tory officer Thomas] Fraser and the cavalry, who were in the back, to push down the road toward the ferry and disperse the rebels. As his dragoons came in front of Marion's ambush line, Fraser saw Marion's horsemen on the causeway in the distance. Assuming them to be Harden's militia, he ordered his cavalry to charge them." The Oller biography of Marion observed that

> [t]he next few minutes may have marked the supreme moment of Marion's career to that point. The twenty-five-year-old Fraser, a Scotsman who settled in New Jersey before the war, was very much in the Tarleton mold—a bold dragoon commander who had been antagonizing the patriots for months. He had routed Sumter in battle, eluded Lee at Monck's Corner, and captured Isaac Hayne. Lately he had been harassing Harden's militia and stealing rice from Whig plantation owners. And now he had fallen directly into Marion's carefully laid ambush.
>
> As Fraser's men entered the killing zone, Marion's shooters let out the first barrage of buckshot, at which the front column of Fraser's horsemen raced forward. It was the only direction they could go. Wedged in together on the narrow causeway, they could not turn around and run into the horsemen charging up the road behind them, as it would have been like going the wrong way on a one-way street. Nor could they charge (or even see) the ambushers hidden in the heavy swamp behind the abatis they had formed. And so, Fraser's dragoons continued moving forward, even though it exposed them to the rest of Marion's men, who shot them as they passed by. Fraser's riders were like people without umbrellas who try to outrun the rain only to be drenched.

Both Marion and one of Fraser's cavalrymen, twenty-four-year-old Stephen Jarvis, used the identical phrase to describe what happened: "running the gauntlet." That specific military term, together with Marion's statement that the enemy ran the gauntlet "through" his men, suggests Marion had placed riflemen on parallel sides of the road. Trapped on the causeway, Fraser's dragoons were forced to absorb the fire along the entire length of the ambush as they galloped toward Parker's Ferry.

Nearly all of Fraser's cavalry and most of their horses were dead or wounded, as were all the Tory artillerymen trapped on the causeway. Von Benning managed to get away with his artillery pieces, but Marion had clearly won this battle, which Greene reported to the Continental Congress, praising Marion's "good conduct, judgment and personal bravery."

Marion could not have known that by late August 1781 his most important battles and actions using irregular partisan tactics were now behind him. What remained was the Battle of Eutaw Springs late that summer, in which Marion commanded the American right wing. Although the Americans departed the battlefield first with great losses, thus allowing British general Alexander Stewart to claim a victory, that victory was pyrrhic at best. Stewart left his dead unburied and the British wounded on the battlefield, uncared for. More importantly, he was now a "spent force" like his British predecessors, Cornwallis and Rawdon.

Marion began performing administrative duties rather than military operations even as a conclusion to the war grew closer. When Light-Horse Harry Lee brought Marion news on November 9 that General Cornwallis and the British Army had surrendered on Friday, October 19, Marion began focusing on the future. He became a state senator in December 1781, returned to military service, and fought his last battle on August 29, 1872, three and a half months before the British left Charleston on December 14.

Marion returned home to a burned house and empty livestock pens. He borrowed money, rebuilt his plantation, married for the first time at fifty-four, helped write the first South Carolina state constitution, and died on February 27, 1795. His gravestone proclaimed Marion to be a man "who lived without fear and died without reproach."

CHAPTER 4

King of the Jayhawkers

It was not the shooting of a few obnoxious persons. The killing was indiscriminate and mostly in cold blood, the victims being quiet, peaceable citizens. None of them, so far as I know, had taken any part in the early disturbances, and none of them were connected with the border troubles during the war. I do not now recall a single military man among the killed . . . The [Kansas] guerrillas shot the men they found, without knowing who they were or caring what they were.
—Kansas militiaman Richard Cordley of Lawrence, Kansas, describing Jayhawker raids into Missouri

The "total war" concept has often been attributed erroneously to General Sherman, when in fact it was created by James Henry Lane, a US senator from Kansas who served simultaneously as a Union general for a brief period of time during the Civil War. During September 1861 Lane waged total war on several pro-secession western Missouri counties with the knowledge and concurrence of the federal government. Lane, a native of Lawrenceburg, Indiana, arrived in Kansas a mere six years earlier, as had the radical abolitionist John Brown. Civil War historian Edward E. Leslie described Lane as a "tall, gaunt, hollow-cheeked, thin-lipped philanderer with a mass of unruly black hair and what had been described by others as 'the sad, dim eyes of a harlot,'" destined to become "the Grim Chieftain of Kansas." Lane, initially a Democrat, started his career in elected office as the lieutenant governor of Indiana.

Lane became a colonel during the Mexican War. Thus qualified, he was elected to the US House of Representatives and threw away his public popularity by supporting the Kansas–Nebraska Act, which most Indiana voters opposed.

Leslie and other historians have noted that Lane came to Kansas with no preconceived opposition to slavery, but a high level of self-indulgence and "an enormous gift for intrigue." Years later, one pioneer discussing Kansans of that era remembered that "He [Lane] talked like none of the others. None of the rest had his husky, rasping, bloodcurdling whisper or that menacing forefinger, or could shriek 'Great God,'" the way Lane could. These qualities brought him much-desired attention from the ladies, as well as more than a few whispers of sexual "impropriety."

He was a switch-hitter in at least one context. Despite his ambivalence on the subject of slavery, he could smell opportunity in the wind. And that smell brought him to the brand-new Free State Party, which opposed the extension of slavery into Kansas and championed individual liberty.

During the July 1861 congressional sessions in Washington, Lane predicted that the institution of slavery would not survive the summer. The Civil War in effect started for Lane seven years earlier, when proslavery Democrats seized control of Kansas Territory. Now, in the first year of the Civil War, while Lane was in Washington, James Montgomery—a religious antislavery fanatic competing with John Brown, and a veteran of 1858–1859 raids on proslavery towns across the state line in Missouri—began organizing the Third Kansas Volunteer Infantry Regiment. The Third Kansas mustered near Mound City, ninety-five miles southeast of Lawrence on the Missouri border. Nearby, William Weer organized the Fourth Kansas Infantry Regiment, while Free State advocate Hamilton P. Johnson raised the Fifth Kansas Volunteer Cavalry Regiment, as described by Alex Wilson Lahasky in his excellent 2017 thesis, "The March of the Union Armies: James Henry Lane, The Union and the Development of Total War on the Kansas–Missouri Border."

The Third, Fourth, and Fifth Regiments, when united under the command of James Lane, became the poorly organized, underequipped, yet highly motivated Kansas Brigade. That motivation stemmed at least in part from developments across the state line, where the Missouri State

Guard took on Federal troops at Carthage on July 5 and decapitated Union general Nathaniel Lyon on August 10 at Wilson Creek, near Springfield. This left western Missouri in rebel hands from Springfield west to the Kansas border and north to the Missouri River near Kansas City.

Now possessing a brigadier general commission and written War Department authorization to raise additional regiments in Kansas, Lane seized control of the Kansas Brigade and moved toward Fort Scott, Kansas, with silent federal acquiescence. Lahasky remarked in "The March of the Union Armies" that "The general acceptance of Lane's command by War Department Officials was indeed unusual but not entirely surprising given the circumstances in Kansas at the time . . . Lane had found a niche not occupied by anyone else. Southeast Kansas was a remote theater of war, connected with the rest of the Union by neither railroad nor telegraph," as noted by Bryce D. Benedict in *Jayhawkers: The Civil War Brigade of James Henry Lane*. Arriving at Fort Scott, some 110 miles due south of Lawrence in late August, Lane assumed formal command of the Kansas Brigade and directed Colonel Charles R. "Doc" Jennison to bring his Seventh Cavalry Regiment to join them. Jennison was a grizzled Kansan with a taste and aptitude for theft, which was excessive even by Kansas standards. The abolition of slavery, Jennison's stated war motivation, worthy cause that it was, only provided pretext for plunder.

Jennison arrived in Fort Scott with his regiment on September 1. Ten days later, after brief battles with Confederate allied Missouri State Guard troops at obscure outposts such as Dry Wood, Kansas, Lane tentatively decided to "march east as far as Papinville, in Bates County, Missouri, and turn north along the Kansas state line through the towns of Butler, Harrisonville, Osceola and Clinton." Jennison's Missouri campaign began on September 11, 1861, with the theft of a wagon, several horses to pull it, and harnesses from the citizens of Butler, Missouri, some fifty miles south of Kansas City. Graduate history student Alex Wilson Lahasky described Lane's raid in a 2017 thesis, asserting that Butler now "suffered a fate similar to that of other towns in Lane's path. The brigade spared most private residences in Butler, but the Kansans again destroyed anything that could prove useful to the Missouri State Guard or guerrillas operating in the area." Lane's troops returned to West Point, Missouri, with "twenty wagonloads of valuables, fifty horses and a column of liberated slaves. Behind it, the [Lane] brigade left a trail of cinders, barren pastures and empty stores."

Lane's Missouri campaign began in earnest during the early-morning hours of Friday, September 13, with a march from Fort Lincoln, Kansas, to West Point, Missouri, in Bates County. Lane used West Point, now a ghost town, as his base of operations for this raid into Missouri. During the next three days his troops liberated some three hundred horses and mules as well as numerous cattle and fifty former slaves from Missourians who were insufficiently pro-Union, or simply unlucky. Curiously, Lane favored emancipation only as a war measure, preferring future colonization of Liberia and South America by American blacks, so as to avoid eventual intermarriage, which he personally opposed.

September 17 brought yet another Lane-directed raid, this time on the Morristown, Missouri, population of 200, which was defended, at least initially, by some 125 raw recruits of the Confederate Missouri State Guard. The Missourians managed to mortally wound Kansas colonel Hamilton P. Johnson, before the brave Kansans occupied and destroyed the town. Kansan Chauncey L. Terrill recorded the day's loot, which included "100 head of horses . . . one dozen tents, a great quantity of camp [gear], saddles, bridles, drugs, merchandise, goods from two or three stores, wagons," and ten prisoners, half of whom were summarily executed without any charges at all being specified.

Emboldened by this military success, Senator Lane issued a proclamation "to the People of Western Missouri, Now Occupied by the Kansas Brigade," encouraging them, in effect, to ignore what had happened in Morristown. "We are *soldiers* [emphasis in original]," Senator Lane proclaimed in the *Liberty Tribune* on October 4, 1861, "not thieves or plunderers or jay hawkers. We have entered the army to fight for a peace, to put down a rebellion, to cause the stars and stripes—your flag as well as ours—once more to float over every foot of American soil." The proclamation continued with a stern warning for rebels, to the effect that "the stern visitations of war will be meted out to the rebels and their allies. I shall then be convinced that your arming for protection is a sham; and rest assured that the traitor, when caught, shall receive a traitor's doom. The cup of mercy has been exhausted. Treason, hereafter, will be treated as treason . . . a traitor will perpetrate crimes which devils would shudder to commit; they shall be blotted from existence, and sent to that hell which yawns for their reception."

Thus, it was Senator James Lane of Kansas rather than General William Tecumseh Sherman who first articulated the concept of total war.

September 19 brought a new Lane initiative. That Thursday morning, Lane chose Osceola, Missouri, as his next objective. The traditional Missouri version of events as recounted by Edward E. Leslie in *The Devil Knows How to Ride* recounts that two days after Confederate general Sterling Price won a September 20, 1861, victory at Lexington, Missouri, Kansas stalwart James Lane

approached the outskirts of Osceola. When his [Lane's] advance [party] was fired on by twenty-five or thirty Confederate soldiers who had concealed themselves in the brush, the fire was returned, killing one and wounding eight. No further resistance was offered, and Lane's troops quickly secured the town. Lane had all the records taken from the courthouse—for some reason he sent them back to Lawrence—then set the building on fire. Since Osceola was an important port on the Osage River, there were many wealthy merchants in residence, and its warehouses were filled with salt, coffee, and a large quantity of other goods. Several appropriated wagons were loaded with loot. The bank was robbed, the take said to have been $8,000 [about $221,000 in modern money]. One hundred and fifty barrels of liquor were found in a cellar dug into a hillside, and because, as Captain Henry E. Palmer put it, "our men were dangerously thirsty," he and some other officers and men were detailed to break in the heads of the barrels and spill this stock of "wet goods" to prevent the men from indulging too freely. The "mixed drinks" . . . ran out of a rear door down a ravine, where the boys filled their canteens and "tanks" with the stuff, more deadly for a while than rebel bullets, and nearly 300 of our men had to be hauled from town in wagons and carriages impressed into service for *that purpose. Had the rebels then rallied and renewed the fight, we would have been captured and shot. The town was fired and burning as we left.*

Leslie adds that "[t]he river of liquor" described above as running down a ravine "caught fire, too. Among the dwelling houses torched was the home of one of Lane's colleagues in the United States Senate, Democrat Waldo P. Johnson," who later served as a Confederate state senator from Missouri. Leslie also noted in 1996 that "More than one hundred houses were burned, along with every store, shop and warehouse. Only a few houses and one livery stable were spared. At least ten citizens were murdered."

In Leslie's estimation, "About one third of Osceola's population was loyal, and many of the men were serving in the Federal army; however, when Lane and his men stole property there, they made no distinction between Unionists and secessionists, destroying or stealing almost everything they could lay their hands on. His [Lane's] personal share of the plunder included a piano, $1,000 in gold, a quantity of silk dresses and a handsome carriage. He would brag of having done a million dollars' worth of damage in Osceola."

Although the population was only about 260, Osceola, near the head of the Osage River, was the very place where lead from mines in the region was collected for the manufacture of bullets, among other products. Two days later, Lane's forces skirmished with two companies of the Missouri State Guard while crossing the Osage River near Osceola, taking five prisoners along as the Federals approached the outskirts of town. The Confederates—commanded by Captain John M. Weidemeyer, a native of Charlottesville, Virginia, who died at age seventy-seven in 1911—were taken by surprise and driven off as flames leapt from several log houses targeted by Kansas artillery. Lane camped for the night on the outskirts of town and entered without a fight the next morning, since most of the male residents left before sunrise.

True to his word, and uninhibited by military opposition, Lane ordered that the town be plundered: "Everything that might benefit the enemy and could not be transported by the troops was destroyed, 'including about two thousand barrels of liquors, thousands of bushels of salt, fifty hogsheads of sugar and molasses' and large quantities of bacon." Although seldom discussed in modern studies of the raid, Lane's men discovered that a musket cartridge factory was operating covertly near Osceola. According to one townsman quoted by the *Lawrence Republican*, on October 3, 1861, "the operation was under the management of Colonel John F. Snyder, the chief of ordnance [officer] under [Confederate] General James Rains's eighth division of the Missouri State Guard." That the depot had served as an ammunition source for Sterling Price's command prompted Lane's men to burn what remained of Osceola, as they adjudged the town "traitorous to the core."

Urban legends of Yankee depredations during the Osceola raid persist to this day. Lahasky noted in his thesis that "Among the most oft-repeated is a tale that claims Lane personally looted the town, making away with, among other things, a valuable piano." Historian Bryce Benedict notes, however, that no reliable primary source exists to corroborate this musical escapade. Benedict also pointed out that "Lane had been outspoken in charging his men that no thieving take place; had he an inclination toward larceny, his takings would have been small enough to conceal from his men, thus at least maintaining the outward appearance of honesty."

In 2017, Alex Wilson Lahasky debunked claims that Lane's men were so drunk that they could not have marched out of Osceola. However, Lahasky did not explain what Union captain Henry E. Palmer might have had to gain in 1905 by describing this episode to the Kansas Historical Society. That said, modern historians doubt that Lane personally snatched $13,000 (about $360,000 in modern money) from the hands of a widow. Even after considering the controversies surrounding many of the Osceola attack details, there is no dispute that during his assault on Osceola, General Lane launched total war practices that General William Tecumseh Sherman later made famous during his late 1864 March to the Sea.

One thing is certain: During the next two years, it was not uncommon for Missouri Confederates to shout *Remember Osceola!* while riding into battle.

CHAPTER 5

The Lawrence Raid: A Kansas 9/11

Five young women were dead—and for no reason. Or so it seemed to many Missourians, whose wives, sisters, and cousins were smothered to death the morning of Thursday, August 13, 1863, in downtown Kansas City.

Some nine to twenty-seven prisoners being held on the second floor of a three-story brick building at 1409 Grand Avenue included Josephine Anderson, who died before she could be extracted from the debris. Her sister Mary, only eighteen years old, bore the effects of her injuries for the rest of her life, as did their youngest sister Martha, whose legs were broken by the same debris that left her face permanently scarred. Three others, namely Charity (Nannie) McCorkle, Armenia Crawford Selvey, and Susan Crawford, also paid with their lives for who they were related or married to. A fifth victim, known to history only as Mrs. Wilson, paid the ultimate price as well.

Union general Thomas Ewing Jr. used the building owned by the estate of the late Reverend Robert S. Thomas as a prison for Missouri women accused of being spies, or other pro-Confederate offenses. Some of the prisoners were awaiting transportation elsewhere.

Historian Edward E. Leslie noted in his seminal 1996 work, *The Devil Knows How to Ride: The True Story of William Clarke Quantrill and His Confederate Raiders* that "The females, none of whom was older than twenty, had been confined on the second floor, and as the building began to shake and walls to split apart from one another, a guard scooped up two girls and carried them outside. Nannie McCorkle leaped out a window. Thirteen-year-old Martha Anderson tried to follow, but according to accounts of survivors, she had annoyed the guards earlier that morning, and to punish her, they had shackled a twelve-pound ball to her ankle."

Union soldiers and Kansas City citizens nearby promptly rose to the occasion, but the dense dust rising from the wreckage was so thick that little could be done quickly enough to help the victims at the bottom of the rubble. Those few women lucky enough to emerge from the top of the wreckage alternated between crying and cursing the Yankees. To their credit, Kansas City residents rushed to dig through the debris toward the groans and screams that seemed the loudest. The rescuers could hear young Josephine Anderson beg for someone to please, please take the bricks off of her head, until she went silent. Preston B. Plumb, chief of staff to Union general Thomas Ewing Jr., arrived just in time to be jeered by increasingly angry bystanders.

All too quickly the expected rumors began to spread. General Ewing, or so it was said, ordered the Union soldiers guarding the prisoners to take away girders under the building so that the prisoners could easily be murdered. According to yet another tale, Leslie recounted: "[A]n aging merchant 'had a store of cheap goods on the first floor—a medley of merchandise, including flashy jewelry, clothing, groceries and liquor.'" Supposedly, just hours before the collapse, the aging merchant had "frantically removed all his stock with the help of the guards. According to Leslie, "It was even claimed that he [the old merchant] was in such a hurry [that] he piled his goods in the street—further 'proof' that the collapse was engineered."

Curiously enough, Kansas City resident George Caleb Bingham, one of the most distinguished American artists of the nineteenth century, conducted a thirteen-year contemporaneous investigation of this mystery. His findings, largely unknown today even to most Civil War buffs, moldered unnoticed in the National Archives for more than a century until historian Edward E. Leslie described them in his 1996 book.

Bingham, talented artist and ardent Unionist though he was, had every reason to blame Union forces for the collapse of the makeshift jail. Border War historian Leslie recounted that "Bingham's second wife, Eliza, was a daughter of the late Reverend Robert S. Thomas, whose estate owned the building and would be reimbursed for its value if it could be established that the Federal military authorities were somehow responsible for its loss." In addition, Bingham also had a long-standing personal grudge against General Ewing.

Bingham quickly established that the key to the collapse was a common wall that the Thomas building shared with the adjoining Cockerel building, which witnesses said collapsed first that day. He also determined that the Thomas building was far from dilapidated. In fact, it was only six years old and overall in good repair. According to Leslie, during the course of the Bingham investigation, "On September 10, 1863, Solomon S. Smith, the mason who built the 'Thomas House,' swore in an affidavit that he had used only the 'hardest and best quality bricks,' and that 'the foundation walls . . . were eighteen inches thick and the partition walls thirteen inches thick,' constructed upon 'solid clay seven feet deep.' Smith stated that he had laid the brick for all the buildings on the 'entire Block' to the same specifications."

Smith added that the walls of the Thomas House were sufficiently thick and substantial to support six stories. Smith also claimed that but for the undermining of the walls or removing the supports, "the Rev. R. S. Thomas Building was a good and substantial building, that the adjoining buildings were also good and substantial . . . and could only [have] given way by removing the columns or by cutting the walls or undermining the foundation in some way."

That very day, on September 10, one Elijah M. McGee, a future Kansas City mayor, gave Bingham an affidavit in which he swore that he had visited the place on August 11, two days before the Thomas House collapse. "He went into the cellar and found that the 'posts or columns' supporting the adjoining wall between the Cockerel and Thomas houses 'had been cut away from the girders . . . and the girders had already sunk two or three feet.'" Afraid that the building might fall at any moment, McGee had hurried outside.

That testimony was corroborated by Charles H. Vincent, McGee's son-in-law, who wrote that "Soldiers cut away and removed the center-posts or columns and partitions, leaving no support for the roof and joists of the Cockerel building." At some unspecified time after the Federal soldiers had removed some center posts from the Cockerel building, on a subsequent visit Vincent noticed that "the girders in the center of the Cockerel building on which the joists rested had given way and the building was about to fall."

And so, within days of the Thomas building collapse, three credible men, living in Kansas City within a few miles of Union headquarters, verified in sworn affidavits to what residents, Unionist and Secessionist alike, had heard on the street from the very day the Thomas building had collapsed. Union soldiers had intentionally removed center posts, which seemingly made the death of the five young women inevitable. But why?

Eleven years after the tragedy, Dr. Joshua Thorne, an acting assistant surgeon who had been in charge of the US General Hospital in Kansas City that August, explained in a sworn affidavit why the critical center posts (girders) in the adjoining Cockerel building had been removed. In addition to the "southern girls" on the second floor, other women "of bad character and diseased" were imprisoned in the Thomas House cellar. Historian Edward Leslie summarized Thorne's testimony: "The [Union] guards cut three large holes in the common cellar wall so that they might gain access to the whores. In no time at all, the cellar had become a house of prostitution," and "the guards in charge very frequently were in there [the Thomas House basement] and together with its inmates in a condition of most beastly intoxication." Thorne described venereal disease among the Union guards as "rampant."

Thorne had warned Union Army authorities that the building was insecure, but they did nothing, for reasons that remain unexplained to this day. Thorne concluded his testimony by stating that on the day before the collapse, he "found many of the female prisoners [in the Thomas House basement] intoxicated—one of the women was cutting with an axe at one of the posts in the basement—which supported a girder and upon which girder the joists of the floor above rested—[and I] reported to the officer on duty the fact of the drunken condition of the women and the danger in cutting away the supports of the building."

Thorne swore that he personally reported this dangerous condition to commanding general Thomas Ewing himself, only to arrive back at the Thomas House on Grand Avenue "in time to see the dust cloud rising and hear the screams."

The significant long-term effect of the calamity arising from this Union Army negligence, in the words of historian Richard Brownlee, cast a "shadow over the rest of the civil war on the [Missouri–Kansas] border," and aggravated what Richard S. Brownlee described in *Gray Ghosts of the Confederacy* as "the ferocious hatred of the guerrillas for the Union forces." According to Brownlee, the Thomas House tragedy "tore the last thin covering of mercy from the hearts of Quantrill's boys. More [seriously], from this moment on, Bill Anderson . . . became insane because of the injury to his sisters, and his attitude toward all men who supported or served the Union was that of a homicidal maniac."

Legend has it that Ohio native and Confederate guerrilla leader William Clarke Quantrill (Quantrell) conducted a deadly August 23, 1863, raid on Lawrence, Kansas, in revenge for the Thomas House collapse. This urban myth survives to this day on the Missouri side of the Missouri–Kansas border.

In fact, Quantrill conducted a war council on the Lawrence raid on August 10, 1863, three days before the Thomas House tragedy. Quantrill, his officers, and other Missouri partisan leaders debated the pros and cons of conducting the operations near Blue Springs, Missouri, a settlement whose founders included an ancestor of this writer. Many of the other partisan leaders initially opposed the raid. "The war council dragged on for twenty-four hours," historian Leslie recounted. "Lawrence was too deep in enemy territory, some argued, and there were too many Yankee troops prowling around; even if they could reach the town [in Kansas] with impunity, they would have to fight all the way back to Missouri."

"The undertaking is too hazardous," one lieutenant supposedly said. Quantrill conceded the point before arguing that "if you never risk, you will never gain." Quantrill supposedly refuted every objection and then turned to Fletch Taylor, a Missouri partisan who had just conducted a reconnaissance mission. Taylor reported that the only Union force in the area consisted of fresh white and black recruits; "The citizens were complacent and the streets were wide and ideal for charging horsemen."

William Gregg, one of the partisans present, "let his mind drift back to January 28, 1862," when Gregg personally witnessed the aftermath of a Kansas militia raid into Missouri. On that day he counted thirteen Missouri houses on fire. Gregg also reminded the group that only eight months before, in January 1863, a squad of Kansans had arrived at a Missouri farm nearby and forced the old woman who lived there "to cook them supper, then burned the house down. A foot of snow was on the ground and it was bitterly cold, but the womenfolk were not permitted to save even a shawl or coat from the flames." The Kansas militia supposedly took a farmer named Sanders "with them, though his wife begged for his life, and shot him soon after." More certainly, they killed a farmer named Jephthah Crawford that very night, supposedly "snatching the lace cap from his wife's gray head and casting it into the flames."

Even as the war council droned on all day, Quantrill knew that everyone present could recite Kansas atrocities that should be avenged. "Quantrill knew what was in their hearts," and made his closing argument, as Leslie recounted, summarizing the two sources of Missouri animosity: "Lawrence is the great hotbed of abolitionism in Kansas," or so Quantrill is quoted, but of even more importance to most present that day, "All the plunder—or the bulk of it—stolen from Missouri will be found stored away in Lawrence, and we can get more revenge and more money there than anywhere else in the state." Even though Quantrill's war council voted unanimously to conduct the raid on Lawrence a full seventy-two hours before the Thomas House collapse, as historian Leslie asserted, "The extraordinary savagery and wholesale destructiveness of the raid may be attributed in part to the bushwhacker's rage and indignation."

General Ewing only aggravated the Missouri hostility by issuing Order No. 10 five days after the Thomas House tragedy, directing his officers to

arrest and send to the district provost-marshal for punishment, all men (and all women not heads of families) who willfully aid and encourage guerrillas, with a written statement . . . of the proof against them. They will discriminate as carefully as possible between those who were compelled by threats or fears [sic] to aid the rebels and those who aid them from disloyal motives. The wives and children of known guerrillas, and also women, who are heads of families and are willfully engaged in aiding guerrillas, will be notified by such officers to remove out of this district and out of the State of Missouri forthwith. They will be allowed to take, unmolested, their stock, provisions and household goods. If they fail to remove promptly, they will be sent by such officers, under escort to Kansas City for shipment south, with their clothes and such necessary household furniture and provision as may be worth saving.

That very evening, on August 18, Quantrill moved his own partisan company to a farm owned by Confederate captain James Perdee on the Blackwater River, the planned staging area for the raid. The following morning, they gathered at the Benjamin Potter farm near Lone Jack, some sixty miles east of Lawrence. This was the very site where, exactly a year earlier, a Union Army disaster had occurred—accomplished in no small measure thanks to troops under Quantrill's command. After dinner, in the evening quiet, the three hundred learned that the target was Lawrence. According to later participant recollections, Quantrill told them that they all might well die, saying that "Any man who feels he is not equal to the task can quit, and no one will call him a coward." A handful of men did just that and rode away.

The next day took the raiders to the headwaters of the Grand River, four miles from the Kansas state line, not to be confused with the lower stretch of the Neosho River, also called the Grand. While riding on toward Lawrence, additional Confederate forces from northern Missouri, as well as some 50 local men, joined them in the late afternoon, bringing the total order of battle to 450 men, "the largest such force ever assembled during the entire Civil War," according to noted historian Albert Castel.

They rode across rolling prairies toward Lawrence, crossing the Kansas border and riding on to Squiresville, a long-abandoned and leveled nineteenth-century resort destination for Union soldiers described by one historian as the Civil War–era Sin City of Johnson County, Kansas.

And it was here that for the first time, at least in some accounts, Quantrill consulted a "death list" of men to be killed and houses to be burned that he had acquired from a Lawrence woman during a personal reconnoiter that Quantrill had conducted sometime before the raid. While most of the men rested, a hit squad selected by Quantrill supposedly visited the nearby home of one Colonel Sims. Since the colonel was not at home, they forced his wife to provide a sumptuous dinner, or so the story goes.

The expedition set off in the darkness for the Santa Fe Trail, which they followed for a few miles before heading north toward Lawrence, killing some ten Unionist men on their own doorsteps, in an eight-mile stretch, according to some accounts. One was a former Missourian, others were German immigrants. Joseph Stone, who lived some twelve miles from Lawrence, was one of them.

Two years earlier, Stone had one of Quantrill's lieutenants arrested in Kansas City. The brave guerrillas clubbed him to death rather than shooting him, for fear that one of Stone's neighbors would ride for Lawrence to alert Union authorities, or so the story goes.

Soon, the expedition rode through Franklin, yet another long-gone Kansas town a few miles east of Lawrence, between the Kansas and Wakarusa Rivers, which should not be confused with present-day Franklin, Kansas, some 136 miles to the south. Ironically enough, seven years earlier, Kansas abolitionists had targeted little Franklin twice for attack, led on the first offensive by John Brown. Now, in 1863, a doctor named R. L. Williams watched the Missourians ride through town just before dawn in a column of four, many tied to their saddles to avoid falling off their horses if they dozed off, hurried along the road by officers trying to arrive in Lawrence before daybreak. After leaving Franklin, the whole expedition broke into a gallop, or so said the good doctor.

Once they reached a ridge overlooking Lawrence, Quantrill sent six scouts forward while he entertained the nervous, reluctant men around him with stories about border ruffians, his experiences with Delaware Indians, and even his love life. Before the scouts returned, several of his men begged Quantrill to call off the raid, which only made him angry. "You can do as you please; I am going to Lawrence!" Quantrill yelled, as he galloped forward. One gallant rebel was heard to complain, "We are lost."

Yet the question remains: Why, of all the towns in Kansas, did the Missouri partisans target this town? Lawrence was the capital of the Free State movement in Kansas, served as one of the more-significant stops on the Underground Railroad, and was a Union soldier recruitment center. Also, "the town had been founded and initially settled by abolitionists and was named after a prominent Boston abolitionist and treasurer of the New England Emigrant Aide Company, Amos Lawrence." Before the war, Lawrencians made raids on nearby "Southern" strongholds to the east in Kansas and Missouri.

Charles Robinson, a leader of the Free State movement, and the first governor of Kansas, lived in Lawrence, as did Kansas guerrilla leader and US Senator James H. Lane. Missouri border Confederates often claimed that goods stolen in Missouri were auctioned at Lane's home, which supposedly contained two pianos stolen east of the Missouri–Kansas border.

Quantrill, it is said, recruited informants to stay at the Eldridge Hotel in Lawrence, which had been erected on the site of the Free State Hotel, burned in 1856 by Missouri ruffians. Frequent rumors of future raids into Lawrence by Quantrill and others prompted Lawrencians to organize a new home guard and demand that the federal government provide weapons. The rusty muskets that eventually arrived in Lawrence were stacked inside an arsenal, and, as a practical matter, therefore rendered useless at the insistence of the mayor, since citizens couldn't carry firearms inside city limits.

This is not to say no precautions at all were taken. Warned in July 1863 that Quantrill was preparing for a raid in mid-August, General Ewing sent one infantry company to Lawrence and another company to "a region of deep, narrow ravines and high hills with steep, rocky slopes thickly covered by dense woods and tangled thickets and pocketed with caves," near Blue Springs in Jackson County, Missouri, a village named for Sni-A-Bar Creek. Many, if not most, of Quantrill's original company came from Sni-A-Bar Township, often simply called Snibar. When mid-August 1863 passed without incident, General Ewing redeployed the Union soldiers away from Lawrence to the Snibar area. This effectively left Lawrence defended only by untrained and unarmed recruits, an opportunity that two Confederate spies, one of whom was black, soon reported to Quantrill.

The removal of Union troops from their midst somehow calmed the Lawrence population. After all, rumors of imminent attack by Quantrill and other Missouri partisans had plagued the Lawrencians for over three years, yet little or nothing had happened. The Lawrencians chose to believe newer rumors to the effect that Quantrill was now operating some fifty miles away.

Congregational clergyman Richard Cordley later remarked that Lawrencians "never felt more secure, and never were less prepared, than the night before the raid." Cordley also complained that "the military authorities at Kansas City, who ought to know, did not consider [Lawrence to be] in danger."

One prisoner taken during the August 23 Lawrence raid asked Quantrill almost in passing why he had not struck two weeks before. The guerrilla leader quipped that "You were expecting me then—but I have caught you napping now."

Several guerrillas peeled away from the column just east of town to kill Reverend S. S. Snyder, who served as a lieutenant and recruiting agent for the 2nd Colored Regiment. Snyder died milking a cow, while others began chasing young John Donnelly and Sallie Young, who had been out on a Sunday-morning ride. Donnelly escaped, but Miss Young was detained to act as a guide.

The beginning of the raid, as described by Edward E. Leslie in *The Devil Knows How to Ride*, seems today like something produced in Hollywood.

> *The guerrillas clattered into town, cutting across vacant lots and down empty streets. Near the center of Lawrence, Quantrill called a halt and sent Holt's company to cover the east side of town and Blunt's men to cover the west. He dispatched eleven men to Mount Oread to act as lookouts to watch for the approach of Federal troops, and then led the rest of the band toward the river. Gregg appeared and showed the way to a camp occupied by twenty-two recruits of the 14th Kansas Regiment. The bushwhackers galloped among the tents, knocking them down and trampling the soldiers under the horse hooves, shooting those who tried to run. Seventeen were killed, five were wounded.*

Nearby, the 2nd Colored Regiment heard the gunfire and fled, just as Quantrill led a wild charge down Massachusetts Street, the main thoroughfare. One frightened Lawrencian couldn't help but notice their horsemanship.

> *They rode with that ease and abandon which are acquired only by a life spent in the saddle amid desperate scenes. Their horses scarcely seemed to touch the ground, and the riders sat upon them with bodies erect and arms perfectly free with revolvers on full cock, shooting at every house and man they passed, and yelling like demons at every bound. On each side of this stream of fire . . . were men falling dead and wounded, and women and children, half-dressed, running and screaming—some trying to escape from danger and some rushing to the side of their murdered friends.*

They dashed along Massachusetts Street, shooting at every straggler on the sidewalk, and into almost every window. They halted in front of the Eldridge Hotel. The firing now ceased and all was silent for a few minutes. They evidently expected resistance here, and sat gazing at the rows of windows above them, apparently in fearful suspense.

What followed was so surreal that it might have been tragically amusing had it been portrayed in a film. When the hotel gong began to ring, Quantrill's men cursed and moved as far to the opposite side of the street as they could, eyes staring into the second-floor windows, from which the raiders apparently expected a torrent of gunfire. The provost marshal of Kansas, Captain Alexander R. Banks, happened to be a hotel resident. He "had been awakened by the gunfire and looked out a front window to see rebels in the street. In the hallway, guests were arguing over what should be done. Some nervous souls wanted to do nothing, to let events take their course and see what happened, but many more wanted to surrender the building if their safety were guaranteed. [Captain] Banks, who knew what the enemy was capable of, pulled a sheet off his bed and waved it out the window, calling for Quantrill."

The guerrilla leader was astride a brown gelding supposedly taken a year earlier from Union colonel James T. Buel of the 7th Missouri Cavalry during a minor engagement called the Battle of Independence, at the future hometown of President Harry S. Truman. A man present later recalled Quantrill wearing "a low-crowned, soft, black hat with a gold cord for a band. His face was sunburned and weather-beaten, and he had a few days' stubble of beard. He wore a brown woolen guerrilla shirt," noted William E. Connelly, which was "ornamented with fine needlework and made for him by some devoted daughter of the South. Four revolvers were stuck in his belt and his gray trousers were stuffed into handsome cavalry boots." Connelly also saw the exchange between Banks and Quantrill.

"What is your object in coming to Lawrence?" asked Banks. "Plunder," Quantrill quickly replied. "The house is surrendered," said Banks, as if he owned the place, "but we demand protection for the inmates." Quantrill agreed, wheeled around on his horse, ordered several men to stay with him, stood up in his stirrups, and then, according to Connelly, ordered, "Kill, kill and you will make no mistake! Lawrence should be thoroughly cleansed and the only way to cleanse it is to kill! Kill!"

Perhaps it was so.

Quantrill then ordered all the guests to leave, allowed some of his men to rob them, and sent others upstairs to ransack the rooms. Topeka, Kansas, judge L. D. Bailey put most of his valuables in a stove for safekeeping, only to learn that the place was going to be burned. Bailey helped carry an ailing Union officer out of the hotel, where he could see that the newspaper offices of the *Lawrence Republican* and the *Kansas Tribune* were already on fire.

Things only got worse from there, according to Leslie:

Men were spurring their horses up and down the street, firing their guns in the air and screaming; the saloons and whiskey shops having been the first places broken into, many of the mounted men were already reeling drunk in their saddles. Some had looted small toy American flags from a store and contemptuously tied them to their horses' tails. A Baptist preacher named Larkin M. Skaggs cut down a huge flag that had been flying from a tall flagstaff nearby and tied it to a long rope attached to his saddle. He raced up and down Massachusetts Street, said Bailey, "putting his horse through various turns fifty feet behind his horse in the deep dust . . . Skaggs's mount galloped close enough to the chair for the flag to be pulled through the major's line of sight. 'There they are, dragging the American flag in the dust! God damn them!'"

Quantrill protected certain other Lawrence residents, personally escorting some of the Eldridge Hotel guests to Nathan Stone's Whitney House, whose owner had done Quantrill a personal favor years before. That said, the Johnson House Hotel was burned to the ground, after most of the male guests were shot to death in the street.

Elsewhere in town, a Dr. Jerome Griswold and his new wife ran a boardinghouse whose residents included the editor of the *Lawrence State Journal*, as well as the owner of a grocery that Quantrill had been charged with burglarizing three years earlier. The bushwhackers shot two Griswold boardinghouse residents, one of whom died. Lane, meanwhile, was making arrangements at his own home nearby.

Leslie recounted that

[a]t the first sound of gunfire, Lane had leaped out of bed and wrenched the nameplate off his front door. He sprinted through his house and went out the back door, hightailing it across a cornfield barefoot and clad only in his nightshirt. He ran over hills and through fields until he came to a deep ravine, where he hid for a time. He started out again, still heading west, and eventually came to a farmhouse where he borrowed a battered straw hat, a pair of old shoes and a pair of trousers. The owner was as short and fat as Lane was tall and lean, so the outfit added to the general's comical appearance.

Eventually, Lane bought or borrowed a plow horse that he rode bareback to warn surprised farmers about the raid. Back in Lawrence, Quantrill soon found the Lane house. Leslie noted that

[c]atching Lane had been a major objective of the raid—Quantrill meant to take him back to Jackson County and hang him—but the only consolation was to burn his magnificent new home. Though her husband was the most hated enemy, Quantrill and his men treated Mrs. Lane with utmost courtesy. Before they torched the house, they let her save many of her possessions and assisted her in carrying canned fruit and preserves out of the cellar. As the flames spread, she wrung her hands over the loss of the piano in the parlor, so they went back inside and cheerfully wrestled with it.

Since the piano was bulky and some of Quantrill's men terribly drunk, they eventually abandoned it. Strangely enough, Quantrill had a seemingly pleasant exchange with Lane's wife, in which he said "with ironic courtesy" that he would be glad to meet Lane. She responded with appropriately cryptic manners that "Mr. Lane would be glad to meet you under . . . more favorable circumstances."

This was not to be. Quantrill's raiders killed some 150 Lawrence citizens that day, leaving over 175 businesses burning to the ground as they left town. Among the more noteworthy participants that day, other than one of this writer's ancestors, were Cole Younger, future partner of Jesse and Frank James. Lawrence Massacre historian Edward E. Leslie credits Younger with saving at least a dozen people. Possibly, more were saved by using secret Freemason hand signals.

After the Massacre, Quantrill led his band, now astride rested, fresh horses stolen in Lawrence, to the southeast along the Lawrence–Fort Scott road even as Senator Lane loped back into town on his borrowed plow horse without a saddle. Lane recruited some dozen men to chase after Quantrill on the very horses the raiders had ridden into town.

CHAPTER 6

The Battle of Commando Bridge

THE JUNE 1940 LETTER TO JOHN SLATER WAS STRAIGHTFORWARD enough. The British Army was looking for men of good physique, able to swim and navigate boats and do hazardous work while demonstrating initiative and leadership. Slater—honorifically renamed Durnford-Slater, but in this chapter simply called Slater—was then serving as the adjutant for the 23rd Medium and Heavy Training Regiment, Royal Artillery, stationed at Plymouth, England, 216 miles southeast of London. He was responsible for all organizational, administrative, and disciplinary matters in the regiment. Slater, then thirty-one, convinced his commanding officer to sign a recommendation for the new mission that Slater himself would write.

Sooner than Slater expected, his commanding officer, Colonel J. V. Naisby, handed him the letter Slater had been hoping for, in British officialese.

CAPT. J. F. DURNFORD SLATER ADJUTANT 23RD MEDIUM AND HEAVY TRAINING REGT. R.A. IS APPOINTED TO RAISE AND COMMAND NUMBER 3 COMMANDO IN THE RANK OF LIEUT. COLONEL. GIVE EVERY ASSISTANCE AND RELEASE FROM PRESENT APPOINTMENT FORTHWITH AS OPERATIONAL ROLE IMMINENT.

Slater learned later that No. 1 and No. 2 Commando did not yet exist when he received the appointment. Originally, both units were intended to be airborne units, but that part of the plan had already been abandoned by the time Slater was recruited. As recounted in his memoir, *Commando: Memoirs of a Fighting Commando in World War Two*, the primary source for this chapter, Slater later recalled with a hint of surprise: "This made me the first Commando soldier of the war. I had wanted action: I was going to get it. I should have been delighted to join at any rank, but was naturally pleased to get command. I was confident I could do the work and made up my mind to produce a really great unit. I owed it to my mother."

His reasoning for that is understandable.

My mother had a strong will. Her father had been in the army and so had her husband. My father, Captain L. F. Slater, was a regular officer in the Royal Sussex Regiment. I last saw him on August 5, 1914, when I was five and a half years old; he had come to join us on holiday at Milton-on-Sea before leaving for France with the British Expeditionary Force (BEF). I remember that just before his arrival I had an encounter with a small boy who told me he was German. I promptly struck him in the nose, drawing blood. I was being led away toward the chastisement I deserved when my father arrived and distracted Mother from her purpose. My father was killed in action a month later, and my mother made it clear to me that I should follow him into the army. She put me down for Wellington, the school with the strongest army tradition in Britain.

Slater entered Wellington, a school in a town of the same name in Somerset, at age thirteen. He developed an initial dislike for everything associated with the Officer Training Corps—the drills, the marching, and even the uniform. Above all, he hated Wednesdays, when he was likely to be yelled at for marching out of step in an untidy uniform. On his all-too-rare vacations back home at Instow in North Devon, the young student listened for hours to neighbors who had returned to the small village after careers in Argentina. He too wanted to raise horses in Argentina, but his mother bluntly told him they didn't have the money. "The army is your best chance" she told him again and again, even though he refused to join his father's regiment, the Royal Sussex. He studied at the Royal Military Academy at Woolwich in southeast London at age eighteen, then was off to India as part of the Royal Artillery in 1929.

He considered the six years he spent there to be "first-rate sport: football, cricket, hockey, plenty of riding and wild boar hunting, known then and there as 'pig-sticking.'" Returning to England in 1935, he found the British Army at a low ebb, and intended to resign—until events at Munich convinced him to stay.

The beginning of the war found him serving as the adjutant of an antiaircraft unit in southwest England, bored to death training troops when he felt he should be knee-deep in the fighting.

All too soon Slater was standing in front of General Sir Robert Haining, deputy chief of the Imperial General Staff, who warned him that he might have to go operational in a fortnight (a British expression, meaning fourteen nights).

Fortunately, he had prior experience in recruiting, which soon paid off. "From volunteers who, like me, had answered the first letter, I made my choice," he recalled. "I wanted cheerful officers, not groaners. A good physique was important, but size was not. I looked for intelligence and keenness."

Slater developed a recruiting method for the Commandos which worked quite well. He looked for men with leadership potential and character "beyond the normal." He automatically eliminated anyone who was boastful, even if that candidate had other strong attributes, such as athleticism. Also, he eliminated anyone who simply talked too much.

On Sunday morning, July 14, 1940, Slater ran into his sister and her husband having breakfast at the Royal Castle Hotel in Dartmouth. The Franklins were there to see their son, a student at the Royal Naval College. Slater was in the area, or so he told them, to conduct some training, when in fact he was preparing to launch the first Commando 3 mission. The operation, prepared in response to a specific request from Prime Minister Winston Churchill, provided for a small-scale raid on the island of Guernsey, an island in the English Channel just off the Normandy coast.

Guernsey had recently been occupied by some 469 German soldiers who had established machine-gun nests all along the coast. Earlier, Slater had been called to London to plan the attack with once-famous film star David Niven, who had deferred his film career to become a staff officer in the Combined Operations Headquarters. Now, at Dartmouth, Slater was called away from breakfast into a hallway, only to learn that the plan for the coming attack had been changed.

"Jerry is too strong," the staff officer told him. "He's been reinforced at some of the places where we intended to land."

Slater and the staff officer planned a new operation on the spot.

"Now we were to land in Telegraph Bay on the south side of the island, just west of the Jerbourg Peninsula, and not on the north coast as originally decided. We were to sail at six o'clock that evening. Our role was still to create a diversion for the Independent Company under Colonel Ronnie Tod, which was to attack the airfield."

They prepared for the mission in a gymnasium at the Royal Navy College, Dartmouth, on a beautiful summer evening. Some of the Naval College students helped them load machine guns. Slater also prepared briefings for the naval commanders and his own men. They left to board a destroyer at about 5:45 p.m.

Slater went over the final details with his officers in the captain's cabin on the *Scimitar*, an S-class destroyer launched in 1918. They had been so busy that entire day, obtaining and issuing weapons, that this was the first opportunity to discuss the newly modified mission together. One party led by Lieutenant Joe Smales was tasked to "establish a road block on the road leading from the Jerbourg Peninsula to the rest of the island, so that [the rest of the men] would not be interrupted by German reinforcements." Slater's own party was to attack a machine-gun nest and put the cable [communications] hut at the foot of the Peninsula out of action.

"Captain V. T. G. de Crespigny, the troop commander of H Troop, with the main party was to attack the barracks situated on the Peninsula, and Peter Young was to guard the beach. Peter did not relish the job, as he wanted more action," Slater recalled.

Slater scratched that itch by telling Peter that if the beach was quiet, he could join in the action. The password for the operation was Desmond. Slater later noted that this operation, like most wartime missions, did not go forward as planned. Problems developed, including the loss of two air-sea rescue launches due to motor and mechanical issues. Still, by midnight, Slater could see the dark, challenging high cliffs on the south side of Guernsey.

"We crept along the length of the island. At about a quarter to one I saw our gap in the cliff, the place where we were to climb to the top. On our right, Telegraph Point reached out into the sea. Our two launches slid alongside the destroyer and we clambered down on rope nettings. The sea was calm. It was dead easy."

From his own launch, Slater watched the other launches silently leave their mother ship and all head in the same direction, exactly as had been planned.

"My own eyes were on the cliffs," he later remembered, "and I was astonished to note that we were heading out to sea in the direction of Brittany." Slater quickly convinced the launch skipper that this was a problem. The boat compass, as luck would have it, had been knocked out of kilter.

Slater ordered his men to go straight in to the beach, and as they did, he couldn't help but notice that a large rock visible in the distance resembled, of all things, a German U-boat. He could hear the launches hit bottom, due to the fact that the operation had been postponed for forty-eight hours, causing them to come in through a high tide which nearly knocked Slater down when he jumped out. Half the men around him were coughing up salt water.

After loosening his uniform with the others to let out the sea water, Captain Slater and one of his sergeants, a man named Knight, ran to the top of their objective, a cliff top accessible by concrete steps that were 250 feet straight up. The captain knew the operation was behind, but at this point there was little they could do, other than listen to a chorus of barking dogs living in several houses nearby. Slater had ordered up an airplane to circle over the prospective battle site and cover over the noises made by his company. When the airplane arrived, Slater could focus more intently on the mission.

The machine-gun post, which was the first objective of my little group, was at the tip of the Jerbourg Peninsula, eight hundred yards from the landing place. I went as far as the barracks with de Crespigny. Just before going into the barracks, de Crespigny broke into a house to get information from the householder. I went in with him through the back door. However, the man we found was so terrified that he had entirely lost the power of speech; all he could do was let out a series of shrieks. We left de Crespigny and began climbing back down the cliff. I sent [several men] to the cable hut. Johnny Giles and I crawled up on either side of the little mound in which the machine-gun nest was dug. I carried grenades and a .45 Webley; Giles, a giant of well over six feet, had a tommy gun. We jumped to our feet and into the nest, a sandbagged circle. We were both ready to shoot, but I found myself face-to-face with Johnny's tommy gun, and he with my Webley.

"Hell!" said Johnny bitterly, "there's no one here!"

The rest of the men were just as disappointed. A man named Knight begged Slater to let him blow the place up.

"No. Apparently the Germans don't know yet that we've come," Slater said. "There's no point in announcing it. Just cut the cables."

Then Slater nearly got himself killed. He and some of his men were checking on de Crespigny when a large hulking soldier approached Slater and put a bayonet in his ribs. Slater recognized one of his men named Gimbert, but barked out "Desmond," the password, as if he'd never met the man.

"Desmond!" I said. Gimbert, recognizing my voice, removed the bayonet quickly.
"All right, Colonel." I thought he sounded disappointed.

De Crespigny didn't find anyone in the barracks, nor had Slater found any Germans in the machine-gun nest he had scouted. He fully expected an exchange of gunfire between the Germans and the Brits, but other than barking dogs, all he heard was silence, as he noticed that it was 2:45 a.m.

Slater and his men lined up using a Guernsey landmark called the Doyle Monument, honoring Sir John Doyle (1756–1834), lieutenant governor of Guernsey. Every last man was disappointed that they had not encountered any Germans. And they had to be back at the beach in ten minutes—or so they thought. While they were running back down the concrete steps, Slater slipped and fell down—discharging the pistol he was carrying in the process.

"This at last brought the Germans to life," Slater recalled. Almost at once there was a line of tracer machine-gun fire from the top of the cliff on the other side of our cove. The tracers were going out to sea, towards the spot where I thought our launches must be awaiting us."

Instead, since they arrived late for the rendezvous and Slater's men went back to the boat in a single dinghy, until that last dinghy washed against the rocks, broke up, and sank, at the loss of at least one Commando. Slater and several of his men had to swim for it, leaving three men who didn't know how behind, with the faint hope that a submarine would come back for them the next morning.

And with that, Slater began the swim. He took off some of his clothes and noticed that several men in the group had stripped naked for the swim, even as Slater carried a cigarette case from his wife and his father's whiskey flask. The trouble was, a strong sea now coming in made the one hundred yards to the launches seem more like a mile, as breakers washed over them. Finally, he felt the helping hands of a sailor on the launch, hauling him on board. The flask and the cigarette case were missing. Worse yet, his watch had stopped. He learned that it was 3:30 a.m., and assumed they had missed their destroyer.

Slater now assessed the positives and negatives of this mission experience. He noted that the men had acted admirably during the difficult swim back to the launches, with no yelling or screaming, and no signs of panic. Likewise, the launch crews had done everything they could to get the tired men back on board with a minimum of trouble. That said, Slater recalled,

With dawn half an hour off, it looked as if we should have to head for home on the launches. This was not a prospect to bring delight. The crews of these boats were brave men, mostly yachtsmen, with no service experience.

At this point, they seemed unable to reach a decision for further action. The second launch had just broken down: ours threw it a line and had it in tow. There was a general discussion of the situation by all hands. Even the engine attendant left his recess to chip in.

"What the hell are we going to do now?" asked the mechanic, bringing [me to my feet]. "For heaven's sake," [I said], or something more profane.

And with that their launch pulled out for sea. They were sure that the *Scimitar* had already left without them, leaving Slater's launch, and a second launch they were towing, to sail back to England across the Channel. Whether or not they would be picked off by German fighters patrolling the English Channel would purely be a matter of luck. Desperate though he was, Slater asked the launch captain for a torch, which he flashed seaward in one last gesture. Within seconds, much to his surprise, a series of answering flashes appeared in the distance. They came from the *Scimitar*, whose captain had decided to make one last sweep, looking for British launches in the few minutes remaining before sunrise would bring the German Luftwaffe, rising from at least a dozen airfields only a few air miles away. There was no hope of British Hurricanes rising to defend them so early in the war.

The three non-swimmers left behind became prisoners for the rest of the war. Slater was both honest and realistic in his assessment of this first British Commando raid, which he considered

a ridiculous, almost comic failure. We had captured no prisoners. We had done no serious damage. We had caused no casualties to the enemy. Even the roll of barbed wire for Lieutenant Smale's roadblock had proved too heavy to lift up the steep steps. There had been no machine-gun nest, and, to all practical purposes, no barracks. We had cut through three telegraph cables. A youth in his teens have done the same.

On the credit side, we had gained a little experience and had learned some of the things not to do. It was very clear that we urgently needed good and reliable landing craft for such an operation. It was equally clear that two hours on shore was long enough to accomplish any worthwhile aim.

Of course, the Prime Minister, whose promptings had largely initiated the Commando idea, had a complete report of the operation in a few hours. He didn't like it. He sent a strong directive to Headquarters Combined Operations.

The prime minister didn't mince any words. "Let there be no more silly fiascos like those perpetrated at Guernsey," he wrote. "The idea of working all these coasts up against us by pinprick raids is to be strictly avoided."

Slater agreed. "Churchill was dead right. He meant that we should go about this Commando business properly." He also "was more than ever determined to mould a unit that would take any raid in stride and bring back results. Only results mattered. I knew that I had a long way to go to achieve them."

Slater learned as he went, during engagements in the Lofoten Islands of Norway. These experiences were a prelude for a perilous Commando landing in Sicily behind enemy lines in mid-July 1943, as he recounted later.

July 13 brought new orders for Slater. He was to meet General Bernard "Monty" Montgomery, as well as General Dempsey and Admiral McGrigor, for some operational planning. While he traveled to the meeting he watched a Messerschmitt turn an oil tanker into a massive fire burning hundreds of feet in the air, several football fields away.

Slater met with the two generals and the admiral in Syracuse, among bombed-out buildings and other ruins. General Dempsey led the discussion: "We've got a new operation for you tonight." This could have been almost anything. "It's an ambitious one," Dempsey continued. Slater recalled in his memoir that "Monty aimed to push right on to Catania," on the east coast of Sicily facing the Ionian Sea, *in one bound. Only one road ran from Syracuse to Catania, and he wanted to cut this at two points so as to disorganize the one and only main line of communication of the Germans and Italians with their bases. There was to be an airborne drop to seize and hold the Primosole Bridge, a few miles from Catania. No. 3 Commando was to land ten miles behind the lines and advance seven miles inland to seize the Punta dei Malati, a bridge over the Leonardo River two miles north of Lentini. Monty's intelligence men, usually unerringly exact, said that only Italian opposition was likely to be met on the beaches. They knew of no German troops in the vicinity.*

Slater thought otherwise. "I have an instinct for danger and was not so sure. That bridge was the only road linking the German and Italian armies with their bases in the Messina area. It seemed likely to me that Jerry would want to make sure it was well guarded."

Monty was confident as usual, Slater recalled. "Everybody's on the move now," Monty said, with vigor. "The enemy is nicely on the move. We want to keep him that way. You can help us do it. Good luck, Slater."

Slater thought that this "was a bold gamble which would probably come off. I didn't mind taking gambles for Monty and Dempsey. We should be out on our own with no one to help us, and it was up to us to look out for ourselves." As they left, Dempsey turned to Slater and said, "If by chance, 50 Division, who will be leading our troops, doesn't get through to you by first light tomorrow morning, clear off and hide up for the day."

Slater later recalled the details.

The landing would be seven miles due east of the target bridge at a small village called Agnone. Slater and his leadership team had less than two hours to issue operational orders and brief the men on the complexities of this mission. They had to land in two flights, and had no air photographs with which to plan, even if they had been given the time to do so.

There were complications, of course.

"Halfway to the place where the landing craft were to be lowered, a German E-boat appeared and fired two torpedoes at us. The Captain went full ahead and torpedoes passed close under our stern." The landing was smooth enough, but Slater recalled, "Before we hit the beach a concentrated crossfire was opened on us from several pillboxes. We returned the fire heavily, but, surprisingly, the enemy continued his machine-gun attack, unlike the wilting fire during the earlier landing. The whole place was lit up with tracer bullets which passed angrily in the air from both directions. A sailor was shooting from just behind me so that the muzzle of his weapon was only a few inches from my head."

Somebody yelled an order not to shoot the colonel, but Slater "found it all most exhilarating. There was a bright moon and we could see men running about on the beach. Johnny Dowling was standing beside me firing magazine after magazine from the Vickers K gun. Streams of tracers were flying in all directions. The noise was too great for me to make myself heard, so I was slapping Johnny's face to indicate to him which way to fire. We continued in good formation and hit the beach."

Once again there were complications.

Slater landed two boat lengths away from the rest of the craft. "The officer carrying the Bangalore torpedo was keen to redeem himself and tried to follow me out of the craft, but in his anxiety, he got the Bangalore jammed across a three-foot ramp leading from the boat." In doing so, the hapless torpedo carrier kept the rest of the men from coming ashore. Slater "was left nakedly alone on the beach for what seemed a very long time. The sand boiled up around me as the bullets struck. Somebody also started throwing grenades down the cliff at me. I thought the bullets were enough without these extras."

The Germans didn't agree.

When all the British boats were beached, Slater heard a cheer go up as the men began working on the wire. The second flight landed as well. Later, Slater learned that Lieutenant G. W. Holt, who minutes before had kept one of the sailors from shooting him by accident, was killed just after the second flight landed, even as Slater himself was looking at a prisoner just captured.

"I looked at the prisoner," Slater recalled. "He was in a German uniform." Of course this was not good news, because the presence of German soldiers instead of Italians usually ensured stiff opposition.

Slater soon "caught up with Peter Young, who was firing a Bren gun against a German machine-gun position." Walter Skrine was "spotting the effect of [Young's] fire. The German machine gun fired back," and Skrine was hit in the leg. Slater sent for help and then moved forward toward the village of Agnone, where, as he recalled, "we had a series of violent little battles. We had to advance continually against machine-gun posts. In one foray, George Herbert was knocked unconscious by an exploding grenade. He was bleeding from one ear. He seemed to recover consciousness."

"How are you George?" Slater asked. Herbert could only groan that he was getting weaker, but as Slater remembered it: "[F]ortunately, he had just had a temporary concussion. In ten minutes he was on his feet and leading the advance in his useful fighting, forceful style," as were three other aggressive Commandos. "We passed Agnone station, and just as we did, Captain Tim Leese, the Commander of No. 1 Troop, was shot through the eye." Then everything seemed to quiet down.

But not for long, for "it was then, in the freshly quiet night, that I heard the drone of many aircraft. Very soon they were overhead and through the night at least a dozen parachutes bloomed in the sky. These airborne troops were dropped at the wrong place, having been assigned to attack a bridge at Primosole."

Half apologizing, Slater told the newcomer that the Primosole Bridge was one hell of a long way off, and directed him to join the Commandos.

"Sorry sir," said the corporal, "I've got my orders." And with that, the corporal led his men off toward the bridge. Slater, of course, had his own problems.

"I was now leading the way along a railway line. It was easier going here. We walked in double line, one file [column] on each side of the tracks. It was absolutely quiet now and there was little cover for an enemy ambush. I felt reasonably secure, for I imagined that the enemy had his troops on the roads. I called a short halt for a troop commander meeting and to check up on casualties. We had 30 men behind on the beach, giving us 160 officers and men."

Slater encouraged his officers to keep up the pace if they could, in the three miles of rough country that loomed just ahead between them and the bridge they had to reach before the Germans retreated there. Soon Slater ordered a change of tactics.

"We struck across country, leaving the railway line behind. We found ourselves in rocky, low hills and forced our way through bramble thickets and over stone walls. Then we came to the Leonardo [River], about a mile beneath the bridge."

One of the men thought the river was shallow enough to cross there but walked in and quickly found himself underwater. Slater and his crew tried several times to find good river crossing north of the bridge they were to attack, in order to preserve the element of surprise. Finally, after several furtive attempts, they found a place they could ford in waist-high water. They quietly moved through some olive trees at about midnight, while watching a German truck cross the bridge with lights off, the driver no doubt hoping that the Allied troops were miles away.

Midnight was upon them.

It was up to Bill Lloyd and his men to clear the pillboxes. I went with him. We walked the road together. The night was as still as it would have been in the heart of Cornwall. Then Lieutenant Brian Butler, commanding the leading section, rushed each pillbox with his men, throwing grenades which split the silence with their reports . . .

. . . There were shouts and loud groans. The pillboxes at our end of the bridge were all cleared in ten minutes. The position was quickly consolidated and we made our dispositions for the events to come. The ground was like concrete.

Despite our efforts, it was not possible in the time available to dig proper defensive positions. The best we could do was to make use of the concrete works constructed by the Italians, mostly pillboxes. We settled in, and I thought we had done well to get there. We were out on our own, ten miles ahead of the Eighth Army, right across the enemy line of communication.

Slater told one of his men to get ready for the hundreds of Italian prisoners they could anticipate taking in the days to come. Almost on cue, the first of them came in, led by a soldier who was yelling and screaming so loudly he would soon give the British position away. Slater had one of his men knock the man out with a single punch, and then he took a quick snooze, much shorter than he had hoped for, interrupted by an enemy mortar round falling all too close to their position.

The Italians were only getting started.

"For the next few hours," Slater recalled, "they literally showered us with mortar bombs, inflicting many casualties." By the time the second British detachment arrived, some fifteen men had been killed or wounded. The pillboxes the Brits had occupied would only accommodate about a dozen of the 350 officers and men on hand.

> There was a clump of evergreen trees beyond the far end of the bridge. Out of it, unexpectedly, a Tiger tank appeared. It started shooting at us with its eighty-eight and its machine gun. I knew then that we were facing Germans as well as Ities [Italian soldiers]. Later I learned that a parachute company had been quartered in the woods the day before. As I was conferring with Charlie Head in an adjacent olive grove, a branch sliced clean off by an eighty-eight shell fell on top of me. A minute later, I felt the wind of another shell parting my hair.

There wasn't time to worry about these close calls, since the Brits were now confronted with a large constant flow of German trucks coming toward them from Messina. Slater stationed some of his men about a hundred yards from the bridge to maximize damage to trucks coming their way. Angered that the casualties in his own unit were higher than expected, Slater charged one of the lorries. Although a large German surprised and nearly killed Slater, one of Slater's men managed to kill him with a single shot.

Herbert told Slater, with respect, that he should get back to the regiment paperwork, just as another German truck drove up. A young British officer named Cave went right up to it, fired his Piat antitank gun into the cab, and died in the resulting explosion. More injuries quickly followed: A mortar fractured one man's ankles; another was killed charging a German machine-gun nest just before one of his comrades lost two fingers in a gunfight. And they still had to deal with the Tiger tank on the far side of the bridge that had yet to be taken.

Slater had to act—and soon. He sent for John Pooley, one of his most dependable soldiers. Slater pointed out a house just in front of their position and told Pooley

> *[to] get our Troop into that house and see if you can shoot up the tank. You may be able to reach it with your Piat mortar.*
>
> *As I was talking to him, mortar bombs were falling around us and John kept diving to the ground. He said afterwards that he thought I was very brave, standing up and not diving every time the mortar bombs burst. I had done plenty of diving early on, but got tired of it and decided that there was just as good a chance standing up . . .*
>
> *. . . John Pooley went off with his Troop in extended line and we gave him covering fire. The tank opened up with its machine gun. I was horrified to see the entire line fall together, then breathed again when they picked themselves up. They had merely fallen over a trip wire which, fortunately, had not been mined. A moment later they were in the house and, using it for cover, fired heavily on the tank with their Brens and a Piat. Unfortunately, the Piat, which could have knocked the tank out, was just beyond its effective range . . .*
>
> *. . . The bridge was about 120 yards long. Eventually, No. 3 Troop, moving under it, was halfway to the other side. Then the German paratroops lining the far bank began to shoot down on them. Taking whatever cover the bridge could give them, they [the Brits] held out for about an hour on the other side of the river. Then I ordered them to withdraw. Of sixty men, eight were casualties. While they were under the bridge they managed to remove demolition charges which the Germans had laid, saving the bridge from being blown up.*

Supposedly, the 50th British Division would relieve them by 4:30 a.m. That didn't happen, because the 50th was unexpectedly engaged in a major battle near Lentini, even as a major battle with the Germans unfolded at the Primosole Bridge. Knowing that he couldn't hold his bridge outright,

Slater moved his men to hills above the structure in hopes he could hold out there.

Troop by troop, they began advancing the operation.

Now our training and discipline proved their values. One section climbed the first hill in extended order, accurately pursued by airbursts from the [German] tank eighty-eight. A shell burst over the middle of the section and a man dropped, but the rest were unhurt. This revealed that our disbursed formations, on which we had insisted during training, actually did minimize casualties. Another shell burst directly behind him, seriously wounding Charlie Head. When [Head] fell, Lofty King picked him up and started to carry him along with the rest of us.

"Drop me and go on," Charlie said to him. "I wouldn't do this for you."

Lofty stopped dead in his tracks. "No," he muttered, "I don't believe you would," and continued to carry him.

They were two big men. They made quite a lump together.

We reached the railway line again. The fragments from the airburst shells made nasty sounds, ricocheting from the lines . . . Shortly we were established, however, in a good position on the hill. The tank had crossed the bridge after us and got busy sweeping the hill with its machine gun. I called for another troop commander meeting.

"It's obvious that 50 Division can't reach us," [I said]. "There's nothing more for us here. We must get back. Our only chance is to split into small parties. Lie up where you can during the day and make your way back to our lines tonight."

Slater hid two men who were too badly injured to move into a house, even as they both assured Slater they would be fine. Then Slater and his remaining men found a good place to hide in some thick olive groves.

After mistaking some German soldiers for his own men, Slater and the rest ran toward the crest of a small hill even as bullets kicked up dry dust behind them. Worse still, Slater spotted Germans just ahead, or so he thought, until he realized that this time he was right. Slater and the rest now found a deep ditch and lay down on their backs in the coming darkness, watching the occasional Spitfire above them flying westward to home after missions.

Slater envied those pilots more than he could admit to himself. "I thought the old game was getting very rough, and wondered how the rest [of my] unit was getting on. I also thought that it was not as much fun being hunted, and that if I ever got out of this alive, I would not go hunting or shooting again," an attitude Slater shared with this writer's own father, a veteran of the World War II Burma campaign.

On a more positive note, Slater had the long period of "quiet thought and contemplation" that his boss in earlier days, Brigadier General Charles Haydon, considered essential for commanding officers in battle.

Soon, however, Slater didn't have much time to think. "From time to time, parties of enemy soldiers came our way." Fortunately for the Brits, none of them looked down in the ditches as they passed by. "Had they done so, they would have had a very warm reception," Slater opined.

When night turned to day, Slater and his men resumed their ten-mile run for safety. He recalled later that "The first two miles, through olive groves, were the most tiring: we were bent double all the way, since the branches were thick and low." Long before they had hoped, Slater and the others were challenged by an enemy soldier guarding the Agnone-Lentini road.

"Give us some covering fire!" Slater yelled to one of his men. Later he recalled: "It was another bright, moonlit night, and I saw him throw his last grenade with great accuracy to the door of the post." It failed to explode. "We ran across the road in groups of two or three. Each time there was a brief burst of enemy fire. Again, we were lucky, and none of us was hit. The rest of the way was plain walking, but plenty of it. Finally we reached an Eighth Army antiaircraft position. After a few hours' sleep, we started collecting No. 3 Commando together again. Small parties were scattered over the countryside, having undergone similar experiences."

Two of his men were captured by Germans. The Germans were in turn captured by the British, who liberated the two short-time POWs.

Not everything worked out quite that well for the British Commandos that day.

"Losses had been severe, and a good many men had been taken prisoner. Most of these returned to us." One man broke out of his POW camp in the middle of Germany and made his way back to Britain by way of the Pyrenees Mountains and the Rock of Gibraltar. Three others escaped from a POW train as it was crossing Brenner Pass and walked six hundred miles to the coast of Italy.

Despite unspeakable German atrocities during the war, Slater recalled that so far as his own men were concerned, "All those who had been made prisoner spoke in very high terms of the 4th German Parachute Brigade. They [the British prisoners] were well-fed and well-treated, and said that the training and discipline of the Germans was very similar to our own."

A number of the Commandos received Military Crosses. Eventually, Slater met with General Montgomery himself. "That was a classic operation, classic," said Monty. "I want you to have [them] engrave 'No. 3 Commando Bridge' on a good piece of stone. Have this stone built into the masonry of the bridge."

Commando Bridge, as things turned out, was a prologue for a particularly challenging campaign in Sicily at a place called Termoli.

CHAPTER 7

An Incident at Termoli

Although I was to remain a Lieutenant-Colonel, the General confirmed my appointment to command a brigade. This consisted of No. 3 Commando [where Slater started], Commando No. 40, Royal Marine Commando, and the Special Raiding Squadron. No. 40 Commando was the original Royal Marine Commando, an entirely volunteer unit, and at that time under the command of Colonel "Pops" Manners. The Special Raiding Squadron, formed from veterans of the desert war, was commanded by an enormous Irishman, Colonel Paddy Mayne. I felt I had a really strong force.

So begins the Slater narrative in his memoir, *Commando: Memoirs of a Fighting Commando in World War Two*, which served as the primary source for this chapter. Slater thought he would be allowed to be in the D-Day landings after the operations in Italy, but Dempsey offered him a brigadier general promotion for staying in Italy with the 13th Corps. Slater courteously turned him down. Later, in his memoir, Slater expressed his frustration with the availability of only one coastal road on which to operate, making it easy for the Germans to delay them.

General Dempsey decided to use Slater's Brigade as an advance force in the offensive to come. Bagnara, a town near the very toe of Italy, was the first landing target. There was no German opposition to speak of, but one yarn told for years afterward mentioned certain women in Bagnara giving out "poisonous" kisses, a claim duly noted in the Eighth Army

Intelligence Summary, or so the story goes. Slater's longtime friend and associate Paddy Mayne landed in Bagnara on September 5, 1943, and "successfully moved several miles beyond it."

"Encouraged by this success, General Dempsey decided to launch a further seaborne attack on Vibo Valentia, some thirty miles further up the west coast. This landing was to be made by 231 Brigade and our Commando Brigade. General Urquart, later of Arnhem fame, commanded the landing."

General Dempsey ordered Slater not to participate in the operation for fear that having a second brigade commander present would only complicate things. Admiral McGrigor, then serving as First Sea Lord, was wounded by a Messerschmitt strafing the shore.

This gave Slater and the men he commanded a few days to rest up before going into battle mode at Salerno, 353 kilometers (219 miles) north on the coast. Slater and his men were not needed as it turned out, so Slater decided to quickly motor over to Bari and begin planning his part of an operation there. The Eighth British Army was moving quickly up the coast, but Kesselring, from all appearances, might make a stand at a good defensive position on the River Biferno. "Monty [General Montgomery] had decided to flank this position by making a landing with our brigade two miles north of the river at Termoli," Slater recalled, "a small medieval town with a useful harbor. With Termoli in our hands, the German armies would be forced to withdraw to the north. The Commando Brigade was moved in landing craft round the bottom of Italy."

Slater found the "trip across Italy was intriguing, as the country had not been properly cleared of the enemy and there were interesting possibilities round each corner. The country was hilly and attractive. In each village, a crowd assembled as we passed through and gave us a cheer."

The British Airborne took the town of Bari just before Slater's Brigade arrived, so there was nothing left to do but go to the Albergo Imperiale Hotel and order spumante cocktails. After some quality time with the local female talent, the Brigade leadership began planning for the Termoli assault. The town was occupied by a garrison of some five hundred paratroopers from the very same 4th German Parachute Brigade which Slater's brigade had engaged before in the Commando Bridge battle.

"We're going to have a hell of a battle," one of the planners told Slater as they looked at the plans for the Termoli assault. Slater thought the man was right, but was totally confident about victory. This was because

[w]e expected to be about twenty miles ahead of the Eighth Army when we landed, and we knew that Monty and Dempsey would make a great effort to catch up with us quickly. We got out an operation order which filled only one sheet of paper. I liked to keep such things simple. An ordinary infantry brigade would have used at least twenty-five sheets for the same operation. It involved the movement of over a thousand men and ten landing craft, 120 miles from Bari to Termoli, the capture of Termoli, and the holding of the town until we were relieved. We had no naval escort, as the navy had not yet caught up with us. This simplified the naval side of the operation.

That evening, Slater told General Dempsey without any reservations or conditions whatsoever that his Commandos would occupy Termoli. That said, he didn't give himself a deadline, since Slater expected strong German reaction resistance. "The plan was for No. 3 Commando to secure the beach about half a mile west of Termoli. No. 40 Royal Marine Commando was to capture the town and the cross-roads west of it, and the Special Raiding Squadron, like No. 3 Commando, was to pass round the western outskirts of Termoli and to secure the area south of town. The Special Raiding Squadron, like No. 3 Commando, had suffered heavy casualties and was badly under strength, so I had to ask 40 Commando to do most of the work. They were a fresh unit, up to full strength."

General Dempsey posed one major challenge to the plan, questioning whether No. 3 Commando unit should be used at all, since they were nearly spent. Slater "wanted to be absolutely sure of the operation," and he knew that the first landing was not always the most dangerous. "Often it took place before the defenses woke up. Also, it would be good to go up the beach with the men I knew so well close behind me." Slater decided to land first himself with his small Brigade Headquarters unit.

Of course, the landing was far from perfect. Slater described what happened next in his 1953 memoir, *Commando*: "The Brigade arrived at Bari by sea on the scheduled night of the operation. The men had come in landing craft which had been inadequately supplied with fresh water. They were tired and dirty." One Slater lieutenant warned that the men hadn't slept in four days and had had a very choppy cruise getting to the embarkation point. The man begged Slater to put the whole thing off for one day. And so, with the concurrence of General Dempsey, they did exactly that. And while they waited, Slater begged the navy officer in charge for the "sailing order," the one piece of paper necessary to launch the operation.

"I'll have nothing to do with this," said the sailor with the pen. "I've heard nothing about it, and I'll not let you go."

The Slater approach to this problem is insightful. "I felt it was not worthwhile arguing the point," Slater recalled.

> *Instead, to give us freedom of movement, I decided to establish our own base at Manfredonia, a good port farther up the coast. Brian Franks wrote out the sailing orders to leave Bari and I signed them. We then moved up the coast. This was somewhat irregular, but necessary, since things had moved so fast that we had outrun our naval liaison, and I did not wish to become entangled in red tape. Later, after a big explosion at an ammunition dump at Bari, I remarked to General Dempsey that it would have been no great tragedy if the naval man there, who was known to the General, had gone up with the ammunition.*

Dempsey scolded Slater for that remark, but Slater had other problems. For one thing they had only a small-scale Italian chart with little geographic detail for their sea assault. The naval commander in charge complained that if they were attacked along the way, their only option would be to run aground. Despite this, on Friday, October 1, 1943, the flotilla "slipped anchor at 11:30 a.m. It was a beautiful day, and we sat on the deck enjoying the sun and the lovely coastline. Soon after nightfall, however, heavy clouds banked up and it became ominously dark. As we neared the mouth of the Biferno, shallow with silt, but not thus marked on our inadequate chart, the entire flotilla ran softly aground. It was not a comfortable feeling to be aground close to an enemy coast at one in the morning, but the naval crews had us free of mud in half an hour."

Of course, other challenges lay ahead. As luck would have it, the sunny weather turned to rain just as they clambered into their small assault boats. That said, the navy positioned them just in the right place, and as they landed in the darkness, the rain stopped. Slater remembered that "The night was dead still. This, the moment before a seaborne attack, with the enemy coastline looming up in the night, was the supreme thrill for me: nothing else could match it."

Slater was among the first to land.

Our headquarters boat beached first, three quarters of a mile west of Termoli. It was 2:00 a.m. Brian Franks and I dashed out [of] the craft. We were followed by four signalers who carried a heavy wireless set on a stretcher. We needed this heavy set, as it had to transmit and receive a distance of at least thirty miles to General Dempsey's headquarters. Another signaler carried carrier pigeons in a basket, just in case the radio didn't work. We climbed the steep sand hills with the four signalers puffing and blowing as they carried the heavy set, slipping now and then and cursing under their breath. Brigade Headquarters was on the move and in action.

Some of the Germans didn't yet realize that the British Commandos had landed: "The large landing craft in which 40 Commando and the Special Raiding Squadron were to come ashore had struck on a sandbank, which [had been unmarked]." Slater turned to a navy lieutenant and asked, "Can you get your small craft going to give them a reasonably dry landing?" The navy man was sure that he could make it happen. Then the shooting began. Slater could hear British and German machine guns chattering not all that far away. "Very soon, our headquarters on a sand dune a half-mile from town was far away from the shifting battle. There was fighting in the streets now, a lot of shooting, plenty of small [arms] sounding crisp, harsh and deadly," Slater recalled.

Slater insisted on moving to where the action was. He jumped into a taxi driven by a German, who did exactly what he was told to do, driving directly to the train station. Slater described what happened next: "The German train never did make its scheduled trip northward. The coaches behind the engine were loaded with German troops, fast asleep." Slater and his staffer Brian Franks woke them up and announced that they were now prisoners of war. "They took a lot of rousing and could scarcely believe what was happening. They thought they were thirty safe miles behind the front lines." Slater established his headquarters in the backyard of a residence near the train station and released several pigeons carrying the good news, but the birds simply circled the yard and came back. In the meantime, sporadic German gunfire from near the train station continued.

No. 40 Commando had cleared up most of the opposition here in the first rush. It was six in the morning. Meanwhile, 40 Commando and the Special Raiding Squadron had moved on. Our opponents were the German parachutists we had encountered before in the Battle of the Commando Bridge. Some of them seemed eager to fight until they died. I saw one lying in an olive grove partly behind a tree about eight hundred yards in front of our position. Although obviously wounded—his actions were stiff and unnatural—he continued to fire at us regularly and accurately. We were unable to move anyone forward to take him prisoner. Instead we returned his fire. He died where he fought, in the olive grove.

The German Parachute Division commander, a General Heydrich, as it turned out, left a long black 1939 Horsch vehicle that the No. 3 Commando found, cleaned up, and presented to Slater. That morning the British ambushed and destroyed a large number of German supply trucks driving through.

Throughout the morning, the Commandos ambushed a dozen German supply trucks trying to drive through Termoli, with long Bren bursts that ran most of them off the road on fire. When the battle was over, Slater called 40 Commando and his Special Raiding Squadron for rest and recuperation.

"That left the perimeter seriously undermanned, but this was a calculated gamble on my part, as these men only had one decent night's sleep in the better part of a week, and I wanted them in tip-top shape in case they were needed. No. 3 Commando was left on outpost duty north of town."

In the meantime, the Commando Brigade Headquarters unit occupied "the best house in the town, a big stucco villa overlooking the harbor. The house belonged to a notorious Fascist who had left with his wife on our approach. The butler who was in charge was typical of his English counterpart, of medium height and distinguished appearance, about fifty years old."

The next day, "The inhabitants began to show signs of being troublesome, and there was a great deal of sniping. A patrol of 40 Commando on anti-sniping duty saw a man leave his house and throw a grenade at a [British] gun position." Slater, who witnessed the incident, estimated that he was killed a half a second after throwing the grenade. That said, he recalled, "The [sniping] incidents continued. Accordingly, I had the entire male population assembled in the town square and spread rumors of a mass execution. They went home in a more cooperative frame of mind. The [Italian] sniping stopped."

Slater shrugged off several reports of German tanks on patrol in the area until he was interrupted over lunch and brandies by reports that if he stepped outside he could see a dozen or more coming over a hill about two miles distant from Termoli. He shrugged off the sighting—at least for the moment—since he didn't have any tanks of his own to intercept the Germans.

Worse still, the next morning while he was shaving, "a dozen low-flying Messerschmitts came over, shooting and bombing. This was unusual, as the Germans were short of aircraft in Italy just then. Just after they had gone it began to rain heavily. I was suddenly acutely aware of impending danger. I had an idea that we were in for a strong German counterattack. There was also the danger of rain flooding our temporary bridge away. This would cut us off from major reinforcements."

He also ordered the 40 Commando and the Special Raiding Squadron to dig themselves into a tight perimeter around Termoli. The rain became so heavy that one of the temporary combat bridges was quickly swept away, as prologue to coming dangers. Slater recalled: "By eight o'clock that morning, an enemy artillery barrage began, consisting of all the Divisional Artillery of the 16th Panzer Division, with a few heavy guns attached. During the night, a German artillery observer managed to infiltrate through our lines into the town—it was a large perimeter with many gaps in it—and set up an observation post with a commanding view. He brought fire on a unit of our troops moving out to the perimeter, landing a direct hit on one truck and killing those inside."

Worse still, the next target was the Commando headquarters.

I was conferring with Brian Franks [the de facto Slater chief of staff] in my office. An eighty-eight mm shell burst in the adjacent room where some of my staff was busy.

"We'd better have a look," I said to Brian. "Let's hope they're all right."

If only it were so.

Tim Leese, who had insisted on coming back after losing an eye in the Commando Bridge Battle two months before, was dead. Alan Peile had been blown out of the window. He was hanging from the sill with a serious concussion, clinging there instinctively. Slater and Franks didn't know until they pulled him in whether he was dead or alive. We moved our office to the ground floor, choosing the room with the strongest walls.

The barrage continued:

The streets of Termoli were, by this time, strewn with broken glass and rubble. Great, jagged holes gaped in the buildings. One shell dropped in a roadway and killed four soldiers walking along the pavement. There were many fires, including several blazing haystacks on the edges of the town. As night fell, they became bright, unwelcome beacons. The battle was not now going in our favor.

The Commando troops, well dug in, had not given an inch, but the newly arrived supporting units, tired from their hurried march and located in badly prepared positions, sometimes could not hold the enemy. By all the accepted rules, the Germans had won the battle, and many of the supporting units started to fall back. They had been beaten by a good enemy [sic] with greatly superior firepower. I had to threaten many officers and men—none of them Commandos—with shooting. Most of them pulled together. Our men refused to be beaten, and I knew that if only I could get the supporting units to hold on, we should win the battle.

Confusion filled that day. With the pontoon bridge swept away, we were completely cut off from reinforcements. Things looked bad. Jerry had a complete Panzer division and supporting troops and tanks against, on our side, one infantry brigade and our Commando Brigade, which was far from being at full strength. We were outnumbered three to two by the enemy. His supply lines were intact. Ours were nonexistent.

The Royal Engineers rebuilding the bridge performed an epic feat. The Germans realized the significance of its reconstruction and showered shells on the sappers [combat engineers] who were hard at work over the roaring river. They completed the bridge by nightfall. Then our tanks crossed in strength and the tide of the battle began to swing in our favor. The weather also changed and we were able to get heavy air support. I now knew that we were sure to win, but that it might take a little time.

We had not yet been able to locate the German artillery observer who had crept into the town. Movement of troops and vehicles, even a part of two or three men, was always a challenge to him and a danger to us. We cursed but could not find him. I sent a party to search for him at noon. Finally, at five, they pinpointed his location in a church tower. They crawled up the tower.

"Come down—surrender!" the Brits ordered.

The German answered with a shot from his revolver and scurried up the roof. Now we sprayed the roof with Bren machine-gun fire, and crawling up a minute or two later, found him there sprawled dead beside his radio set. He was a tough and brave man and while he lived, a great threat to us in Termoli.

Slater remembered only too well how the battle raged on. "No. 3 Commando [Slater's unit], still out in front, were giving, during this German counterattack, what was probably their finest performance during the war. Hammered by tanks, pounded by guns, attacked by infantry, and left exposed and bleeding on their left flank by the retreat of another unit, they did not budge from their positions. I sent them a message that I would get them out of Termoli that night."

Slater remembered the finale of the battle only too well.

Every gun we had, every mortar, tank, airplane and man combined to devastate the Germans. The enemy wisely cleared off in the face of such overwhelming firepower. At last I had a chance to look around. I found that my beautiful Horsch, left behind so kindly by a German General, had been utterly destroyed by a shell outside our headquarters villa. Gears, wheels, upholstery and broken windows were scattered over the street like the parts of a dismantled clock. I tried to console myself with the thought that I was undoubtedly lucky not to have been in the vehicle at the time it was hit.

After a few days' welcome rest, Slater was ordered back to England with No. 3 Commando for the D-Day invasion. He returned with one good story: George Herbert, his liaison officer, spent most of the night before the final battle in the headquarters villa working. In the early-morning hours, he lay down on the floor and nestled with a dog, cuddling it for warmth. Trouble was, in the cold light of dawn, the dog turned out to be a pig.

CHAPTER 8

Escaping Burma

THE ONE HUNDRED LEFT NORTH AFRICA IN SEPTEMBER 1941 KNOWING that they would be conducting a special operation in Burma, but having no idea what it might be. Frederick Charles Goode, age twenty-three, from gloomy Birmingham, England, was among them. Goode left school at age fourteen to become a laborer and joined the Duke of Cornwall's Light Infantry three years later, only to be posted to Lahore, India, before Pakistan was founded. The year 1939 brought Goode's twenty-first birthday and a military transport to Tobruk, Libya, some 3,700 miles away, for action against German and Italian forces. The next year he joined Britain's No. 8 Commando unit, trained at the newly created Bush Warfare School in Maymyo (present-day Pyin Oo Lwin), Burma, some forty miles east of Mandalay.

Some trainees were assigned to Special Service Detachment I (Middle East), while fifty others, including Goode, joined Special Service Detachment II, commanded by fifty-three-year-old Captain Henry Courtney Brocklehurst, who eventually became a lieutenant colonel. SSDI and SSDII shared the codename "Mission 204" and the initial objective of partnering with Australian Army Independent Companies (AAIC) on secret missions to China. There, these joint forces would train local troops in demolition and guerrilla tactics.

On a misty morning in Maymyo, Goode and the rest of SSDII learned that the previous day, Sunday, December 7, 1941, the Japanese had attacked Pearl Harbor, wherever that was. They listened to Franklin

Delano Roosevelt declare war against Japan on the radio. Goode remembered what happened next in his memoir, *No Surrender in Burma: Behind Enemy Lines, Captivity and Torture*, first published by his son in 2014. *No Surrender* is the primary source for this chapter.

Everything changed overnight for Goode and the men he served with. The secrecy was over, even as they learned about the working assumption that Goode and the others would assist the Chinese in China as "civil advisers," fighting the Japanese on the ground. The attack at Pearl Harbor brought Goode the opportunity to cross the border in their own uniforms and own trucks, bearing the Union Jack, rather than undercover. The Aussies would move out first, heading directly to the Canton region to try out their newly acquired Cantonese. Goode himself moved to a town called Taunggyi in the southern Shan State of Burma to set up a base of operations, just in time for the New Year.

Their prospects were not good. The British were playing catch-up, having lost the *Prince of Wales* and *Repulse* to Japanese fighters, knowing that the Japanese had swept other Brits out of the Malay Peninsula, even as, despite all assurances that it would never happen, the Japanese took control over Singapore, long assumed to be "impregnable." Not to be outdone by the Japanese, the Germans were on the move in North Africa, having seized Tobruk and advanced toward Alexandria.

The men of SSDII left most of their gear at the Bush Warfare School and carried necessities, but nothing more. Even so, the trucks in which they traveled were packed to the top with ammunition and explosives, moving slowly through remote bamboo bungalows just outside Taunggyi, the town which they established as a supply base, manned by two Brits. The rest of SSDII jumped back in the trucks and traveled toward a way station to the southeast called Kentuang, and finally, a hamlet called Mong Hsat, where the motor road ended. This meant transferring everything in the trucks to the backs of mules for a march into the late afternoon.

Goode remembered that

[a]round the campfire and after our meal, the Colonel gave us our instructions for the following day. Beginning at dawn we were to split up into parties of five or six with two Chinese muleteers and six

mules. The parties were to set out at intervals of four hours. We were given a reference point on the map, marking an old Buddhist temple about sixty miles from the Thai border, which, without any mishap, should take three days of marching to reach. There we would all collect and wait for everyone to arrive. Our party was the third [to leave], setting off at about two-thirty in the afternoon.

We marched at a comfortable pace with the mules bringing up the rear. We took turns going forward, having two men in front, one link man and two at the rear in close contact with the mules. The British moved on at a pace which some might think leisurely, followed by a herd of mules, with two men in front of the column. They planned the mission so that if any one of them was lost, the rest would know exactly where to go and what to do.

Noon brought them to a river called the Salween, which could only be crossed by using three-man, one-mule rafts guided by three natives. One of them paddled until [the raft] was well into the current, while the other, on the opposite bank, pulled on a thick bamboo rope tied to the rope.

They repeated this process six times or more to get everyone and everything across before the Japanese airplanes could spot them.

Goode remembered later that "After leaving the river and being very pleased with ourselves at crossing without trouble, we camped deep in the thickest jungle, with the knowledge that we would, bar anything going wrong, reach the temple by noon the next day. It was a little after that time that we were met by two of our men who had taken a quiet stroll out of the camp to meet us, 'just in case we had suffered any casualties.'"

When Goode's team arrived, they learned "that we had been most fortunate with our mules, which had behaved well in comparison with the other parties. We heard that some of the mules had just bolted at the river's edge off into the jungle, while others, once their loads were taken off, would not have them back on again. One mule flatly refused to go on the raft, so he and his handler were forced to swim the river."

After three days' rest, "at about ten in the morning, the colonel called us all together. A sand table had been made with two large mounds, which represented hills. The colonel pointed out that these two hills were our objectives for an attack." The colonel told them they would be marching six miles to the border and then about two miles to get close enough to reconnoiter their target before making an attack in the early-morning hours.

"Two gun emplacements cover the whole of an escarpment [steep slope] guarded by Thai and Japanese troops," Goode recalled later. "To get there well before dusk and get a good view, we must set out this afternoon." The colonel designated two separate parties for the mission, leaving five men to guard the camp. Goode's party of eight men would be carrying fifty-pound packages of gelignite, as well as fuses and primer. And with that, they set out, following the colonel toward the target.

"The sun was well behind us as we were traveling in an easterly direction," Goode remembered. "Our path took us up the side of a small mountain and along a grassy ridge, which led us onto a tree-covered plateau. Then after some distance we went down into a valley and up another hill. There we rested. The three officers and the sergeant went on forward in fours, lending us two pairs of field glasses so that we could see the target for ourselves."

Goode could see more hills in the distance, a large hump to his left and another one on his right.

These were our targets. The whole of the range was covered with trees, while below was a rich green valley, the trees and scrub coming only part of the way down, thus giving the defenders a clear view of the whole valley and also the range of hills that we were on. With the aid of the glasses one could make out camouflaged earthworks through the trees on each of the humps.

The positioning of these emplacements had been well thought out, as they could cover the escarpment. We talked among ourselves as we returned to where the rest were waiting. When all of us had seen the targets we set off again, but with ever more caution being taken.

They stopped again.

"This time it was for the two parties to separate," Goode recalled. "Watches were synchronized. The time to move on the targets was set for 2:00 a.m. The colonel led his team off. We had a little further to go to get opposite of our target. It had become quite dark when the captain called a halt. The order was given for no smoking and no talking. We lay in the cover of some trees, awaiting the order to move off."

Later, Goode remembered the trees above him rustling in the wind and the night turning a bit chilly, which he chose to consider a favorable condition that might cover the noise the Brits made during the assault, and encouraging the enemy defenders to keep their heads down for warmth. The whispered "Let's go" meant that the British could huddle against the wind and cold no more—at least for now. Then, Goode remembered, "At the bottom of the hill and moving across the valley to the other side, the signal was passed along to fan out. The captain and sergeant were in the center with two pack men on either side of them." A machine gunner covered both British flanks.

Slowly and steadily we began the steep climb, sometimes on the wet dewy grass. The heavy pack seemed to be pulling me down the slope. We climbed for about two hundred yards before coming to the scraggy brush near the top. Here we halted, for in among the short brushwood, sticking out of the ground and pointed towards us, were shin-high spears of sharpened bamboo. Known as "dragon's teeth," these had not been visible through the glasses and were placed at intervals and not in any straight line. We therefore had to take more care how we went, as there may have been some sort of warning system attached to any one of them. As we picked our way through these spears we wondered if the enemy was in the same predicament, as time was the major factor between success and failure. Should one discharge go off too soon, then the other party stood the chance of being detected before they had even got into position [sic] to set their own charges.

Now it was every man for himself, "moving at their own pace toward the enemy objective, but closed in together at the top and count[ing] heads before attacking. Our target was about twenty feet in diameter and about eight feet high. It had a covering of brush and other material. From where we were, the nozzle of a gun was just visible. Above the noise of the wind in the trees we could make out voices some distance away."

Four men carrying packs were supposed to split into two columns about six feet apart, "dig into the mound about three feet from the ground, fit in the prepared charges, and bring back the fuses to the sergeant, who would be waiting in front of the mound. He would then connect all the fuses together. Then, at the correct time, which was four o'clock [p.m.], he would set out the time pencil."

A time pencil, or pencil detonator, is a time fuse designed to be connected to a detonator or short length of safety fuse. They are about the same size and shape as a pencil. Goode noted, "This should set off all four charges at precisely the same instant." Timing, of course, was everything.

"The sergeant gave me the signal to go," Goode recalled, "and I tapped Jock on my left. We both moved forward. As I neared the large black mound the voices became much clearer. They were slightly to our left and above. Jock came near me. As we got under the mound he tapped me on the shoulder to let me know that he was moving further [a]round."

Goode took his pack off.

The newly grown grass at the base of the mound was wet and quite cold. Then, on my knees, I marked out an area that would be large enough to take the prepared charge. I began to dig away at the earth with the small-handled trench tool. Luckily, underneath the first layer the earth was quite dry and fell away easily. When I thought that I had gone in deep enough, I took the charge from the backpack, which was in a sandbag, and pressed it into the cavity I had made, then scooped up the dirt with my hands and pressed it into the charge. All this time, though it was quite cold, I had broken out into a sweat. I smoothed the dirt. With the fuse wire dangling, I picked up the now empty pack and my trench tool, and with the fuse wire slipping through my fingers, returned to where the sergeant was sitting at the front of the mound, waiting for us. After I handed over the fuse wire to him he waved me to go back to the shelter of the scrub.

After a few minutes, which seemed like hours, the sergeant in charge joined Goode and his partner of the moment, Jock. When signaled to join the rest of the party, all three moved down the slippery slope, doing all they could to not get ensnared in the dragon's teeth.

Goode recalled: "We climbed back up to where we had left Morgan and Scanes, who gave us a wave as we passed them. Then we all took cover among the trees behind the ridge. We were about to settle down to a well-earned rest at just before four o'clock when there was a terrific explosion, followed by some smaller bangs at our left. Then, from where we had placed our charges, came a large explosion, followed again by some smaller ones. We looked towards both directions and could see two pink and red glows in the sky."

They jumped around, exchanged handshakes, and congratulated each other for what they'd done that night, before the captain brought them back to earth. After all, they had to meet the rest of the team as soon as they could get to the rendezvous point, up ahead on the trail.

Of course there was retribution:

It was beginning to get light. The enemy had by this time set up a number of mortars, for we could hear bombs exploding in rapid succession over on our ridge. Then, as the light improved, we heard the drone of aircraft coming in our direction. We lay perfectly still, not even looking up to see what sort they were. The planes dived and began strafing at something and dropping a couple of bombs. The mortars also renewed their attack near where the planes had dived. Eventually the planes separated and went in opposite directions, flying low over the top of the trees, no doubt trying to spot us.

Once the two planes were out of sight, Goode and the others moved out. They heard occasional mortar rounds dropping, but nothing came close to them. The two planes seen earlier made an additional pass, no doubt trying to spot the Brits, without success. Soon, it was 8:00 a.m. Within that hour Goode and the others learned that the other attack party had returned to camp without as much as a banged-up knee. The mission was a total success, which they celebrated until noon the next day, when Colonel Brocklehurst drew them all in to a planning circle. This target was much further from the base camp. They would take mules to carry the gear, munitions, and food, while four men would stay behind to protect their base camp.

Decades later, Goode recalled the night march through deep jungle begun the next morning, in vivid detail.

> *At times it seemed darker than normal as we passed beneath the thick and dense canopy of trees, shutting out even the stars. Then, just as soon, there would be a gap in the trees and there above us once more were the stars and clear sky. We were descending a hill as the grey light of dawn began to creep slowly over the high hills to the east. In the half-light we saw, spread out before us, a lush green valley dotted here and there with large clumps of bamboo and banana trees. As the light got better we could make out tall teak trees on the slopes of the hills beyond the valley, appearing almost black.*

They found a perfect camping spot at the very bottom of the valley by a fast-running stream that meandered through the trees. They watered the mules, slept, and took turns guarding the camp. Even the officers took their turn.

They had covered about thirty miles that first day, and estimated that at this rate, they would arrive at the target after a four-day march. They could not know that on the second day they would encounter more-difficult terrain, not to mention the river they would soon cross in darkness. They detoured around a village, arrived at the target location at noon on the fourth day, camped under trees, and enjoyed fresh water, not to mention all the wild fruit they could eat. Lieutenant Colonel Brocklehurst assembled them at 9:00 a.m. on the fifth day of their journey to say that he and Sergeant Friend would be leaving on an advance reconnaissance of the target. Twenty-four hours later they were back, just as planned, to begin the mission at noon.

On this mission Goode and Lance Corporal Richard Homans were assigned to keep the mules quiet in the jungle near the target, which the rest of their detachment attacked. Sometime after dark on the sixth day of the mission Goode recalled that he must have dozed off with one arm over the shoulder of a mule he was keeping quiet, while holding a stick in his other hand.

"Suddenly, the night came alive with the noise of gunfire," he remembered. "First there came the *rat-tat-tat* of automatics, then some smaller bangs, followed closely by some rapid louder bangs, then more automatic firing. From where we were, it seemed that our party had run into some opposition and was having to fight their way out."

Goode described that night in detail. "The firing continued, together with the *crump-crump-crump* of either artillery or large mortars, which we already knew the Japanese used to good effect. The noise of the firing kept on for what seemed hours to us, and yet it may have been only one or two hours."

Neither Goode nor Homans was wearing a wristwatch, but they guessed that it was about 3:00 a.m. They estimated that the action was about three miles away.

Goode recalled: "As the light began to tell us of the approach of dawn to the east, we heard the slow drone of airplane engines. We kept well under cover and kept hold of the mules. I had my rifle slung over my back, but Homans and I were concerned about not giving our position away more than anything else."

Soon they had other worries.

"The planes swooped down with all guns blazing away at some distant target we could not see. We did see, however, that this time there were three planes. They turned in small circles, going over the same area and also dropping bombs again and again. They swooped low, strafing at something."

But what?

Goode and Homans felt helpless, knowing that their brothers were under fire, but much to their surprise, somebody nearby called for the mules—in Scottish-accented English. Jock Johnson led them deeper into the jungle, where they met Lieutenant Colonel Brocklehurst. Goode made his report: "We have four casualties. Two are able to walk, but the other two are in too bad a shape. We'll have to do the best we can, but I want to get away from here as soon as possible before those damn planes return."

Goode recalled that the prospects were not good.

"The walking wounded had gone on with a couple of others, while the rest of us made two cradles out of bamboo and fitted them onto the mules. After making the wounded men as comfortable as we could, we set off at a steady pace."

They stayed under cover as much as possible.

"When we reached the three men whom we had left to look after the other mules, we wasted no time [in] push[ing] on. The colonel decided that this time we would not avoid the village, but make use of what assistance we could get from there, both for food and to be able to dress and make the wounded more comfortable."

It was then that Goode learned the whole story.

From what the men told us during the march back and in between rest stops, they had not only come across [what] they called dragon's teeth [bamboo spikes], but had also triggered some kind of anti-personnel detonators that were threaded with twine connected to the bamboo spikes. This had signaled exactly where they were, so with guns set on fixed lines in any position, they were almost sitting ducks. They had not had a chance to lay any charges. All they could do was return fire and throw grenades as they withdrew, using the darkness as cover. The [Japanese] mortars had done the most damage. Once again, the aircraft were well off target.

Back in the base camp the group rested for one night, taking care of the wounded before loading them up on litters for the journey to Mong Hsat. "There they would be transferred to motor transport and back to Taunggyi and into hospital," Goode noted. "We had quite a bit of air activity in our area, which came very close at times, but none of the planes were ours."

Three days after they delivered the wounded to Mong Hsat, a mounted Indian soldier rode into camp.

"He brought an urgent message for the colonel," Goode recalled. "We invited him to have some tea and any food he wanted, but he only took the tea since he was a Sikh, and a vegetarian. He then told us that he had met up with the wounded and their escort, and that was how he [had] managed to find us as quickly as he had."

The Sikh also had some surprising news.

"Rangoon [the capital of Burma] had fallen some days ago . . . He went on to say that the Japanese were pushing northward towards Pegu and the oil wells at Prome. This meant that we were almost behind the Japanese forward troops [front line]. Should the Japanese decide to come over the Thai border, we would be in real trouble."

And so once again, they would leave Mong Hsat, this time to avoid Japanese capture.

> *Motor transport had been arranged for us to move out as soon as we were ready. The small town was in utter confusion, and refugees, most of them Chinese, were pouring in from all directions. The fear of what might happen to them showed in their faces. As we walked along the dusty main road towards where our trucks waited, they tugged at our clothes and begged us to help them in some way. There were old men and women, young women, some with four or more young children, all trying to carry what belongings they had managed to grab in the rush to get away from their hated old enemy. Some had hand carts, and some bicycles, with their belongings strapped on the back, but most were walking.*

They used civilian Ford trucks that an army major had found for them, piling their gear, ammunition, and weapons into five three-ton vehicles before heading north.

> *At first, we made very little progress because the road was jammed with refugees. We must have barely gone ten miles when the noise of aircraft was heard. The refugees scattered in all directions. Our convoy pulled off the road and into the cover of the trees. We had guns ready as the aircraft swept down the road, strafing at anything. They turned and came down again. We opened up with everything we had. Some of the refugees had not even made it to the trees and were falling like ninepins, screaming and shouting, both in fear and in pain.*

Small orphaned children were everywhere, but nobody could be seen comforting them.

"We had little time to consider [this] as the planes swept down again," Goode recalled, "one after the other, blazing away with all that they had while we hammered back at them. Finally, the planes flew off. We had a roll call. We did not have one casualty, and yet there were dead and wounded all around us, young and old shattered to pieces. Some were hardly recognizable as human beings, as they had caught the full fury of the attack. We could do nothing but sympathize."

Somehow Goode and the others got into the trucks and rolled into their main base at Taunggyi at two the next morning. They were ready for whatever came next.

Someone shouted "Air raid!" Goode recalled that "[w]e made for our slit trenches well away from where we had stored our demolition and explosives. The drone of the engines came nearer and nearer until they were right overhead. Looking up, we could make out a formation of eight bombers."

The falling bombs were no surprise.

"They fell right across the small town. There had been no warning signal and no antiaircraft fire. From where we were, we could hear the screams and wailing of people who had been injured in the crowded marketplace. We watched as the planes turned, keeping in formation and still keeping their altitude. The planes then turned and went off towards the east."

Goode heard somebody shout, "Come on, lads, let's get cracking!" And with that, the men in his unit began rescuing and helping civilians, too many of whom were dead or dying. While watching an amputation, Goode fainted. After questioning a possible arsonist suspected of setting fires to guide Japanese bombers toward prime buildings, Goode seriously wounded another suspected collaborator while preventing his escape.

Within a few days they were on their way back into combat in four trucks, carrying them toward advancing Japanese at a small town named Psipaw (Hsipaw). "Psipaw was about forty miles from Taunggyi. This meant we had to make a quick dash before turning north-northwest towards the Irrawaddy River, which we hoped to cross." The cattle trail that served as a

> *road was little more than a track used only by cattle carts and mules over many centuries, thus the ruts on either side were of no great help to the trucks as they went from side to side, into one rut and then into the other. There was also dense jungle on either side. Sometimes the trucks were forced to leave the track [road] and make their way the best they could through the jungle. This was done by two or three men going in front and literally cutting a path for them. When the jungle became too dense we had to make it back for the track again [sic]. Our progress was very slow. Dawn was coming when we came near to a village of some four or five bamboo huts. Men from the village came out to meet us. They seemed very agitated and excited as they informed the colonel that they [the villagers] had seen a small party of Japanese to the south of the village before darkness had fallen the night before.*

Goode was among the men who left the convoy to scout for the Japanese.

"After about a quarter of a mile, or maybe less, the [villager] signaled for us to take cover. He with his keen ears had heard something. He told Colonel [Brocklehurst] it was voices. The colonel told three of us to go forward about twenty yards and conceal ourselves, engage the enemy, draw their fire, and then pull back to where the rest [of the scouts] were waiting. The only thing that worried the colonel was how big the [Japanese] party was."

Goode and the others spread out, but kept an eye on everyone in the team as much as possible.

> *I could now hear the swishing of someone brushing against the trees on either side of the track. We looked at each other and gave a nod to let each other know that we had heard. Then I saw them. There were three of them, about twenty-five yards from us. When we opened fire the one in front stopped dead in his tracks, then fell forward. The second threw up his arms and fell sideways. The third man stood still as if in shock*

for a split second. He then turned as if to run, but one of the others put him away with a shot that hit him in the back of the head. There were no moans or groans from any of them, but raising myself up slightly, I could make out the lifeless bodies in among the ferns. All this had happened in a matter of a few seconds, but the jungle had come alive with birds and many other creatures crying out and making some weird sounds. Then, just as suddenly, all was quiet again. We still lay in our positions. The sweat began to run down the side of my face. Flies began to gather and settled on my face and nose. They then tried for my eyes. I began to blink my lids to get rid of them.

Suddenly, the enemy was everywhere.

Giving a nod to my two companions, we crawled through the undergrowth until we were near where our friends were. Then, keeping down and firing from the hip, we joined them. They immediately opened up at the oncoming Japanese, who were shouting and screaming. As I took up a position lying down, I saw one of the enemy in a white shirt push forward with a sword held high, then suddenly stop when a burst of fire caught him across the middle. His white shirt first turned red and then pink with blood as he fell out of sight.

Fortunately, Lieutenant Colonel Brocklehurst had studied Japanese tactics; he knew that

the Japanese always made a frontal attack and then tried to outflank, had to put all the quick firing guns out on our flanks. The first attack stopped. There was an eerie silence, except for the noise of the birds and scared animals. During this short lull the colonel had us move to another position. The second attack came, but with less vigor. As they came at us, we caught them in crossfire. They fell screaming and shouting, then once again, all was quiet. We kept our positions for a few moments, then the colonel ordered us to group up and check for any casualties on our side. There were none. We reckoned there had been about twenty-five to thirty Japanese dead. If there were any survivors, we did not care. We made our way back to where we [had] left our trucks. As we boarded our trucks we looked skyward. Already the vultures were circling high in the sky above, preparing to dive down and take their pick.

Goode and the others returned to Psipaw that night, but left before dawn.

Their next objective was yet another small but strategically important village called Laihka, about a hundred miles north of Psipaw. They made good time, arriving on the outskirts of Laihka after a four-hour trek. Once they saw the hamlet, the vehicle drivers drove hell-bent for leather across the open ground, sending clouds of dirt and dust into the air, as if to alert the Japanese fighters of where they might make some easy kills.

As we neared the trees [just outside Laihka], the drone of aircraft came to our ears. The [British] trucks were pulled well under cover as we dismounted and waited. It was a single Japanese fighter. He had spotted us and was making a run very low over the trees. He came at us with all guns blazing. We returned fire, but he seemed more interested in our trucks than in us. He went out wide and turned for a second run. Again we returned fire. He had set the first truck in [our] column on fire. Again he came around for a third run. Some of our chaps near the burning vehicle were scooping up sand in their hats and chucking it on the fire, stopping only when the plane came down again on its run. After the third run, the plane turned south and went out of sight.

After several days' journey they moved toward Mong Kung, yet another small village that was now a military objective. On the road a number of Chinese troops and Sikhs went missing, because the tables had somehow turned and the Japanese were chasing them. According to Goode, "It was obvious what the Japanese intention was." One Japanese column would push north and join with a second Japanese column engaged with the Chinese near Maymyo.

Their objective was to cut off the Chinese escape route up the Burma Road to China. The British had quite a struggle ahead of them that day. Goode recalled that

> [i]t was very tough going up the track [road] which was taking us in a northeasterly direction and away from the Irrawaddy. The vehicles were showing the strain. The rain of the past few days had not helped either. We were making slow progress over a winding track that took us up and around a mountain when suddenly the [three-ton truck] went dead. Try as we might, we could not get any life out of it at all, so we decided to put all the gear into [it] and push it over the mountain. The truck was only going at a walking pace and it was now so crowded some of us decided to walk. Now and again, those who were riding swapped over with those walking.

There were other problems.

> We still had the mounted Sikhs with us, but lost the Chinese. The Indians and refugees had vanished together. After a time the [three-ton truck] also began to give us trouble. We came to a village, and while scouting around there for food, one of the sergeants found a number of mules. This was reported to the colonel who immediately set about buying all twelve of them, with the [three-ton truck] thrown in as part of the deal. From now on I was all on foot. Where we would end up was anyone's guess. Our whole plan had gone awry. All that we could do was to keep ahead of the Japanese, keep going north and make for the Irrawaddy further on.

Goode and the rest had no choice but to make a run for the Irrawaddy River and hope that they arrived first. They stayed at the little village overnight, loaded up some food, and left at dawn on their mules, walking cross-country instead of on the roads, toward the Myitnge River. After crossing it, they headed for "the ruby mining town of Mogok. The colonel [Brocklehurst] had pointed out that by then we should be ahead of the two Japanese columns that were chasing the Chinese towards the east,"

Goode recalled. "He also pointed out that this was not going to be a picnic; that we must all times be on our guard and not falter. We would rest when we could, but should be on alert at all times, he said, and above all, trust no one else. Some of the others and I had handled mules before, but when it came to crossing rivers with them, it was another matter. I considered myself quite a good swimmer, but with a mule? That posed a problem. Still, I thought to myself that I would worry about that when we got to the river."

They marched on through the night, resting every four hours for half an hour, stopping for their first real break at 8:00 a.m. Goode estimated that overnight they had walked about forty miles, which left another sixty miles before they reached the Myitnge River.

After restarting from our much needed long rest, our route took us once again into the hills. The pace now was beginning to slow down after the hard march of the previous day and night. It was taking a toll on all of us, but we knew that we must try to keep up a steady pace if we were to succeed. The eight Indian horsemen, not being affected by the fatigue, rode on slightly ahead of us [and scouted]. [S]o it turned out, as we approached the Myitnge, the Sikhs warned us that they had seen uniformed troops on the opposite side of the river. With great caution, we went towards it. On closer inspection by a couple of our men who had gone forward, they found that it was a section of [friendly] Gurkhas who had come up the river from the south.

The river itself was more than a challenge, almost as wide as an American football field, with steep banks and fast running water, and the very real threat of being pushed into some jagged rocks downstream if one was not careful. And this was just before a steep, noisy waterfall.

At least the current was in their favor. Goode and the others tied a rope to a small canoe that the current somehow pushed onto the opposite bank. Using this oddity to their advantage, the Brits managed to get across the Myitnge with most of their gear. But then there was the matter of the mules.

The Sikhs were already getting their saddles and equipment off their mounts. So we, who had to get the mules over, stood back for a while to see how they coped with the strong flowing river. [Goode had already stripped down to his gym shorts as] the Indian horsemen began to take their horses over in pairs, swimming alongside them. The first two pairs went over quite easily, but among the next two pairs was a huge grey [horse] who, when just halfway across, decided to turn around. The fast current caught it and turned it over, with its legs thrashing in the air and its head below the water, taking it at a great speed down the river towards the rocks and waterfall. We watched helplessly as the animal was dashed against the rocks and thrown like a log over the waterfall and out of sight. The rider kept on swimming and made it to the other bank. The last we saw of him was running down the bank as fast as he could, no doubt to see if he could save the animal further downriver.

Goode, in the meantime, tried to get his own mule into the water, without much success, having just watched two of the other men and their mules enter the water too close together, causing them to bump into one another and flounder in the strong current. The mules were lost in this mishap, but the men somehow reached the other side. "This made me decide to go further upstream to give both of us [Goode and his mule] a chance." He also waited until everyone else got across to avoid any more mishaps, but had his doubts as to whether his mule could cross the river.

"I picked my spot where we could enter the water," Goode remembered. "When all was clear, I lashed him across the flanks with a piece of brushwood and forced him into the water." Another Commando had told Goode earlier that horses swam leaning slightly to the right, with legs paddling on the left. Of course this meant that Goode could only swim safely on the right side of the horse.

The time to test this out came soon enough.

"The mule entered the water and I plunged in after him. Swimming on his right side I was soon alongside his head. I grabbed the hair on his neck and began to shout encouragement into his ear. We were going very well until about halfway when he [the mule] decided that he had gone far enough and tried to turn around."

Goode grabbed the mule's ear with his left hand and at the same time struck out as hard as he could with his right, forcing the mule in the right direction. Goode remembered that "[h]is head came around as he sensed what I wanted him to do. About halfway [across the river], the current seemed to be pushing instead of pulling, and in no time we were touching bottom and walking up the bank to safety. And then came an oddity. The mule stood with his back feet still in the water, shaking his head and blowing his nostrils. He looked at me and came forward, then tucked his head under my arm and rubbed his nose across my chest, almost pushing me backwards. I am quite sure that it was his way of saying thanks."

While passing through several villages on the far side of the Myitnge River, they discovered that their position was hardly favorable. In fact, the British Commandos were right in the middle of a two-pronged Japanese attack, yet following behind Chinese forces who were looting civilian villages even as they retreated. This meant that Goode and the other Commandos had no way to replenish their dwindling supplies.

We descended the hills and tried to cut through the bottom of the gorge which would bring us into Mogok. As we entered the beginning of the gorge with high, tree-covered walls rising up on either side, aircraft came over and began to bomb the bridge. We did not know whether they were friend or foe. The bombs that missed the target came cascading down into the gorge, causing the ground to shake with the explosions as they burst on the floor of the gorge, sending triple echoes up and down the narrow passage. The noise coming from both sides was deafening. Long after we had left the gorge behind [and] the planes had ceased their destruction, the echoing explosions could still be heard behind us.

At daylight they reached the Burma Road and continued walking, until "the sun was sinking in the western sky." The road looked like a "black ribbon . . . winding its way around the lower hills that would take us into Mogok." Goode and some of the others had been here before to play soccer, of all things. They wondered what kind of a reception they would get this time.

Walking further into the looming darkness, they came upon an iron bridge about three miles from the town. Even though most of the bridge planks had been removed, Chinese armed with rifles and grenades barred the way through, until someone with Goode spoke to the guards in Mandarin.

Most of the Chinese in town were starving, but the Brits found some chicken and even a bag of sweet potatoes, which they cooked and shared with the youngest and oldest beggars among those who surrounded them.

Colonel Brocklehurst began outlining the next objective before the meal was even over, but was interrupted by shouts and shots in the distance. A young Chinese officer came to warn the Commandos that trouble was coming their way. The young Chinaman was shot and killed, muttering "They not listen" just before dying.

Followed by a long line of refugees fleeing the Chinese soldiers, the Commandos left at midnight for a long march, which eventually brought them to yet another obscure village short of Shwegu, their objective on the banks of the Irrawaddy River. They reached the village in time for the evening meal, only to discover that one of their brothers, a soldier named Lacey, had gone missing, God knows where.

The entire crew backtracked and spent six hours looking for Lacey, but found nothing. Colonel Brocklehurst gave Lacey six hours, setting a 4:00 p.m. departure time. Goode was hardly sentimental about leaving Shwegu without him.

Without even a glance down the track [road] to see if he was coming, we set off on what would be the last leg of our long, arduous march. We avoided villages, making slight detours. We crossed rivers by either wading or swimming, after which we took only very short rests and then pushed on again. The colonel was setting a really fast pace now, and we followed him. We were almost running by the time we reached one last river—a river full of leeches, which we had to burn off our feet and legs with cigarettes.

Worse yet, they were hardly sitting down before "the noise of gunfire and light automatic machine-gun fire to the north of us reached our ears. The colonel was first to his feet. 'Come on, lads . . . let's get on.' As we went on, the noise of the gunfire came closer. We glanced at each other, wondering whether we had already lost the race."

They reached Shwegu—their objective, some three hundred yards from the Irrawaddy—at about 1:00 p.m., only to be told by a passerby that the Japanese had been there mere hours before. Soon some British Indian riflemen joined them, even as a reconnaissance team reported that Japanese infantry and artillery were moving into place on the other side of the river.

Within a few minutes, the colonel brought his team together and laid out some options for his men to consider, saying "that it would be best if we split up into small parties and went in different directions." Only one man, Sergeant Friend, voted to keep the entire group together. "Look at it this way, Sergeant," said the colonel. "If we stayed together, we [would] need food and water for over thirty, plus the fact that if we run into trouble, we are all in." That decided the men; they divided into four groups, each of which determined their own route back into India—a trip of over three thousand miles. As a practical matter, each group was on its own.

Two groups attempted the most direct path to India, while the other two groups, which included Goode's unit, attempted a longer route, perceived to be safer. Local villagers helped them, often at great personal risk, but their luck ran out just twenty miles short of Goode's two-thousand-mile race for freedom.

CHAPTER 9

The Galahad

BETRAYED TO THE JAPANESE IN OCTOBER 1942, GOODE AND THE OTHERS were interned in Rangoon Central Jail. Bad luck that, but the Allied Forces launched a special operation campaign known as Galahad in Burma one year later. British prime minister Winston Churchill, of all people, laid the foundation for Galahad during the August 1943 Quebec Conference. Eccentric yet magnetic Major General Orde C. Wingate attended the conference at Churchill's direction to discuss long-range penetration operations behind enemy lines. Wingate already commanded an odd assortment of British, Indian, Gurkha, and Burmese troops, nicknamed "Chindits."

Before the August 1943 Quebec Conference, the Chindits had already conducted significant raids into Burma, damaging Japanese communications as well as the north–south Burma railroad. Despite demands by British traditionalists that the Chindits be brought to heel and confined to more conventional operations, Wingate's confidence, vigor, and presentation skills impressed the Quebec leadership.

American commander George C. Marshall agreed then and there to organize a special US commando force to operate with the Chindits in the months to come. That said, efforts to recruit such a force from among appropriately experienced American commandos were hardly successful. Marshall quickly learned that "few jungle veterans showed any inclination to volunteer." Little wonder then that when confronted with this mandatory call for "volunteers," many American commanders offloaded "personnel who, for various reasons, did not fit with their units."

Once dragged from various posts in the United States and the Caribbean to San Francisco for deployment in Operation Galahad, one cynical American officer, quoted in *Army Special Operations in World War II*—the primary source for American operations described in this chapter by David W. Hogan—observed that "We got the misfits from half the divisions in the country."

Maybe so, but Wingate and his subordinates began training the motley lot in long-range penetration tactics on Halloween morning in Bombay, India. They moved on to Deolali, 170 miles to the southwest, for physical conditioning, and then to Deogarh, in central India, for advanced training in scouting, patrolling, stream crossing, demolitions, camouflage, small unit attacks, and airdrops, among other subjects.

Now it was time to meet the Chindits. The combined British-American training group began a weeklong maneuver in December of 1942. The prospects for successful operations were not considered good, at least initially.

"From the beginning, the unit was hard to handle," military historian David W. Hogan observed. "[W]hen it moved by rail from Deogarh to the Ledo area, one officer found his men shooting out the windows at Indians as if they were riding through the Wild West in the 1870s. Nevertheless, for all its disciplinary problems, and Colonel Charles N. Hunter's belief that it needed more training, theater headquarters decided that Galahad would be ready for combat by February 1944."

And ready it was—but Wingate would not lead the men of Galahad into battle. Determined that the only US combat troops in the theater would not serve under a British officer, General Joseph Stilwell chose one of his intimates, Brigadier General Frank D. Merrill, for that role. American news correspondents soon dubbed the new unit "Merrill's Marauders," but that was not the only change. The commando firm of Stilwell and Merrill had an entirely different concept of how this special operations unit should be used. Stilwell and Merrill "envisioned Galahad's proper role as strategic cavalry, conducting [operations] deep into the Japanese rear while Stilwell's two Chinese divisions advanced on the enemy front. Their opponent was the veteran Japanese 18th Division, which had conquered Singapore."

The Marauders proved their worth from their very first operation.

After a 140-mile march from the Ledo area to their jump-off point near Shingbwiyang, the Marauders enveloped the right flank of the 18th [Japanese] Division. Screened by three intelligence and reconnaissance platoons and supplied by airdrops in the infrequent jungle clearings, the three battalions followed obscure trails to a pair of positions near Walawbum, astride the expected Japanese line of retreat. The Chinese division commanders, under orders from Chiang to minimize casualties, failed to press their attacks, putting the Americans in an awkward situation. Taking advantage of the slow Chinese advance, Lieutenant General Shinichi Tanaka, commander of the 18th Division, launched heavy attacks against the Galahad roadblocks.

Even though mortars were all they had to counter Japanese artillery, the Marauders inflicted eight hundred casualties on the Japanese, while sustaining two hundred themselves.

"As Chinese reinforcements began to arrive on March 7," Hogan noted, "Merrill withdrew his weary men from their positions. By then, the enemy had bypassed the roadblocks and had fallen back to a line along the rugged Jamba Bum range near Shaduzup."

Stilwell resolved to capture the Jamba Range before the June monsoon season would likely bring all offensive operations to a halt, and so directed resumption of the offensive on Friday, March 12.

Accompanied by the Chinese 113th Regiment, Galahad's 1st Battalion outflanked the Japanese right, negotiating steep slopes and bypassing Japanese positions by slowly hacking its way through the dense undergrowth. In the course of the march, the battalion crossed one stream fifty-six times. Early on the morning of March 28, the [Marauder] advance surprised an enemy camp south of Shaduzup and established a roadblock. Farther south the other two battalions moved to cut the road at Inkangahtawng, but the 2nd Battalion had no sooner established a blocking position than both battalions received orders from Stilwell's headquarters to head off a major Japanese drive against the flank of the American advance. Abandoning its prepared positions under fire, the 2nd [Marauder] Battalion moved east to an isolated ridgeline at Nhpum Ga. Up to this point, Stilwell's headquarters had used Galahad as a flanking force that would only hold blocking positions for brief periods of time. As the official history points out, the change to a static defensive role at Nhpum Ga represented a radical change in the concept of Galahad's employment.

The 2nd Battalion, surrounded and isolated at Nhpum Ga,

withstood heavy attacks and shelling, while the 1st and 3rd attempted to break through to them. Within the perimeter, lack of water and the pervasive stench of mule carcasses tortured the defenders; only a few supply drops made their position tenable. The defense was aided by the presence of Nisei [Japanese-American] interpreters who overheard enemy orders and frequently confused the enemy by shouting directives in Japanese. Meanwhile, Merrill had been evacuated after suffering a heart attack, leaving Hunter in command of Galahad. Supported by artillery air-dropped to them, the 1st and 3rd Battalions finally reached the 2nd and 9th on April 9 as the Japanese withdrew south.

However much they deserved a brief rest, the 1,400 surviving Marauders, supported by Chinese regiments and Kachin irregulars from the Kachin Hills in northern Burma, were ordered to seize an airfield at Myitkyina. "The American commander recognized the poor condition of the Marauders but believed he had no alternative if the Allies were to capture Myitkyina before the monsoon," Hogan observed. He promised to evacuate Galahad without delay if things went as he anticipated. Now the tired but determined Marauders began a sixty-five-mile march over the formidable 6,000-foot Kumon mountain range toward Myitkyina. One officer described the mission launch:

We set off with that what-the-hell-did-you-expect-anyway spirit that served the 5307th [Galahad] in place of morale, and I dare say served it better. Mere morale would never have carried us through the country we now had to cross. The saw-toothed ridges would have been difficult enough to traverse when dry. Greased with mud, the trail that went over them was all but impossible. Mules fell off ledges to their deaths below. Marauders left their packs by the side of the trail; straggling was rampant. Despite all the obstacles, the Marauders and their allies surprised the defenders of the air base on May 17, seized the strip, and probed toward Myitkyina itself. Lacking a plan to follow up its initial success and reliable intelligence on the strength of the Japanese defense, the task force faltered in its attempts to take the city.

Worse, the Japanese promptly rushed reinforcements to the Myitkyina airfield.

Physically exhausted, the Marauders desperately needed to be replaced by rested, more heavily armed line units, but Stilwell lacked fresh troops and politically could not afford to remove the Americans from the battle while other nationalities continued to fight. The results were inevitable. By May 25 the Marauders were losing 75 to 100 men daily to malaria, dysentery and typhus. Merrill was evacuated after his second heart attack. Morale, already low, plummeted when desperate staff officers, trying to hold down the rate of evacuation, pressed into service sick or wounded troops who could still walk. Along with broken promises of relief, the episode confirmed Galahad's self-image as the maltreated stepchild of higher headquarters.

Colonel Hunter, deeply embittered, was relieved of command on the very day that Myitkyina fell to Allied forces. The Marauders as a whole were equally embittered, but

grateful for the aid received from the Kachins. When Galahad had first marched into northern Burma, the Kachins . . . provided information, guided patrols and screened [protected] American movements from the Japanese. Kachin villages even placed their cargo-bearing elephants at the disposal of the Marauders. Later, Kachin patrols served as flank guards for the advance on Myitkyina. Despite a serious snakebite, a young Kachin guided the Marauders to the edge of the airstrip, making a surprise attack possible. During the siege of Myitkyina, Kachin guerrillas cut communications between the city and the Japanese 56th Division on the Chinese border, forcing the enemy to divert a battalion to that region. Other Kachins ambushed Japanese troops attempting to flee the city by floating down the Irrawaddy River on rafts. With the support of the Kachins, the [Marauders] could feel that the jungle was on their side. Many Marauders would later volunteer for service with the Kachin guerrillas following their campaign.

Colonel Hunter believed that Galahad could not have succeeded without the Kachins. In early August 1944 the Galahad survivors were consolidated into the 475th Infantry for further service in Northern Burma, even as Fred Goode and his SSDII brethren languished in the Rangoon jail.

The previous March cholera had broken out among the British, taking a significant toll. Goode recalled the details of that tragedy while writing his memoirs. "By the second day of the infection four men [British prisoners] had died, two in each compound. We could not bury the dead," Goode recalled, "because the Japanese would not allow us outside the prison. All they allowed us to do was wrap the dead bodies in sacks, open the gate of our compound, carry the bodies to an unoccupied compound and leave them there." June 1944 brought a crop of American prisoners with news of Allied initiatives in the Pacific Theater on land and sea.

"All of this gave us a new lease on life," Goode recalled. "Working parties did not cease altogether, but they were certainly curtailed. The Japanese themselves seemed to be getting friendlier. It was also noticed that the crueler elements of our guards had moved away. There were fewer beatings for minor offenses. Out on the working parties were the odd arrogant Japanese who still thought that they were invincible. It was these who gave the odd kick and slap now and then. But on the whole, the majority of them [the Japanese guards] must have realized that the end was coming."

And come it did. Despite nearly being killed by a falling Allied bomb on November 23, 1944, Goode survived to be marched out of the

Rangoon POW camp toward another prison. Allied fighters periodically strafed them, not knowing until it was too late, if they knew at all, that their targets were Allied prisoners. In late August a British Spitfire killed a British brigadier general, not knowing any better.

The Japanese liberated Goode and the other British prisoners, in a manner of speaking, on the evening of Sunday, April 29, 1945, by simply releasing them from their long march, with a letter directing any other Japanese forces who the British might encounter to simply let them go. In late August, during their long march to freedom, a British Spitfire killed Goode's commanding officer, a British brigadier general, not knowing any better. Goode's rescue came not far from the small village where the brigadier had been killed. Years later, he remembered the details with exactitude.

The sound came from my left. Slowly, I sat down among some brush and turned my head, first to the left and then to the right, in an effort to catch another sound, but there was none. All was silent again. After a while I decided to go towards where the sound came from. I moved slightly to my left, going as carefully as I could and moving from tree to tree until I came to some open ground. The only light was coming from the stars. I dropped down on my stomach and lay flat for a time, not moving a muscle. I could see before me the black outline of trees against the skyline on the other side of a paddy field. As I lay there viewing what was in front of me, I saw some figures pass across my vision. I was almost sure they were wearing British steel helmets.

My heart gave a flutter, but I still hesitated. I was not going to throw caution to the wind. Not now, I thought. I did not want to get this far and then miss the boat, like the brigadier. Keeping flat, I edged myself over the paddy bund [embankment] and began to wriggle forward. Stopping now and then, I must have gone thirty yards on my belly when I heard voices again, this time more distinct, and I was sure that they were either Hindi or Urdu. I was about to go on a bit further when there was a prod in the small of my back. I went hot. I went cold and I began to shake. I kept perfectly still, lying flat on my stomach with my hands outstretched in front of me. The thing was still pressing into my back. Sweat was pouring from me. Then a voice in broken English said "Get up and keep your hands above your head."

Goode was at last free.

CHAPTER 10

The Lure of Adventure

THE KOREAN WAR WAS RAGING AND THE CHINESE COMMUNISTS WERE doing their damnedest to defeat the Americans and their allies, filling American Mobile Army Surgical Hospital (MASH) facilities with casualties at an unbelievable rate, only two years after driving the Nationalist forces led by Chiang Kai-shek off the mainland. These efforts were so successful that the Americans had to consider their options.

Some US strategists thought that the great (Chinese) Nationalist Army should be sent into Korea to fight the Communists. Others, however, judged that in addition to insurmountable political and diplomatic obstacles, the forces that had been evacuated from the mainland to Taiwan were still licking their wounds, were ill-equipped and poorly trained, and would likely have to be evacuated from the mainland again.

There were other options worth considering. In his seminal 2018 book, *Raiders of the China Coast: CIA Covert Operations during the Korean War*, which served as the primary source for this chapter, Frank Holober noted:

Another more modest solution was to consider aiming a diversionary sortie at China's soft underbelly, the coastal area lying opposite Taiwan. Assuming that the Communists had assigned their most astute and seasoned generals and troops to the Korean venture, military and political action along the coast might encounter something less than crack troops and serve to drain away the forces needed to fight [the Americans and their allies] in Korea.

As fate would have it, the means were at hand. Along the China coast lay as many as fifty large and small islands, which were either in Nationalist hands or protected by Nationalist naval vessels, a relatively competent and well-trained force. On these islands lived thousands of natives of the coastal areas, organized as irregular guerrillas, who had fought the good battle until forced to hop in their junks [Asian sailboats] and fishing boats and eke out a living in the islands, fishing, smuggling and pirating.

Somehow these forces managed to maintain a semblance of military organization, partially armed, sometimes well led, and decidedly anti-Communist. At the same time, the newspapers carried frequent accounts of guerrilla action on the mainland itself, carried out by perhaps half a million or more Nationalist irregulars, who, like the French Maquis of World War II, were persevering as best they could, awaiting the fulfillment of Chiang Kai-shek's promise to retake the mainland. Unfortunately, news of mainland guerrilla action generally originated either with the Republic of China's Ministry of National Defense (MND) or the Ministry of the Interior, both of which had little credibility in the world, and were suspected of ulterior motives involving money and position.

The US government—driven by the Korean War and the Nationalists— was anxious to both obtain the hard data necessary to pinpoint genuine anti-Communist guerrilla activity, and to render appropriate assistance. To avoid the possibility of broadening the conflict by either the Chinese Communists or the Soviet Union, President Truman ruled out bombing staging areas in Manchuria or elsewhere in the mainland, and in June 1950, "neutralized" the Taiwan straits by ordering the US Seventh Fleet between the warring parties.

Holober observed that "Once elected, President Eisenhower changed all that by reversing the Truman doctrine, thereby freeing the Nationalists to act as they thought right. That said, the situation was complicated, as often seems the case to Americans operating in Asia." According to Holober,

Technically the islands were outside the [Truman] policy and could have been attacked at will by the Communists without provoking a US response. On the other hand, a Communist attack on Quemoy at least would have resulted in a spirited Nationalist defense, including reinforcement by regular forces on Taiwan. Furthermore, Major General William C. Chase, head of MAAG (Military Assistance Advisory Group) on Taiwan, and various political figures in Washington had hinted more than once that an attack on the islands, especially Quemoy, with its large contingent of regular forces, would be considered as a prelude to an attack on Taiwan itself, and would be dealt with accordingly. Most observers at the time, however, felt that neither the Communists nor the Nationalists had much inclination for large-scale hostilities in the straits.

That said, no serious observers at the time expressed any fear that either side wanted a confrontation in the straits. "Whatever the US policy, it was treated as a nonevent by all except the US government, which organized its search for anti-Communist support on the islands and on the mainland under the cover of a civilian import-export firm called Western Enterprises Incorporated (WEI). The implication was that guerrilla action along the coast was outside official policy and could proceed without restraint, following the precedent set with the 'civilian' Flying Tigers prior to Pearl Harbor and the formal entry of the United States into World War II."

The WEI origin story is largely unknown today, since official documents that might reveal it are still under wraps. However, Holober noted: "The need for intelligence on the exact number of guerrillas and their locations was a matter of urgency once the Chinese Communist armies appeared in Korea. Once located, they would immediately receive unlimited support. One early proponent of action on the American side was no doubt General Claire Chenault of Flying Tiger fame, then living in Taiwan, who would expound on the subject to anyone who would listen, publicly or privately, especially congressmen, senators and members of the administration."

Madame Chiang Kai-shek was equal, if not superior, to Chenault in influence. She was "a power behind the [Nationalist] throne and true Mother of the Guerrillas, who personally and through Wellington Koo, the Chinese ambassador in Washington, encouraged the Americans to do the right thing. Allen Dulles, brother of Secretary of State John Foster Dulles and a high-ranking OSS operative in Europe during World War II was certainly a player."

WEI was incorporated in February 1951 and maintained headquarters in Pittsburgh, Pennsylvania.

As Holober observed, "It was standard procedure for all new WEI employees to pass through Pittsburgh to sign their contracts . . . before applying for passports and visas. Having already been trained in parachuting, explosives and other appropriate aspects of commercial life, the first WEI recruits came to Pittsburgh in February 1951."

A motley crew of Americans from various backgrounds were soon on their way to Quemoy and other lesser-known islands nearby. Few were surprised to learn later on that the Central Intelligence Agency was directing them. This was because "the military action was irregular and the US government, for its own reasons, wanted to hide the activity under the rubric of deniability. WEI was an amalgam of CIA paramilitary types: World War II Office of Strategic Services (OSS); and operatives, intelligence specialists, seconded [temporarily detached], retired and active army, navy and marine officers; smokejumpers, and newly recruited college graduates, including several football stars. Some had short-lived careers, coinciding only with a tour with WEI. Others rose to high military or diplomatic position."

Later prominence had little relationship with what these men did in Korea. Frank Holober observed that contrary to public perception, the CIA of that era served several functions: "A common assumption is that the CIA was full of spies who would rather chew on a lethal tablet and expire with a calm, defiant, patriotic smug smile than identify their true employer. Not so. Most employees were working in overt [as opposed to covert] positions, acting as analysts, translators of newspapers and periodicals, monitors of foreign broadcasts, interviewers of travelers to exotic places, all able to say with a proud smile to friends, relatives and real estate agents, 'I work at the CIA, and here is my office telephone number.'"

Of course there were others who Holober and many others have described as "spooks." "Members of the Clandestine Service, these operatives either worked under suitable cover, carried fake ID cards and gave out phone numbers that always seemed to have a mechanical or human message-taker at the receiving end, or existed precariously in a twilight zone, mumbling unintelligibly when asked where they worked and what they did. These were all 'agents,' those who collected information from covert sources, worked to overthrow or redirect governments, or otherwise led adventurous lives only imagined by ordinary mortals."

Holober recalled a distinction between "those with eyes and ears—the spies—and those with ham-like hands and bulging biceps, the political-action and paramilitary types. The former were viewed by the latter as effete Ivy Leaguers who could cover themselves as diplomats without a seam showing."

That said, "The spies' true employer was a part of the CIA ambiguously called the Office of Special Operations, or OSO. The latter were viewed by the former as square-shouldered, jock-like creatures of limited intelligence, also college graduates, but rarely Ivy League, for whom the Defense Department would provide a more appropriate cover. Sometimes called 'knuckle draggers,' these agents were employed by . . . the Office of Policy Coordination, or OPC."

The politics were complex, but whether part of the Office of Strategic Services, Office of Strategic Operations, or Office of Policy Coordination, the Americans at that time frequently worked with legendary Chinese Nationalist General Mao Jen-feng, who once served as an aide to Chinese Communist guerrilla General Tai Li. Frank Holober noted in *Raiders of the China Coast* that "General Tai had been a major liaison figure with the American military during World War II as head of the Sino-American Cooperative Organization (SACO) with Navy Captain Milton E. 'Mary' Miles as his deputy. Operating behind Japanese lines, SACO's members, both Chinese and American, performed heroically and effectively. This history was not lost on the leaders of WEI, who were faced with launching a similar effort from Taiwan just six years later."

The organization led by Mao Jen-feng on Taiwan was called the Secrets Preservation Bureau, and

claimed continuing contacts with agents and guerrilla units on the mainland, as well as the loyalty of guerrilla units on the offshore islands. Because less than two years had elapsed since the establishment of the People's Republic of China on October 1, 1949, the sheer number of these remnants on the mainland could have been substantial. Continued contact was difficult at best; radio traffic would have to be sporadic and brief. Getting couriers in and out in the face of the ever-tightening controls over life on the mainland had become increasingly risky. Good morale could be maintained only if such stay-behind assets were occasionally resupplied and if they could be convinced that the Nationalists would make good on their promise to "fight back to the mainland." As time went on, the reliability, even the existence of these remnants, became impossible to verify.

That said, "fierce ethnic horsemen of the far west of mainland China" and guerrillas mainly hiding on coastal islands, controlled as both groups were by the PMC, proved to be exceptional assets.

Early June 1951 found Frank Holober, author of *Raiders of the China Coast*, flying across the Pacific aboard a Philippine Air Lines DC-6 sitting next to another WEI agent named "Robert," flying into Taipei, the capital of Taiwan. Holober remembered forty-eight years later that

[t]rue to his covert training, [Robert] was so full of sly glances and knowing smiles that he might as well have had a "spy" sticker attached to his forehead.

When he verified that I [Holober] was indeed a member of WEI, he insisted that we share a two-bedroom suite so that we could compare notes. On the elevator he casually flicked a fiver [$49 in 2019 dollars] to the bellhop and asked him to please deliver a tender young thing to his room. Evidently, Robert had passed through Manila before and knew the right passwords to get special room service.

With the efficiency that only private enterprise can boast, a timid knock sounded on the door in about ten minutes. Robert opened the door to admit a slim, demure looker who appeared to be every bit of sixteen summers. But then, many Asian women looked like teenagers well into their thirties. He gallantly waved her into his adjoining bedroom, where his good looks, charming manners, adroit small talk, and the appropriate denominations in US currency, all combined to work their magic.

Holober and his new friend "Robert" soon arrived at the WEI headquarters in Taipei, at the guesthouse within the Grand Hotel complex. Holober checked in with the WEI leadership and the Chinese officials with whom he would soon be working. Holober remembered nearly five decades later that "I next went heavenward into the WEI nerve center. There were no guards, and one did not have to show a badge to gain admission. It was an inner sanctum but open to all the brotherhood. Despite the lack of signs on the walls leading up to the stairs, it was quite clear that the local staff was to stay on the first floor. I made my presence known to the medics, the keepers of the treasury, the [command] staff, the administrative officer, the operations chief, the intelligence chief, and anyone else wandering the halls."

While those early days went by, he met a beardless Santa Claus named "Uncle Rod" Gilbert and other veteran China hands while waiting for his first mission. He couldn't help but notice that

[i]n the early fifties, the scent of decay pervaded the air of Taipei. In the minds of my cohorts and myself, the Soviet adversary had a charging horse for an ally, while we were vainly trying to prod a dead one into action. In the face of the Communist challenge, the Nationalists were waiting for the Americans to destroy the enemy in Korea, praying for a saturation bombing of Manchuria and dreaming that an American-led crusade would sweep over all of China, finally ending with prostrate Communists forming a red carpet for the "Fight Back to the Mainland" crowd.

However elusive and impractical these Nationalist Chinese dreams might have been, Holober soon found himself on an island named Quemoy. Holober described Quemoy in the early autumn of 1951 as

a county by itself; it was large, flat, kidney-shaped, and measured about 10 by 5 miles, lengthwise running east and west. The perimeter of the island with its twists and turns measured as much as 120 miles. There was plenty of space on the southwest corner in a place whose Chinese named translated as "Bordering Stream Village" to house the sixteen hundred or so guerrillas either originally taking refuge on Quemoy, or brought in from other nearby smaller islands for the specialized training soon to be given by the Americans. The south side of the island was taken up by a large bay . . . protected by a long, curving, sandy beach on the opposite side of the island from the mainland and therefore hidden from the prying eyes of the Communist enemy.

The large bay "was thus most suitable as an anchorage for the small guerrilla fleet when the boats were not out on the seas patrolling, fishing, or smuggling, and as a loading area for guerrilla forays against enemy targets along the coast. The Americans soon discovered a cove just north of the bay, within a few minutes' walk of the village, which was largely unused by the locals for recreational purposes. The cove was a most pleasurable location for jogging, sunbathing, and ocean swimming."

When Holober wrote his memoirs, published in 1999, the cove was called Hsi-pien Bathing Beach. Despite this peaceful, idyllic setting, real dangers existed here. "Less than two years earlier, the Communists [had] made a determined effort to seize Quemoy as part of their thrust southward [on mainland China], which succeeded in 'liberating' all of Southeast China," much to the embarrassed surprise of

armchair strategists who confidently predicted that the Communists, with their rapid advances, would run out of steam in the mountainous areas of this part of China. These analysts recalled the problems that the Nationalists had in dislodging the Communists from mountainous "border regions" and forcing them into their famous "Long March" to safer havens in North China. They were wrong elsewhere but certainly right about Quemoy. In October 1949 the Communists launched a furious assault, using fifteen thousand troops aboard motorized junks. Since the Communist east coast port at Amoy was essentially blockaded, at least for military action, the [Communist] "liberation" fleet set sail from Swatow in northern Kwangtung [on the Chinese mainland]. The Communists landed on [Quemoy], igniting a three-day battle that resulted in a crushing defeat of the Red troops, three thousand of whom were captured. The landing junks were completely destroyed.

This victory laid the groundwork for a series of CIA-sponsored actions by Chinese Nationalist guerrillas largely based on Quemoy. Two Chinese Nationalists who Holober identified in his 1999 memoir as "Little Huang" and "Fat Wang" initiated a mission to kidnap a so-called Chinese Communist "purge team" that intelligence sources indicated would soon arrive in Quemoy to capture and try certain "counterrevolutionary" (e.g., non-Communist Nationalists) stationed there.

"The raiders left before dawn and arrived back the same afternoon," Holober recalled, "carrying with them a few recruits, some militia weapons and several souvenir flags and banners. The local [Communist] party headquarters had been blown up. Because the [Communist] purge team got wind of some turmoil on the beach and fled to safety, part of the mission had failed. However, the [Nationalist] raiders intercepted a packet boat bound for Hong Kong loaded with mail."

On the surface, this was a moderately successful mission. However,

[b]ecause the guerrillas had been trained in the importance of picking up documents that might contain valuable intelligence, without hesitation they brought back the letters [bound for Hong Kong] instead of deep-sixing them. Edward Smith Hamilton, the CIA station chief dubbed "the Dragon," immediately sent the mail on to Taipei to be perused for useful information. Uncle Rod seized on them with glee. He arranged for an anti-Communist leaflet to be inserted into each letter, which was then carefully resealed and reinserted into

the normal mail pipeline out of Hong Kong. The implication was that anti-Communists rampant on the mainland had somehow managed to carry off this caper. Articles to that effect began to appear in the local Chinese and native press in Southeast Asia, reprinted or alluded to in major Hong Kong and Singapore newspapers and, eventually, newspapers in other parts of the world, sometimes innocently, sometimes helped along by media "assets." It was a media coup that made the palms [of people] like Uncle Rod sweaty and their eyes dance.

And this was only the beginning.

[Huang and Wang] next selected a small island not too far up the coast. It was not a large target in either political or population terms, but it did have attractions. For one, the island had many friends and relatives of the two companies selected for the raid. Second, it apparently was guarded by mostly local militia, who in case of trouble would expect to be reinforced by motorized junks from the nearby mainland. Third, the raid would give everyone concerned a chance to learn from the master, Ed Hamilton, code name Dragon, the one-eyed West Pointer himself, how to plan, organize and carry out a military operation his way. Last, the operation would give all concerned the opportunity to see if the new training and equipment would translate into greater efficiency on the ground as the guerrillas prepared for larger and more complicated operations. The Americans wanted to see if their newly adopted comrades in arms were truly motivated by a fierce and well-placed anti-Communism. Would they live up to their elegant designation as the (Fukien) Anti-Communist National Salvation Army? The Fukien (Fujian) Province on the east coast of China includes a number of offshore islands.

The preparations for the raid were meticulous.

Three days before the raid, in October 1951, the Dragon asked that WEI's friendly Civil Air Transport (CAT) cousins send a fully loaded C-46 over an uninhabited area in the southeastern part of

Quemoy and award the two companies an airdrop of new hardware and ammo to carry with them into the battle. It would also give the troops practical training in the organization of, and reception at, a DZ [drop zone], in case they did one day manage to establish a base on the mainland. It was a bit of a tricky mission, in that the Communist coastal city Amoy was so close that if enough front-porch lights were left on, the lucky residents might find themselves armed with the latest and best in surplus weaponry from around the world.

Another danger was that at the sound of a plane droning that close to Amoy at night, the Communists would finally arrange to put in a couple of runway lights on or near Amoy, install one honest-to-goodness advanced fighter plane and shoot down one of our resupply planes, day or night, or shoot up the landing craft being used to bring all types of supplies for the populace and regular military on Quemoy. Certainly, if the Communists had used their own eyes and ears and talked to local fishermen all along the coast, they should have known there were Americans on the island [Quemoy] up to no good. Then why did the Communists not send in a specially trained commando unit one night, land on the warm sands of His-pien Beach—where the Americans basked almost every day, and which was only a couple of hundred yards from their residence—and pick up a few round-eyed specimens? One can only speculate, and there were good reasons for a do-nothing policy (massive retaliation in and around Amoy, for example), but it remained a small mystery why no reaction was ever felt. It was almost an insult. Wasn't this mosquito worth swatting?

These speculations aside, conditions for the operation launch couldn't have been better, in the sense that clear skies illuminated the American landing zone.

Right on schedule, at about 2000 hours [8:00 p.m.], the drone of propellers was heard. A small team in the landing area lit a long slit trench shaped like a cross into which had been sprinkled a copious quantity of gasoline-soaked brush and wood, and then raced for the hills. Almost at once, long heavy boxes drifted toward the landing zone, slowed by parachutes and silhouetted first by the heavens and then by the flames. When the first box hit, Fat Wang could resist no longer. He hoisted up his corpulent body and raced into the landing area, risking life and limb, though that was normal for him. He ripped open a cracked case and, raising aloft a new rifle in each hand, he bent his mouth into a wide smile and began yelling in South Fukienese.

Serious preparations began the next morning. Holober recalled in the late 1990s that he and another American had constructed a sand mock-up of Mei-chou (the eastern Chinese coastal city and mission target) some three feet square. The Dragon had calculated logistics and reviewed all available intelligence, with special attention to possible opposition and reinforcement. He then closeted himself for a couple of hours while he consulted with his military angels and composed a practiced five-paragraph field order, a slim document that gave everyone his marching orders and coordinated all elements of the campaign in one elegant whole. The same afternoon, a call for a briefing went out to the six platoon commanders; the two company commanders; raid commander Colonel Wu; Little Huang and Fat Wang (for the guerrillas); and Captain K'ang Chao of the Nationalist Chinese Navy, who would serve as host, and whose destroyer escort (DE) would provide covering firepower for the operation as required.

The planning process Holober recalled is insightful: "Ed [Hamilton] took everyone step by step through the tactics of the entire operation, beginning with landing areas, routes to be taken by the individual platoons, policy toward prisoners, necessity for consulting the local people before taking any action against local officials, sparing the conscientious and punishing the tyrants, and timing the entire action down to the exact minute for [leaving]."

Of most significance, in Holober's view:

It was not a one-way lecture. The guerrilla commanders obviously had a feeling for their personnel and seemed to have no difficulty placing themselves on the ground and running through the operation as it unfolded. Their questions were to the point, clarifying as they went exactly what was expected of them both militarily and politically. They seemingly recognized at once the psychological warfare aspects of the raid, the potential effects of their performance on the future of the guerrilla program, and the potential ripple effect on the Communist and Nationalist military, locally on Quemoy as well as Amoy/Foochow, and possibly even Taipei and Peking. The Americans tended to view this raid as not a throwaway perhaps, but something whose outcome was reasonably assured, as a warm-up for the real things to come. It was not to be taken so seriously that everyone should get uptight and maybe screw up. The Chinese, however, took it very seriously, though Fat Wang's usual exuberance could be expected to keep everything on an even keel.

The dawn landing was largely uneventful, as was the rest of the operation. Midnight found the Nationalist guerrillas sleeping in their tents after a special celebration meal. That, of course, was not the end of the story. During the debriefing the next day the Dragon gave the platoon and company commanders some constructive criticism for use in future operations. That said, the raid "was obviously a success. Some unpopular officials had been punished; friendly casualties were limited to a dozen wounded—none seriously; neither the navy nor the air force had to fire in anger; and the Communists had clearly been taken by surprise and had no time to commit regular forces. Coming back with some twenty militiamen, many of them slightly wounded, was of doubtful value, since they never could be considered reliable recruits and had no intelligence of value to speak of."

Holober noted that a few family members defected with the militiamen. The Americans didn't really ask many questions about what would happen to them, since they were already thinking about the next mission for these Quemoy-based Nationalist guerrillas. "Now that the island guerrillas [Nationalists on Quemoy] had proved themselves in battle, the next target selected was Nan-jih Island, a county-sized island certain to have a sizable contingent of regular forces training daily for the possibility of an aggressive strike by their [Nationalist] guerrilla enemies. The skilled attack on Mei-chou must have alerted them that the war in

Korea was to have a spinoff much farther down the coast, their adversaries being not hated foreigners, but Fukienese brothers with a grudge."

Holober recalled forty-eight years later that "Serious preparations for a major raid began in the early days of December 1951, about a week before the operation was scheduled to begin. By this time the thoughtful people at company headquarters (CIA was for some reason called "the company") had provided not just a flat contour map of the target . . . but an actual plastic mold, itself three-dimensional. Not only were all contours shown, but place names and special geographical features were marked on the map as well. A person half-expected to see signs designating which government buildings would be targeted for demolition," Holober recalled, with some irony, adding that he had assessed the enemy order of battle (strength and numbers) himself. Ed "the Dragon" Hamilton prepared

> *his usual measured and authoritative five-paragraph field order, suitably translated. All guerrilla officers from platoon leader and above attended the ensuing briefing, as well as representatives of Hu Lien's headquarters, the navy and air force. The briefing did not break up until everyone was thoroughly familiar with both his and everyone else's role. They then dispersed to pass along the good news to the individual squads. The process was a little more complex than the Mei-chou operation because this time, the whole [Nationalist] guerrilla complement, roughly the size of a regiment, was to be involved, and the junk transports took on the appearance of a small armada. Little Huang, Hamilton, Cracy and I went along as observers.*

Holober recalled that "Command of the forces was split. While at sea, Fat Wang was firmly in command. Once the troops hit the beaches, command shifted to General Li Kuo-jan, whose official position was Fat Wang's aide-de-camp and heir apparent. Handsome and affable, Li was no doubt everyone's favorite dinner companion."

The Chinese Central News Agency reported that 450 Communist troops had been killed or wounded, adding that "[t]he results of this raid included the confirmed sinking of twelve motorized junks, each carrying one hundred troops, of whom no less than three hundred found a watery grave. On land, enemy losses totaled four hundred, including killed wounded and captured. A large number of weapons and ammunition were also taken." The News Agency went on to report that "The price paid by our forces was on a ration of twenty to one."

"The first thing that comes to mind was the colossal bravery of Fat Wang," said Holober, in his memoir, *Raiders of the China Coast*. "His [Fat Wang's] junk, loaded with troops, was in the vanguard as his fleet headed for shore. Was he sheltering himself behind a bulkhead, to avoid being shot by the marksmen on shore who were waiting for his men in slit trenches and foxholes? Not only was Fat Wang on his feet, seemingly the only man on his boat, but he had mounted a six-foot ladder attached to the mast and was gesticulating wildly, all the while shouting to the winds, cursing the cowardly demons on shore and wishing them a quick entry into purgatory."

Perhaps this was so, but, Holober continued,

[a]t the same time, he [Fat Wang] was exhorting his own forces to speed up their racing motors and hit the beaches as rapidly as possible. His corpulent body made such a great target that all rifles seemed to be pointing at him. Bullets flew around his profile and even took splinters out of the ladder, but he, father of eleven, came through unscathed, threw his charges onto the shore, and then turned back out to look for any enemy junks that may have ventured to leave the mainland with the intention of raining on his parade. Fat Wang was one determined gentleman. Fukien lost a great politician when it turned Communist.

There were, of course, complications and losses, as Holober recalled:

After about an hour observers on the DE noticed a small flotilla of motorized junks approaching from the mainland. Most of the flotilla was engaged by Fat Wang's crews, but the real punisher was the DE, the only one with the firepower to do the job. One junk must have had a Mao-crazed skipper who obviously felt he would go to Communist nirvana if he could only neutralize that big bully DE. He headed directly for us, machine gun blazing away, and its bullets forming a perforated line on the surface of the water. The DE blasted it with several rounds, waiting in between to see if the firing stopped. The junk pressed forward, machine gun still firing. Suddenly, the Dragon [Ed Hamilton] and I, standing on the front deck, observing the action, heard the pop of a mortar. The shell cleared the deck and fell in the water on the other side. The DE gunner was clearly not amused and soon left the junk floundering in the water, guns finally silenced. No human had ever been seen [on the junk]. Those junks were obviously built to take punishment. No one was cheering for the unlucky inhabitants of the junk, but the feeling was obvious that the poor, misguided fools had at least displayed a lot of courage. . . .

When the raid was half over, the Chinese [communications] operator on shore sent word that General Li had been wounded and was being sent to the DE. It was more than a wound. While directing the action, he had peered over a large rock to survey the situation and had taken a round right in the middle of his forehead. H was killed instantly, which dealt the guerrilla cause a terrible blow.

Holober attended a Buddhist ceremony honoring Li the next day. During early October 1952 the Americans and their Chinese Nationalist counterparts planned a second raid on an island named Nan-jih. Intelligence suggested that "the island was guarded by thirteen hundred regular PLA troops, plus a sizable militia force drawn from the local population of thirteen thousand. A force of this size would be beyond the scope of guerrilla operations. In fact, even though the entire Nan-hai [Nationalist] contingent eventually participated and WEI was called upon to prepare an intelligence annex [supplemental plan], target selection and planning had been done" by the Chinese Nationalist guerrilla General Hu Lien and his leadership cadre. From Holober's perspective, "The plan was full of surprises. Even though the islands were technically outside Truman's order to the Seventh Fleet to 'neutralize' the Taiwan straits, General Hu went against the intent of the order by employing four thousand of his crack regulars, adding one thousand guerrillas. The raid was supported by several [US] navy ships stationed at Quemoy, including a destroyer and an LST [Landing Ship, Tank]. In all it was the largest naval operation since the Nationalists [had] evacuated the mainland in 1949."

Holober considered the "Nan-jih Two" operation plan a masterful success, "executed flawlessly." He recalled in 1999 that "After a furious seven-hour battle in which all defense was quelled, Hu Lien ordered a partial withdrawal, designed to draw in Chicom [Chinese Communist] reinforcements which were then in turn clobbered. Hu's forces remained on the island for three days, at which point it was clear that the Communists were amassing a force large enough to make a continuing operation too expensive," in lives and material. The Chinese Nationalist forces returned to Quemoy on October 14, "with hordes of prisoners escorted off the LST. The official number of prisoners was 720, although newspaper accounts went up to 811. A total of 596 able-bodied prisoners" were sent to Taiwan.

Late 1952 brought an unexpected defection from the Nationalist military leadership. Holober's friend "Little Huang somehow lost his political sure-footedness and took off for a clandestine life in Hong Kong," much to Holober's surprise. Holober recalled that "I met him there in the spring of 1953 while on R&R. He looked prosperous, so the spy business must have been rather good."

Frank Holober went on to a long and distinguished career in the Central Intelligence Agency. General Robert H. Barrow, in his insightful foreword to *Raiders of the China Coast*, wrote that the American–Chinese relationship Holober wrote about was marked by "significant behavioral differences. The Americans tended to be informal, impatient, outspoken and often uninhibited; the Chinese, mannerly, patient, circumspect and concerned with saving face. With few exceptions, the relationship worked, cemented by common purpose."

However, General Barrow admitted that in retrospect, "Any contribution to the Korean War was modest at best. Any real success was local, mixed with failure, and of short duration. Early on, lofty expectations gave way to the lure of adventure."

CHAPTER 11

Hey, Blue

WHAT BEGAN AS A TRICKLE INTO SOUTH VIETNAM ALL TOO SOON became a deluge.

At its April 1959 15th Plenum, the North Vietnamese Communist Party Central Committee voted in secret session to return covertly to South Vietnam thousands of Viet Minh veterans. These infiltrators were to work with party cadres who had remained in South Vietnam to execute a conquest intended from its inception to be deniable and thus undercut any rationale for foreign intervention. To infiltrate on such a scale, the Central Committee created a special Army unit, the 559th Transport Group—the numbers commemorating its May 1959 founding—which in tandem with North Vietnam's Trinh Sat secret intelligence service would train people and move them southward. From his headquarters in North Vietnam's Ha Tinh Province, the infiltration commander, Brigadier General Vo Bam, cautioned, "This route must be kept absolutely secret." Therefore, when the first group headed south in August 1959, they wore untraceable peasant garb and carried captured French weapons.

So wrote John L. Plaster in his groundbreaking 1997 nonfiction work *SOG: The Secret Wars of America's Commandos in Vietnam*, which serves as the primary source for this chapter. The term SOG stood for Studies and Observation Group, the unit created in January 1964 to conduct strategic reconaissance in the Republic of Vietnam (South Vietnam). These grizzled Viet Minh veterans tried to cover ten miles every day, working their way around North Vietnamese combat engineers, tediously following a series of meandering footpaths through a mountain chain called Truong Son. The route wound through North Vietnam, Laos, and Cambodia into South Vietnam.

That very year, in 1959, William Colby—an upscale Catholic Ivy Leaguer whose suit and bow tie would have been more appropriate in a corporate boardroom—became the CIA station chief in Saigon. However out of place his wardrobe, his résumé for this assignment was impeccable.

"In 1944," Plaster wrote, "then-Lieutenant William Colby had parachuted into Nazi-occupied France as one of the OSS's most elite operatives, a Jedburgh officer to help the Resistance disrupt German defenses behind the Normandy beaches. A year later he was sabotaging Norwegian rail lines to prevent German units from reaching the Reich before its collapse. While several of his OSS colleagues became founders of US Special Forces, Colby joined the new postwar civilian intelligence agency, the CIA."

These experiences served Colby well fifteen years later in Saigon. According to Plaster, he "found gathering information about the Truong Son Route difficult. Indeed, this landlocked Laotian wilderness was largely unmapped, with misty valleys so blanketed by jungle that flyovers and aerial photos disclosed nothing." Colby and his CIA associates "recruited French coffee planters at Khe Sanh on South Vietnam's northwest frontier to travel every few weeks along Route 9 to the quiet village of Tchephone, Laos, 30 miles away. Despite keeping their eyes peeled, the planters brought back little intelligence because infiltration parties were small."

They traveled Highway 9 at night when visibility was quite limited. Kennedy administration officials upped the game by expanding "Colby's covert effort to detect Communist infiltration and insinuate an expanded network of CIA saboteurs and agents into North Vietnam. National Security Memorandum 52 authorized the CIA to employ Army Green Berets and Navy SEALs to train and advise the South Vietnamese who would execute Colby's covert missions."

According to Plaster,

Technically, the Green Berets and the SEALs weren't working for the CIA—they worked for CAS, an innocuous cover whose initials stood for Combined Area Studies. At the seaside resort town of Nha Trang, American Special Forces trained South Vietnamese 1st Observation Group (1st Group) commandos to explore the growing Ho Chi Minh trail; during 1961 and 1962, the 1st Group mounted forty-one recon operations into the Laotian infiltration corridor, but its teams were too cautious to learn much. The CIA-funded Mountain Scouts penetrated Laos too; however, these courageous but illiterate Montagnard tribesmen could not comprehend map reading and couldn't associate what they discovered with a recordable location.

No matter; progress was being made elsewhere.

Meanwhile in Da Nang, the SEALs trained junk crews to land secret agents in the north and organized a civilian raiding force, the Sea Commandos, for hit-and-run coastal attacks. Soon the Sea Commandos began across-the-beach raids on North Vietnam, to plan a clever weapon designed by SEAL Gunners Mate Barry Enoch. Enoch rigged a pack-board [backpack with wooden frame] with four cardboard tubes—each containing a 3.5-inch antitank rocket-wired to a delay mechanism, so a raider could slip ashore at night, aim the pack-board toward, say, a radar station, activate the timer, and then paddle back to a waiting boat. The raiders would be long gone by the time the North Vietnamese got their sunrise surprise.

Despite this innovation, American-financed raider junks were soon intercepted on a regular basis by North Vietnamese patrol boats, prompting new tactics. The CIA began a search for faster boats and turned to aerial infiltration via a new South Vietnamese Air Force Unit.

And of course, this meant a search for capable pilots. The top candidate Colby turned to was *a flamboyant pilot with a thin Clark Gable mustache and a penchant for black flight suits. [Then] only thirty years old, already he was a colonel and commanded Saigon's Tan Son Nhut Air Base, and seemed willing to fly anything, anywhere—but did that include piloting unmarked C-47s deep into North Vietnam, Colby asked? The pilot smiled and said, "When do we start?" The gutsy flyer eventually would head his country's Air Force and go on to become South Vietnam's president. Nguyen Cao Ky recruited his best pilots, but months of training would precede their first operational flight. To help them, the CIA brought in Nationalist Chinese instructor pilots with hundreds of missions over mainland China very similar to what Ky's men would fly—100 feet above the treetops, at night, under 30 percent moonlight.*

The best CIA air experts available in the southeast helped Colby plan the North Vietnamese aerial penetrations, "[w]ith 90 percent of the North's population arrayed along its coastal lowlands and Red River Valley." The CIA experts "could see that any approach from the Tonkin Gulf—the 'front door'—was certain to be met by MiGs and antiaircraft guns. Therefore, he planned aerial infiltration routes through the less-populated mountainous border with Laos, the 'back door,'" where terrain masking and electronic confusion were most effective. The air force officer coordinating this strategy "had Air America planes in Laos climb to 5,000 feet, where they would appear on North Vietnamese radar, fly a 'back-door' approach, then descend to low level below radar and turn back to Thailand. After dozens of false alarms, the North's air defense network would stop alerting fighters and antiaircraft units and wouldn't be able to distinguish" between the American feints and the real infiltration flights that were soon to begin.

Meanwhile, the agents to be inserted were being instructed at Camp Long Thanh, twenty miles east of Saigon, where Green Berets and CIA officers taught them intelligence and sabotage techniques, rough-terrain parachuting, weapons handling, Morse code, and survival—skills to sustain them for years in North Vietnam. Plaster observed that "By late spring 1961, the graduate agents were ready to join Agent *Ares*."

Several months earlier, in February 1961, a bobbing thirty-eight-foot junk, wood-hulled and two-masted, built in the Vietnamese tradition, navigated through high seas in North Vietnamese waters. According to Plaster,

Like all North Vietnamese fishing boats, [it] displayed proudly Communist red sails; they were her only propulsion. And because she lacked modern navigational instruments, her captain steered as his ancestors had for ten generations, by the stars. But in tonight's overcast it was not his knowledge of the heavens but his familiarity with the towering limestone islands around them that allowed him to steer closer to the seaside town of Cam Pha.

Two nights earlier they'd passed the glowing horizon that was Haiphong, North Vietnam's major port city, and this evening, during a quiet sunset, they could almost see the hazy mountains of Kwangsi Province, China, some 40 miles northward. No other fishing boats braved tonight's squalls or teased the darkened reefs and shoals. On so miserable a night, surely no government craft could come to their rescue if they were swamped.

That said,

neither would a Communist Swatow-class patrol boat stop them and make difficult inquiries, which actually was their main concern. Despite its authentic appearance, this junk had not been built in North Vietnam, but [rather] 800 miles away, at Vung Tau, South Vietnam. And while the men who made and manned her were once simple fishermen, in more recent years they'd become refugees who fled the Communists; and even more recently, they'd been trained by CIA paramilitary officers who also had financed this entire operation.

When at last his junk reached calmer, leeside waters behind a jagged island, the captain called up a thin, middle-aged man from below. Several crewmen lowered over the side a small woven basket boat crammed with a radio and provisions, and off he went; Agent

Ares, the CIA's first long-term North Vietnam–based operative, had been successfully landed.

The later operatives were not as successful or as lucky as *Ares*. "The first airdropped group, Team *Atlas*, never came up on its appointed frequency; the plane that delivered them disappeared. Colonel Ky personally flew the next airdrop mission, inserting Team *Castor* deep in North Vietnam. Three months later, Hanoi held a much publicized trial for three *Atlas* survivors. Then Team *Castor* went off the air, and CIA handlers realized Teams *Dido* and *Echo* were under enemy control, so they were played as 'doubles.' The last team parachuted into North Vietnam in 1961, Team *Tarzan* was presumed captured."

Altogether, during the three-year program that began that year, SOG dropped some twenty-two teams into North Vietnam, of which only five, *Ares, Bell, Remus, Easy,* and *Tourbillon*, remained intact.

Despite these setbacks, SOG began to book operations using the assets available. Eventually, thirty-eight-foot Norwegian PT boats complete with Norwegian skippers began to replace the Vietnamese junks initially deployed. Vietnamese boats and crews eventually replaced the Norwegians. In July 1964 alone the SOG teams demolished five targets in North Vietnam.

Just after a July 30 SOG operation in which five radar sites near Haiphong were demolished, "Word came that North Vietnamese PT boats had attacked the US destroyer *Maddox* in what became known as the Gulf of Tonkin incident. The first US Marine combat forces waded ashore at Da Nang on Monday, March 8, 1965."

Seven months later, "American newspapers were reporting the 1st Air Cavalry Division's violent clash with the NVA 66th and 33rd Regiment in the Ia Drang Valley, the first major US ground combat of the war. But no one would read about the momentous top-secret doings that day near Kham Duc in Laos."

John L. Plaster described that momentous operation in detail:

At 6:00 p.m. the helicopters lifted off, Cowboy in the lead chopper with Mustachio in the second bird. The third Kingbee, a chase aircraft to retrieve crew and passengers if Cowboy or Mustachio or a Huey gunship went down, carried only Larry Thorne, who was not about to stay behind at Kham Duc. In his lap he cradled a bolt-action Springfield M1903-A3 rifle, an obsolete weapon in this era of AK-47s and M16s, but he'd always gone into combat with a Finnish Mosin Nagant or German Mauser, so a bolt-action gun felt natural in Vietnam too.

If there was a song on anyone's mind as the three unmarked Kingbees cranked their engines, it had to be the current Johnny Rivers hit, "Secret Agent Man," whose first line, "a man who leads a life of danger," so fit [the men on this mission].

. . . Indeed, each had been given a number and had his name taken away. Not only that, but Green Beret Team Leader, Master Sergeant Charles "Slats" Petry and Assistant Team Leader Sergeant First Class Willie Card, had turned in their dog tags, military ID cards, even their US cigarettes, which were replaced by Asian brands. If they were killed and their bodies captured, the US government would deny their identities.

Wild river, jungle, and hills were everywhere "as the Kingbees and Huey gunships flew along. The weather proved especially hazardous, forcing them to weave between thunderheads and sunbeams, avoiding sporadic .50 caliber machine-gun fire. They took no hits."

What happened next illustrates the joy and misery of combat in Vietnam.

The Kingbees spiraled into the appointed slash-and-burn, roared away and it was done.

The weather worsened. Thorne sent the first two Kingbees back while he orbited near the landing zone in case RT [Recon Team] Iowa ran into trouble. Cowboy and Mustachio reported low-level visibility so bad that they climbed to 8,500 feet, above the clouds, and made it back to Kham Duc, followed shortly by the O-1 Bird Dog and the Huey Gunships. Larry Thorne stayed until the team radioed that they were safe, then Thorne radioed that he too was headed back.

Larry Thorne was never seen again.

SOG noncommissioned officers (NCOs) had a tradition of sorts for dealing with losses. When an NCO died or went missing, Plaster observed, "There were drinks, some toasts, a few funny stories," and music, namely the singing of "Old Blue," a nineteenth-century folk song changed to honor the names of the men who were lost.

The fall of 1966 brought new SOG assignments, missions, and tactics.

"When SOG [reconnaissance] teams packed their rucksacks to go north and support the Marines," Plaster wrote, "they carried along a new item: wiretap devices. Over the past year, SOG teams had discovered dozens of enemy telephone lines along roads and trails, but until now they didn't have wiretaps and cassette recorders. These taps could produce intelligence of inestimable value because landlines often carried messages too sensitive to transmit by radio." Also, "they might yield important clues for decrypting radio messages." Eventually SOG wiretaps were recognized as "incomparable intelligence sources."

That said, "the NVA ability to detect taps electronically was so great that at least initially, any team that planted a tap was living on borrowed time." Eventually the CIA supplied induction tap devices, which used rubber-coated pads over the wire to glean a recordable signal from its electrical field. The CIA wiretap was not electronically detectable.

In the meantime, another mission—this one a matter of life and death—arrived at the SOG doorstep.

Lieutenant Dean Woods looked down from the top of a tree the evening of Wednesday, October 12, 1966, hoping against hope that no one had seen exactly where he had landed. His "crippled A-1 Skyraider had limped within sight of the South China Sea," but the US Navy pilot realized he had run out of time, pulled the yellow handle beneath his seat, and launched himself into the air a few seconds before his crippled aircraft exploded in full view of any enemy soldiers who might have been watching. He was on a dense jungle forest ridgeline halfway between Hanoi and a town called Vinh, some thirty miles from the South China Sea, between "two bomb-pocked highways that carried supplies from" the Haiphong docks to the Ho Chi Minh Trail and the lesser-known Mu Gia Pass.

"Both roads, he knew, would be crawling with troops," Plaster observed. "Woods distanced himself from his parachute and waited for Thursday. It looked hopeful the next day," if only briefly. "Escorted by A-1 Skyraiders and high-flying Navy F-4 Phantoms, a Sikorsky SH-3C Sea King helicopter whirred above the ridgeline until, at last, the crew chief could see Woods waving his arms beneath the heavy canopy. While the A-1s strafed approaching enemy patrols, the hovering Sea King lowered an extraction rig from its winch, but the harness kept snagging in the trees. By the time it was clear that this [technique] would not work, there was not enough daylight left for the helicopter to return to sea to refuel and finish the operation."

The next day brought clouds and, worse yet, fog. That evening, Seventh Fleet Commander decided to bring in SOG for the first "Bright Light" top-secret rescue mission attempted in North Vietnam. They arrived aboard the USS *Intrepid* that evening, but the weather problems continued. The situation became worse, if that was possible. Plaster recounted that "Beneath the shielding cloud cover, the North Vietnamese continued searching for Lieutenant Woods, who was now suffering through his third day without food. Enough time passed that the NVA had trucked in additional 37mm and 57mm antiaircraft guns to engage American rescue helicopters when they came, as the enemy knew they would. Several companies of NVA had arrived to reinforce the local militia."

Navy Sea King helicopters returned to the rescue site at dawn the morning of Saturday, October 15, with Master Sergeant Dick Meadows's Recon Team (RT) Iowa aboard.

As the North Vietnamese coast took shape, there was an uncomfortable realization that ahead was a modern air defense system whose radars already were tracking their approach and alerting antiaircraft units and ground forces who'd had four days to prepare for them.

When the helicopters crossed the coast, the sky exploded with antiaircraft shell bursts, but the Navy pilots expertly weaved between the worst of it. Minutes later they could see the heavily forested ridge where [at] that very moment the NVA were converging on the downed flyer. After several false insertions to confuse the enemy, one Sea King inserted RT Iowa about 800 yards from Lieutenant Woods's hiding place.

Meadows ran for the ridge.

Nearby, "Lieutenant Woods could hear buzzing planes, helicopters and the booming of antiaircraft guns," but his concerns were more immediate, since he could hear North Vietnamese soldiers within yards of where he was hiding. A few minutes later, the navy notified the SOG rescue team that Woods was in North Vietnamese hands, just before Sergeant Meadows watched an NVA officer and three enlisted men come walking toward him on a trail. Meadows leveled his AK-47 and killed all four before they could level their guns. Although all six SOG rescuers escaped, Lieutenant Woods spent six years as a POW. Years later, Meadows gave Lieutenant Woods the very Tokarev pistol Meadows had taken from the dead NVA officer.

In the years that followed, SOG did not rescue a single American POW, but fared much, much better in stand-up gunfights with NVA regulars who frequently outnumbered them.

One such incident in late 1967 illustrates SOG accomplishments.

The drifting rain squalls were annoying, but didn't stop the Reconnaissance Team Maine incursion into southeast Laos somewhere near Highway 165. The H-34 Kingbee made its way to a slash-and-burn clearing as reinforcements in the form of additional troop helicopters, gunships, and A-1 Skyraiders lingered nearby, just in case they were needed.

Team leader David Baker; Mike Buckland; Sherman Miller, the radioman; and five Montagnard tribesmen watched the helicopters fly away—just before the fun began. "Baker headed for a wood line," Plaster recounted, "and then froze—everyone froze; just ahead were bunkers and milling groups of NVA. Baker backed away, turned toward another wood line, and saw that it too bristled with men and heavy earth-and-log bunkers—NVA soldiers were *everywhere*. [The RT] was totally surrounded on an open LZ, outnumbered perhaps twenty to one by an entrenched enemy, and overlooked by heavy machine guns whose bolts they now heard slamming shut. By any reckoning, Baker and his seven men had about ten seconds to live."

Buckland tersely radioed, "Have inserted into a major unit and not yet engaged. Stand by." However inexplicably, "the NVA just stood there watching, some only 20 yards away. Baker made a shrewd observation: the NVA had bomb shelters, not fighting bunkers. These [bomb shelters] lacked firing ports, so the NVA couldn't shoot from inside and had to climb out even to see, silhouetting their heads and shoulders like targets in a shooting gallery." Plaster described what happened next:

Meanwhile, a half-dozen enemy leaders marched from deeper in the bunker area with an indignant "we'll-get-to-the-bottom-of-this" air about them. Perhaps, just perhaps, RT Maine's unmarked Kingbee had been mistaken for a similar-looking Soviet-made Mi-4, used by the North Vietnamese. Mike Buckland smiled, waved and called out reassuringly in Russian.

More NVA were standing atop bunkers now, craning their necks like gawkers at a traffic accident. They didn't even point their AKs at the team. Baker, Buckland and their point man kept their CAR-15s low and let the NVA officers approach to the edge of the wood line, only fifteen paces away. Then all three opened fire and snuffed [the NVA] out in two seconds. The NVA command element was gone.

The surviving NVA machine gunners were too stunned to fire their heavy 12.7mm machine guns, giving the Recon Team the time they needed to kill them all. The NVA were so astounded by what they saw that the SOG men fired a full ten seconds before any of the enemy fired back. And with that came the slaughter.

"More NVA climbed into view, and RT Maine cleaned the bunker tops again, this time dropping twenty men. But their luck was almost gone. Seeking cover, Baker hustled his men a few steps into a knee-deep depression, just enough to lie belly-down in, while the heavy fire crisscrossed above them."

The NVA that survived began shooting at each other in their confusion.

Staying as low as they could, "the SOG men shot low to ensure hits while the confused NVA fired high, hitting each other. Newly arriving NVA didn't understand at whom or what they were supposed to fire. Baker called in gunships and told them to strafe any tree line." That's when things might have become dangerous.

"Manned by replacements, the two 12.7mms fired, but they'd been emplaced as antiaircraft weapons and their muzzles couldn't be depressed low enough to hit RT Maine—they were pummeling their own bunkers. A pair of A-1 Skyraiders rolled in with cluster bombs and 20 mm cannons just as an NVA squad assaulted the SOG team"—or tried to; "the NVA were dead before they'd gone 10 yards."

Of course, that wasn't the end of the firefight.

"On a shouted command, another NVA squad rushed out, but made it only 20 yards before CAR-15 fire knocked them all down. Covey offered to attempt an extract, but Baker said no, not until the NVA were dead or pushed back."

The incoming was closer and closer.

Bullets smacked into the rucksacks behind which Maine's men had taken shelter, and then a bullet tore a URC-10 radio from Baker's hand. The NVA launched three human-wave assaults, and each time they got closer before Maine's fire cut them down; Baker told Covey to bring napalm in close or they'd be overrun. Another fifteen NVA jumped to their feet, shouting and dashing and firing just as an A-1 rolled.

The bounding 750-pound napalm canister split apart so close it spewed petroleum-smelling globs on RT Maine's rucksacks and weapons and on Mike Buckland's hand and shirt. An instant later the napalm burst hot orange all around them and set ablaze rucksacks and a Montagnard CAR-15. They felt the air sucked away as black smoke blocked the sun, and inside its shadow fifteen Vietnamese human torches staggered and collapsed, "a horrifying sight," Buckland called it.

During this gunfight, the Skyraiders took out most if not all of the heavy machine guns, forcing the NVA to fall out. And with this, "A

Kingbee nearly out of station time snatched away RT Maine; Baker's men had been on the ground forty-two minutes, had fired nearly four thousand rounds and had thrown fifty grenades. They'd been too busy fighting to count, but a likely fifty enemy lay dead and twice that many wounded. Against this heavy loss, Baker alone was wounded, superficially, by grenade fragments."

In describing this mission, Plaster paid particular attention to the difference between history and Hollywood.

> *Contrary to how Hollywood depicts such things, [an] SOG operation was not laid out in a thirty-second huddle aboard an aircraft en route to a target. The process began a week before insert with a warning order that gave the One-Zero [team leader] an execution date, target and mission description. Later the team's Americans sat through a formal briefing, then the One-Zero overflew the targets to select LZs, shoot photos and get the lay of the land. Next came days studying maps, intelligence reports and aerial photos. Then the One-Zero formulated a detailed plan that he briefed back to his FOB commander. The One-Zero had tremendous latitude, a freer hand, thought Major Henry Gole, a SOG staff officer, "than most senior officers in conventional forces." And there was pre-mission training: If it was a wiretap, for instance, the team brushed up on operating tap gear and rehearsed security formations they'd use during the tap. Finally came the draw of mission-specific gear, packing it all up, followed by the One-Zero's equipment inspection, then a quick weapons test firing.*

In summary, "Every aspect of SOG recon procedures was intensely thought through to push out little edges, a thousand little edges that cumulatively yielded the kind of decisive advantage that brought RT Maine out alive. Recon men had to outrun, outshoot, outmaneuver and outthink the best Hanoi threw at them."

But of course, in the end, each mission depended upon the men who answered to the leadership. Their habits in Vietnam are worth examining even today.

*Every item a recon man carried was deliberately positioned. Reload
magazines went on his left side, grenades on the right, compass on the
left wrist so he could extend his arm away from a steel weapon for an
accurate reading without taking his right hand off the grip. Reload
magazines were positioned so that even on the move he could drop an
empty magazine with one hand, pull a full one with the other, slam it
into his CAR-15 without even looking, slap the bolt release with the
left palm and continue firing. With practice, reloading took less than
three seconds.*

Everybody took precautions, thinking "worst case" all the time.
"Recon men straightened grenade pins and wrapped them once with tape
so that even if wounded in one arm they could pull pins with their teeth,
just like in the movies. And every bit of gear was muffled with tape or
rubber bands so it generated no rattle, clank or noise of any kind. There
was a rule, a lesson, a reason, for everything they did—*everything.*"

The most demanding SOG missions were enemy prisoner snatches.

"By hook [or by] crook, by trickery and device, by technology and
technique, SOG men aspired to perfect their kidnapping craft, developing
more skill in this artful science than at any time in previous military
history. Rewards and accolades were heaped upon successful snatchers,
and with good reason: There is no intelligence source as fruitful as a
freshly snatched prisoner."

That said, during the entire Vietnam War, SOG teams, as skilled as
they were, snatched fewer than fifty prisoners from Laos and Cambodia.
The efforts were most successful in the early years; twelve targets were
captured in 1966, ten the next year, but statistics tumbled to one solitary
snatch in 1968 when the NVA initiated counter-reconnaissance teams
and expanded security forces in Laos and Cambodia.

Snatch techniques debated constantly by SOG principles boiled
down to three options: "disabling the candidate with a carefully placed
gunshot, knocking him senseless with explosives, or just grabbing him."
One mission illustrates the difficulties in the "shoot and grab" method:

"In early 1969, Master Sergeant Norm Doney, One-Zero of
RT Florida, took careful aim with a .22 High Standard at [an] NVA

approaching him on a side road near Laotian Highway 110 . . . Minutes earlier, Doney had positioned a three-man Nung security team in a curve 50 yards down the road, telling them to block any reaction force so he could disable and capture a passing NVA."

An unfortunate NVA appeared all too soon.

"Doney let him come to within 10 feet, and then plugged him in the thigh; he collapsed, dropping his AK. Perfect! But unknown to the One-Zero, around that curve a long line of NVA troops followed visible to Doney's security men, who, instead of shooting to buy their leader time, turned and ran so noisily that the NVA column opened fire."

Doney and his team standing over the wounded NVA hardly noticed the rest of the team rushing past them. Within seconds the ARVN sergeant and interpreter assigned to Doney made a run for it too.

"Then an exploding RPG rocket knocked Doney to his knees, peppering him with shrapnel. The would-be prisoner leaped for his AK but Doney groggily managed to shoot first, popping him several times with the suppressed pistol, killing him. With NVA advancing up the road, Doney rejoined Joe Morris and ran to an LZ, where they found the rest of their team. While waiting [for] extraction, they heard a truckload of troops drive up; an air strike destroyed it. Then Hueys swooped in and pulled them out."

Since the mission was almost successful, Doney decided to try at that very spot one month later. This time he arrived with an extra American on the team, just in time to encounter a single NVA who they killed instead of kidnapping.

Several weeks later, another recon team returned to the same spot, hoping that the third effort would be successful, only to see that the NVA had posted a "Danger Zone" sign. "And sure enough, the team noted, whenever enemy troops passed Doney's ambush site, they'd fire a few magazines into the bushes like kids whistling past a graveyard on a spooky night."

John Plaster, author of *SOG: The Secret Wars of America's Commandos in Vietnam*, wrote of his own participation in a kidnap effort,

when I went into northeast Cambodia with RT Illinois to assess one of [Secretary of State] Henry Kissinger's so-called secret B-52 raids, in hopes that if we came upon a small party of bomb-disoriented NVA, I could dispatch all but one and we'd take him prisoner. Instead, we bumped head-on into an NVA unit, exchanged fire and had two of our indigs [indigenous Vietnamese] hit bad. Ben Thompson, our One-Zero, dragged them toward an LZ while George Bacon, my other US teammate, and I delayed the enemy. When George fired his CAR-15, enemy soldiers ducked and dove; when I fired my silenced Swedish K, it virtually had no effect. They didn't know I was shooting. But that wasn't all.

After Plaster rejoined the team, "a lone NVA suddenly popped up and almost got me, but I dealt him a solid torso burst and he went down. When a Huey landed to evacuate our wounded, I rushed past where the NVA had fallen and saw that he [had] crawled away with his AK."

During yet another SOG snatch mission in the "Fishhook" region of Cambodia, just three hours after insert, Plaster and several Americans came to a series of high-speed trails. "Cargo-laden bicycles rolled past and loud voices called out from several directions; they found a bundle of communications wires 2 inches thick." The team leader "figured they'd better attempt a snatch immediately and get away fast." While Bryan Stockdale radioed a nearby FAC (Forward Air Control), another American arrayed the team along a trail and cocked his Grease Gun. They'd take the next NVA coming down the trail, even as some fifty miles away USAF Green Hornet helicopters took off.

Plaster remembered what happened next:

RT Hammer hadn't lain there five minutes when along came a lone enemy soldier, his AK slung because his hands were full of canteens. When he was just 10 feet away, Mackay took aim at his [the NVA's] leg, squeezed the Grease Gun trigger—but the bolt lurched to the magazine lip and jammed there, making a loud thunk. The startled NVA dropped his canteens, but just as quickly two RT Hammer Yards [team members] pounced on him and, with Stockdale, dragged him into the bushes, handcuffed and blindfolded him. Mackay came over to help and set down his errant Grease Gun—and the bolt snapped forward and popped one shot into Stockdale's leg, under the knee. Stockdale felt the pain, thought he'd been hit by some distant gunman, and then he noticed smoke wisping from the M3 suppressor. He soundly cursed out his One-Zero. However, he found just a grazing wound; he could walk and, fortunately, no one had heard the shot. Soon, the Green Hornets were overheard and RT Hammer escaped without a hitch.

The SOG war went on "into the fall of 1971, as teams documented the continuing NVA buildup. By October, seven of every nine missions had teams fighting for survival, yet they were always ready to go back, as if it were 1965 and America was fighting to win."

NVA tanks were spotted in southern Laos that month, even as command in Saigon seemed increasingly reluctant to heed SOG warnings, focusing instead on nitpicking and minimizing field reports. According to Plaster, this emerging conflict among Americans came to a head during a briefing for General Creighton Abrams.

Chief SOG had just presented recon team reports of tanks and tank trails coming out of Laos, when a staff officer began demanding arcane details before the intelligence could be accepted. Abrams grew furious, slammed his fist on the table, and barked, "I don't know what you want these soldiers to do! Do you want them to personally bring back the battalion flag so you can see what the hell his unit is before you believe? Because goddamn it, I send these guys there, they have the worst job in this command and do it brilliantly, and they bring back intelligence and they risk their lives and you guys sit on your hands and say, "We don't believe this shit."

Plaster marked this as the end of Saigon nitpicking.

The last SOG recon team went out to the Ashau Valley that December. They tracked down air strikes on some NVA trucks and escaped, bringing the SOG combat role in Vietnam to a quiet end. The most highly decorated combat unit in Vietnam was the sixty-man SOG reconnaissance unit at Kontum, whose men earned five Medals of Honor.

CHAPTER 12

Non Sibi Sed Patria

Andrew R. Finlayson bounded onto the makeshift stage at the US Naval Academy football stadium in Annapolis for the prize that had consumed the last four years of his life. That day in June 1966 "marked the end of four frustrating and largely unhappy years of academic struggle," according to his memoir, *Killer Kane: A Marine Long-Range Recon Team Leader in Vietnam, 1967–1968*, which serves as the primary source for this chapter.

Worse still, his parents were concerned about his decision to serve in the most dangerous military branch of service, the US Marines Corps. After some time off back in Merchantville, New Jersey, he drove a brand-new Triumph TR4 roadster some 187 miles southwest to Quantico, Virginia. First stop was the Basic School—a twenty-two-week endurance test to see if Finlayson measured up to the required standards for a marine officer. Later, he recalled, "I found myself thinking of some of the useful training I had received prior to graduation from the [Naval] Academy. During some informal evening classes for Naval Academy students seeking a marine career, Major Jarvis Lynch taught how to organize a standard issue Marines Corps pack and what to put in it; how to care for the equipment we would be issued at Basic School, and how to maintain and tune a PRC-10 radio." Finlayson recalled in his memoir that one "of the most valuable lectures he arranged for us was given by a Marine First Sergeant with more than twenty years' experience in the Corps who told us what to expect from a Marine Corps Staff Noncommissioned Officer

(SNCO) and how to deal with [an] SNCO so we worked as a team, each of us with separate responsibilities and tasks to perform."

Late January 1967 found Finlayson on his way to Vietnam after calls to his parents and a former girlfriend, identified only as "Jane" in his memoir. The next morning he joined a friend and some two hundred other marines for the flight to Okinawa. Several days after they arrived there, Finlayson carried a B-4 flight bag and footlocker onto a US Marine Corps C-130 transport plane bound for Vietnam. Thanks to an alarm-clock malfunction, or so the story goes, Finlayson nearly missed the flight, a breach of military etiquette tantamount to going AWOL. Upon arrival, a marine truck transported them to an Officers' Transient "Bachelor Officers' Quarters" (BOQ) a few miles west of Da Nang.

Finlayson's recollection of that occasion is insightful. "The trip from the airport to the division headquarters was a short one, about fifteen minutes. As we drove along, I eagerly took in my new surroundings. Just outside the airfield perimeter fence, we passed the village of Phuoc Tuong, better known as Dogpatch to the Marines."

The original Dogpatch was the Arkansas hometown of a cartoon character named Li'l Abner until 1977, when the forty-three-year-old comic strip created by Al Capp ended. Phuoc Tuong was a "ramshackle village of huts and garish shops [that] had once been open to Marines on liberty." A few grim episodes resulting in the deaths of several marines prompted commanders to place Dogpatch off limits.

Finlayson's next stop was Camp Reasoner, one of the marine encampments on or near Hill 327. Finlayson spent the next four days getting ready for his first patrol. He busied himself drawing (getting possession) of his field equipment, studying old patrol reports that might be helpful in the missions to come, running three miles a day, "reviewing my Basic School notes on field communications and the use of supporting arms," and talking to the other officers in his hootch (quarters) about what he needed to know for his first patrol.

Nor were his evenings free. In his memoir Finlayson recalled that "In the evenings I spent my time . . . monitoring the progress of patrols in the field as they reported in via radio and tracking their progress on a large map of the Da Nang area. In the dim light amid the crackling of the radios and the intermittent clapping of a typewriter, I tried to digest as much information as I could about the area I would be making my patrols in."

Over the next ten months Finlayson spent hour upon hour doing the same thing: trying to find out all he could about where he would be going. "I was never sorry I did this. It was time well spent."

The day before his first patrol a Sergeant McDonald invited Finlayson to

join the other members of the patrol, code-named Brisbane, so I could be introduced to them. I could tell that every Marine in the patrol was sizing me up and wondering whether I would be a help or a hindrance on the patrol. They did not say anything, but I could read the apprehension in their eyes. They knew I would soon become a patrol leader for one of the platoon's two patrols [code-named Brisbane and Killer Kane], so their interest in me was not casual or insignificant. I was determined to make the correct impression and to do everything possible to assuage their apprehension, but I knew this would take time. These first few minutes were important since they were my only chance to make a good impression. Sgt. McDonald asked me if I wanted to say anything to the team. I did not feel it was the time or place for any long-winded speech, so I merely stated that I was very proud to be among them, and that I realized I had a lot to learn about reconnaissance patrolling. I asked them to share their knowledge with me and always feel free to talk to me if they had any ideas about how I might improve the conduct of a patrol.

Finlayson marveled at the detail in the patrol reconnaissance order prepared by Sergeant McDonald for this, his first mission. He could see the confidence that the whole patrol had in McDonald. Turning to the mission, they would be

patrolling Charlie Ridge, a large, jungle-covered mountain southwest of Da Nang that was notorious for the many enemy contacts made there by our reconnaissance teams. He also told us about the weather and terrain and what enemy units might be encountered. He went over the general conduct of the patrol, but he also carefully informed each man of his job on the patrol, what equipment and ammunition we were to take with us and how such items as Claymore mines, demolition kits and binoculars would be apportioned among the patrol members. He went over the radio call signs and frequencies we would be using, the artillery positions that would be supporting us, the locations of nearby reconnaissance teams and friendly infantry units who might come to our assistance and a myriad of other details.

That afternoon the patrol test-fired their weapons, practiced drills rehearsing their movements during the mission, and reviewed procedures for securing prisoners with parachute cord. After lunch Finlayson and McDonald conducted a reconnaissance helicopter overflight. Finlayson recalled that the reconnaissance helicopter "pitched violently and descended until we were only a few hundred feet above the trees on Charlie Ridge. All I could make out were tall, dark, 100-foot-high trees with thick foliage. The noise in the helicopter made talking very difficult, so Sgt. McDonald resorted to sign language most of the time. Sgt. McDonald pointed to his map and pointed out the [right side] of the C-46, indicating the landing zone on his map was we passed over it."

They also flew over two alternative landing zones before returning to Camp Reasoner. Finlayson didn't sleep much that night.

I was going on a combat recon patrol with seven young Marines and a Navy corpsman into an area controlled by the enemy and known for danger and death. Only our training and luck would protect us and prevent the enemy from detecting us. It seemed as if morning came just an hour after I went to sleep, but my traveling alarm clock indicated I had been in bed for six hours. I was not hungry, so I did not eat breakfast, a mistake I would not make again. Instead, I put all my patrol gear on the back porch and waited for the insertion helicopters to arrive.

Weather and operational issues delayed their planned early-morning departure into midafternoon. Finlayson recounted every detail in his memoir:

Our ride to the insertion zone lasted less than thirty minutes. I watched as Sgt. McDonald left his pack on his seat and moved into a position between the pilot and copilot of the CH-46 helicopter. He pointed to the map and showed the pilots the Polaroid picture I had taken of the LZ [landing zone] on the overflight the day before. They nodded and then Sgt. McDonald returned to his seat and put his back pack on. Seated next to me, he placed his mouth close to my ear and shouted, "We are going into a false LZ first, so don't move from your seat until I tell you to." . . . The helicopter began a rapid, spiraling descent that seemed to force my stomach into my mouth. As we descended, I saw the trees come into view outside and heard a distinctive cracking sound. I suddenly realized that we were taking fire from somewhere near the LZ. The helicopter briefly touched down in some elephant grass and then with a shudder it began to rise up out of the LZ and gain altitude. Sgt. McDonald again put his mouth to my ear and yelled, "That was a false insertion. We did it to fool the enemy into thinking we had actually landed there. It was a good thing because they were waiting for us. That was the shooting." The thought struck me: This was the first time in my life someone had shot at me, and I thanked God that they missed.

[The chopper] circled another LZ not too far from the false insertion zone while Huey gunships prepped the LZ with machine-gun fire. After prepping the LZ, the gunships flew in beside our helicopter and followed us down as we again began to spiral toward the earth in what appeared to me to be "crash mode." As we descended into our LZ Sgt. McDonald instructed all of us to take the safeties of our weapons off and get ready to exit the helicopter. The helicopter shuddered violently as it lowered into the LZ.

When we exited the helicopter, we had to jump off the rear ramp because the CH-46 could only get partially landed in the small zone. I was the third person off the ramp and I dropped about four feet through the elephant grass onto the hard ground. The weight of my 70-pound pack made my drop seem like the height was a lot higher than four feet, and it sent a shock through my spine. Our eight-man team scurried to cover in the dense jungle while the helicopter shook itself loose from the bounds of earth and lifted slowly into the air like some huge, primeval insect, sending dirt, grass and other debris into the air around us.

As the helicopters flew away and the sound of its rotors became more distant, we huddled in silence, straining our ears for any telltale signs that the enemy was near. Sgt. McDonald told me that the enemy often waited until the helicopters and the fixed-wing escort planes departed to hit a recon patrol, so we stayed on alert in a small circle facing outboard, our ears and eyes straining to pick up any sound or movement that might indicate the enemy had seen us land and were preparing to attack us. We wondered if the VC who fired at us during the false insertion would attempt to find us in our new location.

McDonald waited twenty minutes or so and then had his radioman notify the base camp that the patrol was safe and would soon begin their mission. "When the message had been passed to one of our radio-relay stations, Sgt. McDonald used hand and arm signals to order the patrol to move out in a column, moving through the jungle in an uphill westerly direction."

Finlayson recalled being somewhere in the middle of the column. He stayed right behind McDonald to take in how McDonald handled himself. "The patrol, which had developed its procedures through trial and error over time, began to move slowly through the thick secondary growth at a pace [I] initially thought was excessively slow." All too soon Finlayson realized that this particular pace was designed for one thing: silent movement.

"The point man, Lance Corporal Bart Russell, set the pace. He would often stop to take out his K-bar knife so he could slowly and noiselessly cut vines and small branches that impeded our way or might make a loud noise if someone caused them to spring back after passing. Every twenty minutes the patrol would stop and sit down with each man in the patrol facing outboard in staggered fashion so all 360 degrees around the patrol was covered."

All was silence. Nobody talked or even used hand signals.

"During these stops, we listened to ascertain if we were being followed. After each ten-minute rest period, Sgt. McDonald would signal us to continue. We struggled to rise under the weight of our packs, which made us walk in a stooped fashion and often caused us to stop and hitch our packs up on our backs to gain comfort from the weight."

Finlayson remembered later that

> [w]ithin minutes, I was perspiring profusely and the heat and humidity seemed to sap my strength. It was the heat of the day when we inserted, and after two hours of struggling uphill through the tangled undergrowth beneath the thick jungle canopy, I was near exhaustion. However, I was determined not to let the other members of the patrol see my discomfort or to ask them to stop and allow me to rest. Nervous tension and my concern about how other members of the patrol would view me made me push on without complaint, secretly anticipating the next ten-minute respite the patrol would be taking as a security break.
>
> As light began to fade, we stopped and formed a circle with each man facing outboard. Sgt. McDonald came over to me and took out his map. I took out my map also and he showed me where we were and told me to watch him as he wrote a Situation Report (SITREP) that would be sent via radio back to base, informing them that we were stopped for the day and soon would be occupying a night harbor site. Sgt. McDonald showed me the SITREP, which he had written on yellow message paper, and whispered to me that the harbor site location was approximately 100 meters from our present location, and that we would move to it as soon as it became dark. In this way, if the enemy had spotted us and wanted to attack after dark, they would hit our present location and not the real harbor site 100 yards distant. We would have a distinct advantage using this technique.
>
> While the radioman whispered the SITREP over the radio, Sgt. McDonald signaled to us to eat. We carefully and noiselessly took a

can of C rations from our packs and then quietly and slowly used our P-38 [John Wayne] can openers to open the cans. Sgt. McDonald did not allow his men to cook their meals since the smell of cooking food traveled far in the jungle and it could give our position away. He also did not allow anyone to smoke on patrol, which resulted in most of the men chewing tobacco.

Finlayson tore into a can of beans and franks for a slow, surprisingly good dinner, as he remembered it. "In the days ahead this meal would always be my favorite one among the culinary offerings of C rations," or so he remembered. The team collected the empty cans so one man could shovel leaves over them. After finishing dinner they moved toward their harbor site, even as Finlayson realized they had only traveled 500 meters (547 yards) from their landing zone.

This was easily explained on reflection. First,

The very careful and slow pace over rough terrain with frequent stops every twenty minutes greatly reduced the distance the patrol would cover. It was not uncommon for a patrol to cover less than 1,000 meters in a full day of patrolling in the jungle. That said, there were several advantages to using this tactic. Rapid movement in the jungle was loud and could easily alert the enemy if they were nearby. Second, any loud movement prevented the patrol from hearing the telltale noises that indicated the enemy's presence. Sound, especially man-made sound, traveled far in the jungle. Third, a slow pace did not tire the patrol members or make them careless. Finally, a slow pace allowed the patrol to take note of all surroundings so that later, during the patrol debriefing at Camp Reasoner, the area covered could be accurately described. Such information as trails, streams, ambush sites, enemy bunkers and the like could be described in detail so future patrols or infantry units would have a good idea of the terrain and enemy activities in the area covered by the patrol.

My first night in the field in Vietnam passed quietly. Our harbor site, which we crawled into on our hands and knees because it was so thick with tangled foliage, was ideal, since anyone trying to get close to us during the night would make an awful racket fighting their way through the thick brush, thus giving us advance warning of their approach. We slept in a tight circle with our feet facing inboard and our heads and weapons facing outboard next to us, so we could quietly retrieve them in the darkness if needed. The patrol's two radios were placed in the center of the circle so any one of us could use them during the night. Sgt. McDonald assigned each member of the patrol a one-hour radio watch, and these assignments went in a clockwise direction around the circle of men so it would be easy for the man on watch to quietly wake up the man next to him and pass him the radio set.

McDonald arranged the schedule so that just this once, Finlayson could get a full eight hours' sleep.

Three days later, near the end of daylight, the patrol moved toward their extraction landing zone (LZ), covering a one-thousand-meter uphill walk in three hours. "Along the way," Finlayson recalled, "we found an unoccupied enemy company–sized harbor site with a dozen bunkers made of logs.

"When we reached our extraction LZ, Sgt. McDonald instructed the patrol to search the area around it to make sure there were no booby traps or enemy fighting positions. It was a larger LZ than our insertion LZ, capable of easily accommodating two CH-46 helicopters. We kept watch on the zone until it was nearly dark, and then we moved 100 meters into some thick secondary growth and established our night harbor site."

"VC lights," Sgt. McDonald whispered to Finlayson after darkness had fallen. Finlayson watched fifty or so lights in a row descending a nearby ridge, parallel to the marine patrol position, 500 meters (547 yards) away and moving away from them. McDonald reported the sighting but didn't order artillery because he couldn't calculate exactly where it should be placed. In good time, two CH-46 gunships came for them, ending the uneventful patrol. Other than a missed opportunity to ambush three NVA soldiers, Finlayson's first three patrols were uneventful, a far cry from the rest of 1967.

On Saturday, March 25, Finlayson's friend and roommate Eric Barnes was killed during a patrol into the inexplicably named Antenna Valley that he could have skipped, along with Thomas Dodd. This prompted the First Force Recon group, known as Killer Kane, to become more aggressive in their patrol efforts. Later Finlayson recalled, "That evening as I lay in my bed, sweltering in the heat, I vowed that I would make the enemy pay for what they had done to Tom, Eric and Sgt. Godfred Blankenship. For hours that night, I thought about how I could take revenge on the enemy. The answer would come the next morning."

Sergeant Roy Watson woke Finlayson up the next day with an urgent request.

"Lieutenant, our team is angry about the deaths of Capt. Barnes and Sgt. Blankenship, and we want to avenge their deaths. We need you to help us do this." Watson laid out the specifics:

We want you to lead a combined patrol of the men from Countersign and Killer Kane, so we can go back to the Antenna Valley Pass and ambush the bastards who killed our friends. Our team talked it over, and we decided we want you to lead this patrol because we know you are not one of the patrol leaders who just goes out and hides from the enemy. You ambushed that Caucasian guy in Elephant Valley, and you were not afraid to try to ambush some VC on your last patrol. Your team says you are aggressive, and that is the kind of team leader we need on a mission like this. Besides, we know you request patrols, so no one would be suspicious if you requested a patrol near the Antenna Valley Pass.

Finlayson almost turned them down.

At first I thought the idea was a bad one. I knew it would be risky to go back into an area that was mined, but I was also aware of the dangers of ambushing [along] a well-used trail far from any friendly units. I also did not like the idea of taking Marines from another patrol along with my men, since I would not know these men and how they would react under my command. I also was aware of the eccentric and manipulative character of Sgt. Watson. My initial reaction to his idea was to reject it, but then I felt the rage well up inside me about Tom

Dowd's and Eric Barnes's death. Despite my misgivings, I told Sgt. Watson to come with me to the hooch, where I took out one of my maps of Antenna Valley so the two of us could study it. He pointed out where Team Countersign had been inserted on a ridgeline north of the pass and the path they had taken before they hit the land mine that killed Capt. Barnes and Sgt. Blankenship. I noticed that the Antenna Valley Pass was both long and very narrow, with steep mountains on the north and south sides, which would make it an ideal place to establish ambush sites.

The more I studied the map with Sgt. Watson, the more I liked his idea of setting an ambush in the pass. I told Sgt. Watson to choose four of his best men from Team Countersign, and I would pick three of my best men to make up the combined patrol using my call sign of Killer Kane. I also had him swear to secrecy about what we intended to do on this patrol. He waited for me on the back porch while I went to the S-3 office to request a patrol for Killer Kane that would take us into the Antenna Valley Pass area.

Next, Finlayson dropped by the S-3 office and casually suggested that his next patrol focus on the south side of Antenna Valley, near "the old French fort," a long-abandoned concrete blockhouse that may have dated back to the First Indochina War. After listening to Finlayson's pitch, the marine officer making the go/no-go decision only said one thing: "Lieutenant, you need to be careful here because Capt. Barnes's team hit that land mine on the north side of the pass, and there may be more mines there. I recommend you stay off the ridgelines and that trail below in the valley or you might end up getting killed."

Now that the patrol was approved, Finlayson and Watson met for a planning session. Finlayson recalled in his memoir,

I included Cpl. [Robert] Garcia in our conspiracy because he had impressed me with his skills as a point man, and I knew with the danger of land mines it was essential that he be mentally prepared to avoid them when we moved to the valley floor for our ambush. We decided that the best approach was to be inserted into an LZ on a ridge adjacent to the one that Team Countersign had used on its tragic patrol. We would then . . . avoid any trails and ridge lines [en route] to a position where we could observe as much of the trail as possible, but low enough so we could quickly get down to the trail to establish an ambush. We looked at the contour lines on the map and a few black-and-white aerial reconnaissance photos of the pass that I had obtained from . . . the S-2 shop so we could plot a good patrol.

The three of them were the only marines who organized and planned the proposed ambush.

Now Finlayson began mentally selecting the rest of the team.

The next day, Sgt. Watson and I went over the particulars of the patrol so I could write my patrol order and arrange for an overflight. We paid particular attention to the equipment we were to carry. In addition to the two PRC-25 radios, we included an M60 machine gun, two 7x50 binoculars, an M79 grenade launcher, and one of the new, experimental Stoner carbines. We also made sure that each man carried 300 rounds of ammunition and two M26 fragmentation hand grenades and one CS tear gas grenade. Since we were going on an ambush patrol, we wanted to have all the firepower we could carry.

Finlayson also prepared for other contingencies. "We took along several three-foot parachute cords that we could use to secure any captured enemy and a few extra field bandanas to cover their eyes while we transported them back to base. Mentally, Sgt. Watson and I walked through the patrol route, the selection of the ambush site, the occupation of the ambush site, the conduct of the ambush and the search procedures for the killing zone."

And they weren't through yet. Next came an overflight.

The more time I spent on overflights the better I became at finding terrain features on the ground that I had previously plotted on a map. Using my wrist compass to orient my map, I was able to find terrain features on the ground from a helicopter with relative ease. I could then talk to the pilots over the headset and direct them to the LZs I wanted to observe. As part of my routine on an overflight, I took along a Polaroid camera so I could photograph the insertion and extraction LZs. These photos could then be used to familiarize the team members with the LZs and to brief the insertion pilots prior to liftoff on the day of the patrol.

On this overflight Finlayson and Watson wore headsets so they could guide the pilots through the reconnaissance. "Sgt. Watson already knew exactly what the terrain looked like," Finlayson recalled, since he had covered it only a few days earlier.

The next day, after dealing with other important operational details such as the patrol order, Finlayson recalled that

[w]e went down to the helipad area and test-fired all of our weapons with the exception of the grenade launcher. Then we went over the hand and arm signals we would be using on the patrol because our team was a combination of two teams from separate platoons, and I did not want to find out during the patrol that we used different hand and arm signals. Since we rarely talked on patrol, these hand and arm signals needed to be understood by each member of the patrol. It was essential that everyone could quickly and accurately communicate in silence. We also positioned everyone in their respective positions for the patrol and rehearsed our quick reaction drills for countering an ambush and breaking contact.

Other briefings, coordination meetings with the mission pilots, and a review of the latest available intelligence followed. During the early-morning March 31 flight, Finlayson changed the planned landing zone at the last minute. The pilot "did not question my change of plans," Finlayson recalled, "but simply nodded his head, took my map, examined the location of the new LZ on the ground, and we began our descent. We began a steep dive, giving the team just enough time to take their weapons off safe and prepare for our landing. As we drew closer to the ground, the air in the helicopter changed from cold to cool and then hot, all within the space of a few seconds."

When they stepped out onto the narrow ridgeline and made their way through the elephant grass, Finlayson remembered, "We were met with a blast of hot air, like stepping into the mouth of a furnace. We moved off the LZ into some thick brush as the helicopter rose and joined up with the chase bird and the gun ships. The pilot radioed us and asked us if we were all 'secure.' I replied that we were on the ground, had not taken any fire and had seen no signs of the enemy."

Finlayson recalled that "we spent 20 minutes sitting quietly, our ears straining to pick up any indication the enemy had spotted us and were moving toward us. During this time, all we heard were the normal sounds of the jungle, the chirping of birds, the hum of insects and the whistling of the wind in the tall elephant grass."

The next two days were relatively uneventful, but on the third day Finlayson ordered most of the patrol down onto the floor of their destination valley to set up an ambush, while Finlayson and his five-man Operation Post (OP) team remained on high ground to watch for the enemy. "As I scanned the terrain below," Finlayson recalled, "I found that I could see anyone approaching from the west as far away as 1,000 meters and track their advance right into the killing zone. We had one radio with us in the OP, and Lt. Williamson took the other radio with him down into the valley. With this arrangement, I could use our radios to inform the ambush team well in advance of any enemy moving along the trail toward their ambush."

Only a few minutes later one of the OP team members whispered to Finlayson that he saw Vietcong (VC) some 500 meters (546 yards) away on the trail, moving west toward the American ambush.

"I quickly scanned my binoculars to where he pointed and saw three VC," Finlayson recounted. "They were all dressed in black pajamas and carrying packs and weapons. Two of them wore the distinctive pith helmets of the Communist forces. I took the radio and contacted Lt. Williamson, informing him that three armed VC would enter his ambush in approximately five minutes. I then had the four Marines with me get into good firing positions so they could fire into the killing zone, adding our firepower to [that of] the Marines below."

And then all became silence.

What seemed like an eternity passed before we saw the lead enemy soldier walk into the killing zone below us. A second enemy soldier, following the first by about ten yards, entered the killing zone and we heard the sharp report of Sgt. Watson's M14 rifle, followed almost simultaneously by the rifle fire of the other [American] members of his ambush team. I aimed at the lead enemy soldier and fired five or six rounds at him. He stumbled but did not fall. He disappeared into the high elephant grass on the far side of the trail, and I continued to fire at him although I could not see him. I could see one body in the killing zone, but no others.

They found a pith helmet, pack, and a blood trail leading into the high elephant grass, but instead of searching for the dead VC, covered up the blood trail and waited for more enemy soldiers. Only one ventured by, but Finlayson let him go in the hope that others would soon follow.

The next day, April 3, 1967, the team killed two more VC. Finlayson recalled:

Since I had not seen the VC we had killed until after the ambush had been triggered, I did not know what they looked like or what they were carrying. As it turned out, we had obtained some very valuable intelligence from one of the two VC we had killed. Both VC were dressed in a combination of khaki and black clothing, and both carried weapons and packs. One of them, however, was clearly different. He appeared to be an officer or [part of a] senior Communist cadre. He was the older and taller of the two, and he carried a pistol and a dispatch case, two items that indicated he was an officer or a party official.

When we returned to the OP, we began to take an inventory of the weapons, equipment and documents found on these dead VC. The smaller of the two VC had an NVA rucksack that contained assorted clothing, green plastic material, sights for a 12.7mm heavy machine gun, [and] several black-and-white photos of him and his family. He was also carrying a Chinese Type 50 submachine gun. The taller VC, the one who appeared to be an officer or senior communist cadre was carrying a US Marine Corps haversack.

Killer Kane returned to base where Finlayson took a major-league ass-chewing for deviating from his orders to set the ambush in Antenna Valley. No matter; his friend Eric Barnes, Tom Dodd, and Godfred Blankenship had been avenged. Finlayson could remember with pride what the Latin phrase *Non sibi sed patria* inscribed on his Naval Academy ring meant: *Not for self, but for country*.

CHAPTER 13

The Labyrinth

THE SHY, ELEGANT WARLORD WALKED DOWN A ROAD IN PAKISTAN WITH his American adviser, plotting and scheming the seemingly impossible task of freeing Afghanistan from the Taliban. Hamid Karzai, forty-four, wore a long, flowing nightshirt that evening, or so it would seem to most Americans; in fact, his *shalwar kameez* marked his gentility and personal importance. Karzai carried no weapon despite the danger that he faced. Jason Amerine, a tall, skinny captain in the US Special Forces, had an M9 machine pistol tucked in his belt, just in case. He wore a coarse brown beard that helped him blend in with the local population near Jalalabad, Pakistan. Kabul fell that very morning, November 13, 2001, to a combined force of Americans and Northern Alliance fighters who shared only one common trait: hostility to the Taliban. So Eric Blehm described the situation in his seminal 2010 book, *The Only Thing Worth Dying For: How Eleven Green Beret Fought for a New Afghanistan*, the primary source for this chapter.

Karzai and Amerine now discussed the next step—a bold venture that had been planned earlier at high levels. The following night, Wednesday, November 14, an eleven-man "first-string" American team called Operational Detachment Alpha (ODA) 574 would sneak into Southern Afghanistan, link up with allied (more or less) Pashtun tribal leaders, and destroy any Taliban they found in Kandahar, a critically important city. Most importantly, these efforts would hopefully unite Southern Pashtuns with Northern Hazaras, Uzbeks, and Tajiks behind Karzai. "The Northern

Alliance was on course to topple the Taliban," Blehm observed, "so unless the Pashtun joined the fight, they would be frozen out of the government that would rule after the Taliban." Karzai believed that if this happened, Afghanistan would descend into yet another devastating civil war.

The American pondered all of this as they walked along, remembering that "Karzai was not the warlord Amerine had expected. To the contrary, he was dignified, cultured and gentle. Still, Amerine had thought, *that doesn't mean he's trustworthy*." Incredible as it might sound eighteen years later, Amerine, age thirty, alone and relying only on his own judgment, would decide whether the Karzai southern initiative against America's enemies was worth gambling the lives of American servicemen. There was no doubt that Karzai was both bright and knowledgeable. According to Blehm, "Nine days before, on the first of their nighttime walks, Karzai had posed some obvious yet awkward questions." Foremost among these, Karzai asked, "Who will govern Afghanistan after the terrorists and the Taliban are defeated? What are the US Government's long-term plans for Afghanistan?"

If only Amerine knew. His educated guess was that other than hunting down the 9/11 terrorists, the American government really didn't have any specific plans for dealing with the military, economic, and political consequences of this tragic new era. Having no other option, if he were to build and keep Karzai's trust, Amerine simply blurted out the truth. At least telling the man "I don't know" was honest.

Karzai carefully stated the outcomes he wanted to see rather than pitching himself as leader of Afghanistan. He wanted to help bring about a *Loya Jirga*—that is, a grand council in which tribal leaders from across Afghanistan would decide what was to be done. That brief, self-effacing statement convinced Amerine that he could trust Karzai in the days to come.

The next morning, "The eleven-man A-team gathered in the meeting room in their safe house," in the Jacobabad District of Sindh Province Pakistan. Their clothing was a "mixed bag of desert camouflage pants, dark civilian fleece or down jackets over thermals," and Vietnam War–era hats and baseball caps with Harley-Davidson and Boston Red Sox logos. Nobody had shaved after leaving Fort Campbell Kentucky about a month before.

Blehm described what happened next:

Amerine watched as his weapons sergeants laid out enormous piles of weaponry and ammo as well as two laser targeting devices and began to discuss the distribution of their loads. The only non–Green Beret on the mission, an Air Force combat controller (CCT) named Alex, joined the communications sergeants Dan and Wes, in making final checks on all radios, laptops and batteries. Victor, the engineer responsible for the load plan, paced back and forth between the two groups of men and their piles, ready to re-weigh the equipment for the helicopters that would fly them in. Every passenger and every item they carried had to be weighed and logged. Assigned to the team at the last minute, Ken, the medic, was leaning up against a wall with the medical supplies organized in front of him, laying out small but ominous morphine injectors that he would issue to each man.

Everyone had checked their gear several times by noon.

Each would carry an M4 carbine, an M9 pistol, grenades, ammunition, food, water, minimal clothing in shades of desert camouflage, a mid-weight sleeping bag, and a waterproof jacket. Each man would also carry gear specific to his job—communications equipment, medical supplies, extra weapons—that added another fifty-plus pounds per pack. They had no body armor or helmets; for this unconventional warfare mission, the team would share the risk with the [friendly] guerrillas they would lead. If Karzai's followers did not have body armor, neither would they.

An officer from Air Force Special Operations Command (AFSOC) arrived to brief ODA 574, as well as the men from the Central Intelligence Agency who would be infiltrating with them, on the flight and escape-and-recovery plans. As the officer spoke, Amerine felt an eerie connection to the three-man Jedburgh teams—considered the predecessors to both Special Forces soldiers and CIA agents—that parachuted behind Nazi lines to assist resistance fighters during World War II. Those teams received similar briefings. How many made it back alive? Not many, thought Amerine. Casper, a CIA team leader, sat next to Amerine's team as he explained that they would be flown by Air Force Special Operations Command pilots from a nearby airstrip to a clandestine one near the Afghanistan border on two MH-53 Pave Lows, the Air Force heavy-lift helicopters.

Once they arrived at the clandestine landing zone, five MH-60 Black Hawk helicopters—piloted by the 160th Special Operations Aviation Regiment (SOAR), specialists in low-altitude night operations—would take them into Afghanistan.

The plans all changed at 3:00 p.m., just as they began loading gear onto trucks for the short trip to the first helicopters. A Special Forces operator insisted that three Delta Force men would be taking the place of three ODA 74 teammates, whether ODA 74 liked it or not. Amerine soon learned from the Delta Force guys that this change had been a CIA decision. Minutes later they were airborne.

"The two helicopters hugged the rolling hills of the Pakistani desert for an hour before coming upon an airstrip just south of the Afghan border," Blehm recounted, "which appeared like a mirage on the horizon. They landed when it was still light enough to see squads of Army Rangers patrolling the perimeter. When the helicopter ramps dropped, some of the Rangers ran over to help the teams unload their gear, and then the Pave Lows immediately lifted off, blanketing everyone in dust."

And now they waited.

The thump, thump, thump they heard next could mean only one thing. The rotors beating against the wind, announcing the arrival of their next ride: five Black Hawks to carry the men in groups of four and five on a western heading into Afghanistan. The Rangers helped move the gear on the helicopters, which lifted off into the night sky in a tight combat formation—staggered, with a distance of one rotor disk between them. Two more Black Hawks beefed up with heavy weapons flew on the flanks. Thousands of feet above, heavily armed jets escorted the formation. At the border of Pakistan and Afghanistan, the flock turned north. If all went well, they would cover close to two hundred miles before setting down on Afghan soil for a few seconds to unload their passengers.

The pilots searched the horizon for wood fires that would signal the "all clear" for them to go on. "The flight held a northerly course toward the Hindu Kush Mountains. Two hours in, during a midair refueling, Amerine's helicopter—first in the formation—filled with jet fuel flames," and, of all things, the scent of flowers. It wasn't the right season for poppies, and Amerine had no idea what poppies smelled like anyway. "A few moments later, the Black Hawk bucked and jerked in an evasive maneuver," Blehm recounted. The right gunner squeezed off some rounds as Amerine looked over at the SOAR commander, who gave no indication at all of concern. Minutes later, Amerine heard over his headset that the gunner had mistaken the laser beam from his own weapon for ground fire.

Even as they flew toward the landing zones, there was no indication from the advance surveillance planes that signal fires had been lit to welcome them in. Amerine decided to continue the mission anyway. Finally, four lit fires appeared.

The landing zone was in a small valley as long as a football field and slightly narrower. As the helicopters swooped down into the rugged mountains, the fires marking the four corners of this smooth barren patch of earth were extinguished so as not to blind the pilots. Less than two hundred feet above the ground, the five Black Hawks drifted gracefully into a straight line. Amerine's helicopter descended first, with the others following close behind like boxcars tethered to a locomotive. As the helicopter dropped, its powerful rotors stirred up fine sand and dust that billowed into the air like a volcanic eruption, creating a brownout that shrouded the landing zone and threw the tightly synchronized formation into disarray. Amerine's helicopter set down gently, its crew and passengers unaware that they were now invisible to the pilots above.

Amerine and two of his team members, as well as one of the CIA guys, watched as the helicopter lifted off. And then the other three helicopters came in. "The second helicopter, descending quickly after Amerine's group, nearly collided with a rocky right wall. The men squinted up in disbelief as the mechanical monster seemed about to crush them—then it suddenly lurched to the left, regained stability, and landed gently as well."

And this was not the end of the trouble.

"The third helicopter dropped rapidly through the dust, its pilot determined to land despite zero visibility. The Black Hawk hit the ground hard. While Karzai, Casper, another spook named Charlie and two of the Delta operators scrambled out, a gunner crawled underneath to inspect the landing gear. It was undamaged, and the helicopter lifted back into the air."

Even more surprising, the fourth helicopter came down inside an enormous cloud as the occupants choked on dust. "The main rotor blades, throwing sparks from the static created by their proximity to the sides of the cleft, looked like giant sparklers." The men inside the chopper braced for impact with the ground. Instead, the Black Hawk somehow powered up and out of the brownout, banked away and disappeared into the night. Since the choppers weren't able to land in a straight row, the men

were scattered in small groups around the valley, each setting up its own defensive perimeter.

And there was movement: a half-dozen armed Afghans milling next to a string of undersized donkeys a hundred yards away, near the eastern edge of the valley, and a solitary figure striding through the dust toward them.

Hamid Karzai, who was to make the initial linkup with the Pashtun tribesmen, had immediately sprung forward to meet them, the white leather tennis shoes he'd been given by the CIA in Pakistan practically glowing beneath his shalwar kameez and looking as if they were walking themselves through the darkness. The Americans aimed their carbines at the tribesmen, the beams from their lasers invisible to the Afghans.

One of the team members wondered whether there were spies or assassins among the Afghans, worrying for Karzai's safety. If there were any spies, they didn't act—at least, not yet.

After the men from the ODA and CIA had dropped their rucks [rucksacks] next to the donkeys, JD set them all in a tight perimeter with every man lying prone and facing outward to form a circle half the size of a basketball court, with Amerine and Caspar along with Karzai at its center. Then he approached Amerine.

"We're missing four men . . . Their helicopter must have headed to an alternative landing zone."

"What does that mean?" asked Karzai.

Amerine told him the Americans had some men lost in the mountains.

Not good. Caspar and Amerine told Karzai that they would be moving to higher ground to search for the lost men. The radio guy stretched out a long antenna and began listening intensely to his radio for any sign that the missing men were still alive. After a dull, chilling silence, he turned to Amerine.

"I can hear them now—they're trying to reach us, but they can't hear me at all. They need to get to higher ground."

Worse still, somebody noticed that Caspar, the CIA operative, had snuck off on his own to find the missing men. Worse yet, he had taken Karzai with him. They had taken small, low-powered radios that wouldn't be of much help. One of Amerine's men wisecracked that CIA stood for "Children in Action." Later, they learned that "The fourth Black Hawk had drifted more than two miles west from the landing zone as its pilot searched for a suitable place to set down. In desperation, he briefly flicked on his spotlights, flooding the valley below in white light, drawing an obscenity from one of the Special Forces guys, urging the pilot in plain profane English that they needed to land somewhere else."

The pilot searched the horizon through clouds of dust for a few seconds, then announced they were going in.

"He dropped the helicopter like a rock, determined to land before the dust storm could swallow the Black Hawk. They bounced hard, and then settled on a massive shelf with mountains rising to the east. To the west, the flat terrain rolled off into either a sloping hillside or a cliff—it was impossible to tell which."

The highest-ranking sergeant on the chopper, known as "Mag," told the pilot, "Radio my team with these coordinates so we can link up," just before jumping out. Within two minutes they spotted light on the horizon. Mag and another man searched around in the darkness for a decent fighting position, just in case they needed one.

What happened next was pure luck.

"About eighty yards out, they practically fell into what would suffice as a fighting position," Blehm recounted, "a depression at the base of a slight embankment. They hurried back to get the others, and the men concealed their gear as best they could in the bushes."

That Wednesday evening, "in the mountains of Uruzgan Province, the single flashlight was joined by three others, each beam sweeping across the landscape." Mag and the three others, "lying as flat as possible," could now make out four men, each wearing a *shalwar kameez* and carrying a Russian assault rifle over his shoulder. Garbled voices could now be heard in the distance. The Afghans had been there too long to just be passing through. Soon, "What had been incomprehensible chatter became shouts." One of the team members recognized the language they were speaking to be Pashto, just as the flashlights seemed to stop, which meant the Afghanis were coming right toward them. That captured the attention of the entire American team.

Shifting slightly, they steadied their aim at the group 150 yards away and closing. Infrared laser dots from their carbines covered the chest of the lead man, several yards ahead of the other Afghans, an easy kill. "Dead man walking," whispered Mag. "Let him come in," somebody said. The Americans held their fire, allowing the group to advance. Their training taught them to anticipate the worst and engage the enemy only if they had the upper hand, and these four men might only be a foot patrol sent out by a much larger Taliban force close by.

A single gunshot would reveal the American position. For now, their only advantage was to remain invisible.

Almost at the same time, Karzai, the prospective leader of the entire Afghan nation, was still wandering around in the darkness with Caspar, the CIA spook, looking for Mag and the rest of the lost boys. In the meantime, Amerine chose a high position "to provide his senior communications sergeant the best radio signal vantage overlooking the mountains that spread out below them like a starlit relief map. Amerine knelt on the cold, hard, wind-scoured ground, hoping for the best."

Losing perspective wouldn't be too good for Afghan Prime Minister Karzai's career.

"Four Afghans were now between the Americans and their gear, about sixty yards away and closing in; each of the Afghans was tagged by a laser dot from an American carbine." One of the men alternated his aim between the head and chest of his designated target, just to steady his nerves.

And then the incident was over before it had begun.

The approaching Afghan "hostiles" shouted, "Don't shoot!" in Farsi, and "Americans," and then began to make noises and move around in a manner that told the Special Forces that these might not be Taliban fighters.

"Are you a friend of Karzai?" one of the Americans shouted in Farsi.

"Yes, yes, we are friends of Hamid Karzai," came the response. Next, the Afghans claimed they could take the Americans to the Afghan leader. Having few options, the Americans accepted the offer, hoping for the best.

This time the Afghans were telling the truth. Soon the ODA 574 operators were back together, "following Karzai and his Pashtun tribesmen—the first of his supposed three hundred guerrillas." Their next target was a town called Tarin Kowt, where Karzai had a strong base of support, despite Taliban occupation.

November 16 brought good news for Amerine.

I know we were just getting settled in here, but we're leaving in three hours. The people of Tarin Kowt killed their Taliban governor last night, so that speeds things up for us. We're going to help the locals hold the town. Karzai is getting vehicles—it's a four-hour drive—and there are some twenty villages on our route that should be on Karzai's side. That said, we'll get some air [support] to escort us. Somebody asked a good question: what exactly was the route to Tarin Kowt.

Amerine pulled out his survival map, which he'd folded so that Uruzgan Province [where they were then] was on one side and Kandahar Province on the other. He traced the route with his finger for the team to see.

"Hamid [Karzai] says we'll head north along the river to Deh Rawood and then cut east through these mountains to Tarin Kowt. All our maps are fucked—we don't know if these roads still exist, so we'll play it by ear, but this is the basic route. I expect a counterattack in Tarin Kowt within twenty-four hours. Hopefully we'll get there before that happens."

One doubter asked what had happened to the several hundred Afghanis who were issued American weapons that very day. "They disappeared back into the mountains," Amerine admitted. "It was understood that some of them were being armed to protect their villages, but it appears that Hamid is still lacking credibility, or there would be some guys hanging around, looking for something to do. Hamid says he's been promised all the men we need in Tarin Kowt once we get there."

"That sounds familiar," groused one American wise guy.

The combined American-Afghan force was ready to go by sunset. The convoy consisted of station wagons, minivans, Toyota trucks, and even a shuttle bus, crowded together on the streets of Haji Badhur Cove. Two pickup trucks from Tarin Kowt were full of (pro-Karzai) guerrillas armed with RPGs and assault rifles and would lead the convoy back there. Karzai and the CIA team—including one injured guy hooked up to an IV—boarded the shuttle bus for the trip in.

Karzai told Amerine that the Afghans talking in a group nearby owned the vehicles and intended to drive them, a detail which did not bode well with the Americans. Nobody trusted the [Afghan] drivers to

*react calmly if they drove into an ambush or were stopped at a Taliban
checkpoint. Amerine balked, but Karzai explained that there was no
other option—in Uruzgan, vehicles were hard to come by, and the
Afghans would not relinquish theirs. The team could have bought its
own trucks in Pakistan and had them airlifted with the weapons the
night before, but Karzai wanted to be as inconspicuous as possible, and
promised to acquire trucks for ODA 574 in-country.*

The men of ODA 574 went over their plans and agreed among
themselves that this time, the "never leave a man behind" rule would be
deep-sixed. One man summed it up well: "If I'm killed and we're going
to be overrun, don't die trying to bring back my body. Save yourselves and
tell the story."

Their proposed route would follow the Helmand River some fifteen
miles, turn east at a place called Deh Rawood, and cross a thirty-mile
small mountain range to arrive at Tarin Kowt after four hours on the road.
Two F-18 jets flew interference ahead of the convoy—just in case.

The convoy arrived at the compound in Tarin Kowt at about 11:00
p.m.

"Karzai said a few words to one of the four armed men in the
compound, then led Casper [the CIA agent] and Amerine into the
dwelling. He quickly showed the two rooms [ODA 574] would stay in,
and then the three men returned to the driveway where the Americans
were unloading their gear from the trucks."

That's when Karzai drove off alone to the former Taliban governor's
office for a meeting with the resistance. He sent for Amerine and Casper
forty-five minutes later.

The guerrillas drove them into a residential area, past a pair of rusted-
out Soviet infantry carriers, to a modest concrete building where Karzai
delivered the bad news. "A large convoy of Pakistani Taliban is on its way
from Kandahar to retake Tarin Kowt, the very place they were staying.
How large was the convoy?" Karzai was somber: "There are reports of one
hundred trucks carrying one thousand men."

Hours later, while Amerine and the others planned out the coming
battle, the first report of enemy movement came in. "Sir, the F-18s spotted

eight trucks bearing north from Kandahar." Amerine knew immediately that this was only the advance element of a much larger force even as he green-lighted an F-18 attack.

"The room went quiet. Every man looked at Amerine. He visualized the valleys and roads, pictured the mountains and what the pilots were seeing. According to Karzai, a force like this coming north could only be Taliban. If a thousand men were closing in, they had to slow them down to gain time for Karzai to rally his men. These air strikes would also be crucial to defending Tarin Kowt. Without further consideration he [Amerine] gave the order: 'Smoke 'em.'"

Amerine went up on the roof to watch what he hoped would be a devastating air strike.

"A thousand men are coming to this place, Amerine thought. Horrible odds, just as there had been during Operation Safe Haven, when he was a second lieutenant fresh out of West Point, stationed in Panama on the first assignment of his career." Thanks to restrictive orders from higher-ups, men under Amerine's command in Panama had attempted to quell a riot inside a refugee camp with inadequate weapons and paid the price. Would this be another debacle?

Karzai soon returned from the governor's palace with bad news. Instead of the massive Afghan defense force everyone had hoped for, only a few local men had volunteered to help Karzai and the Americans. They would arrive within the hour. Twelve Americans and thirty-five Afghans overflown by American F-18 air support would face some one thousand Taliban.

The planning went on. They would face the thousand Taliban at a good defensive position some twelve miles outside of town. So far, the F-18s had not spotted any enemy convoy. That gave them more time to plan the best use of their limited resources. According to Blehm, "Amerine planned for the worst," telling Karzai, "If Tarin Kowt gets overrun, my team will come back for you."

Blehm noted that "The thirty guerrillas arrived an hour late, at 4:00 a.m." The men of ODA 574 quickly loaded their gear—which now included two machine guns, along with ammunition, hand grenades, and RPGs—into a couple of trucks. Everybody in the ODA 574 marked the compound on their personal GPS systems, but had to wonder whether it was realistic to hope that they would have any chance at all of returning.

On the way out of town the Americans watched one of their convoy drivers fill his truck with gasoline without turning off the engine—a sure invitation to an explosion. Just outside Tarin Kowt, their path descended from a sloping plateau into a cluster of ridges and hills, as if the skin of the desert had wrinkled, creating a maze of passages that became dead ends, goat trails, or circles.

The road through this hilly labyrinth was dotted with simple compounds and led to Tarin Kowt Pass, a gash in the mountains twelve miles to the south. ODA 574 and Karzai's guerrillas would conceal their trucks there and lie in wait, ready to call in air strikes on the enemy convoy they expected to arrive on the road below. On the map, the location seemed perfect, but Amerine knew that terrain analysis is more art than science: It depends on intuition and eyes—on consideration. Despite all the maps and modern technology at their disposal, it would come down to what they would find on the ground.

Only five hundred yards outside of town, the convoy passed "a hillside dotted with hundreds of slender stakes, their colorful cloth streamers fluttering in the breeze, like a pincushion, covered with threaded needles." Then, they entered the labyrinth, heading toward the high ground they'd identified on the map.

On the way there, Amerine spotted several Russian armored personnel carriers (BTRs) just before things got worse. "The convoy looked like a snake slithering out of the pass. There seemed to be no end; it just kept coming, its numbers obscured by the dust storm it created as it advanced across the flat desert floor." Amerine admitted to himself how much trouble they were in. "If there are a hundred trucks on the other side of the pass, we don't have enough bombs to stop them all. Once they reach our ridgeline, we'll either stop them there or we'll have to retreat back toward Tarin Kowt." Now, ODA 574 watched an F-18 air mission take out several Taliban trucks and let out a cheer, only to realize that most of their Afghan allies were gone. Two of the Americans attempted to block their retreat, but the Afghan guerrilla trucks were rolling back to Tarin Kowt, as their drivers urged the Americans to get in.

"There was no interpreter to explain what was going on to the guerrillas. They had never witnessed American airpower, but they knew all about the atrocities the Taliban were capable of committing. Yet the people of Tarin Kowt would be slaughtered if ODA 574 didn't stop the convoy."

ODA 574 had to follow the guerrillas and bring them back. In the meantime,

> *When the first bombs hit the lead trucks, the Taliban drivers might have considered the explosions to be lucky hits from old Soviet mortars the townspeople were firing from somewhere up ahead. They did not know they were being targeted by American soldiers. The first contingent of F-18s had dropped its small complement of bombs and left to rearm, creating the illusion that the artillery barrage had ceased. Unable to hear or see the [American] aircraft high overhead, the convoy drove faster, racing along the road on the valley floor past the burning wreckage of four vehicles toward the ridge abandoned by ODA 574.*

Somehow the Taliban truck drivers consolidated the convoy and began moving up the road toward the ridgeline they would have to pass to reach Tarin Kowt. They were not alone. The F-18 pilots were able to see well enough despite the dust to provide ODA 574 a preliminary assessment of what they were up against. Fifty trucks probably carrying five hundred Taliban fighters were coming through Tarin Kowt Pass. One of the trucks towed an artillery piece. Across Afghanistan, American forces learned that "[a] lone team of Green Berets was in contact with hundreds of Taliban fighters. Flights were diverted from other missions in Afghanistan and aircraft were scrambled from their carriers to the Arabian Sea, all of them heading to Tarin Kowt."

So was ODA 574, as if they had any choice, given that their Afghan allies insisted on driving away from the labyrinth into Tarin Kowt. Alex, the ODA 574 air support coordinator, sat astride the gear in the bed of a moving truck. Holding on for dear life, he continued "to direct the US aircraft from all over the country; F-14 Tomcats, in their final months of military service, joined their replacements, F-18 Hornets, all staying above 30,000 feet. Below them the pilots saw dust clouds from the Taliban convoy approaching Tarin Kowt along three roads through the labyrinth. The F-18 pilots saw the Taliban convoy converging on the pair of trucks sitting just outside town and notified ODA 574.

" 'That's us,' said Alex. 'You mean, that's *all* you've got?'"

The pilots could now see that on the flanks, smaller columns of the Taliban attack were moving slower than the main force in the center. Amerine directed the F-18s to put everything they had into an attack on the middle. Alex, the ODA 574 forward observer, counted the planes as they checked in. "Amerine calculated how much firepower they had available: three aircraft, carrying a total of eighteen bombs, to take out at least fifty vehicles coming their way. Not enough," Blehm observed. Even as they heard explosions in the distance, Alex and Amerine both knew instinctively what the F-18 pilots confirmed: "The Taliban were halfway through the labyrinth, still coming on strong."

The arrival of more planes brought Alex some help. One of the pilots was Airborne Forward Air Control–qualified, and capable of directing dozens of aircraft from the sky. "Aided by the AFAC, Alex coordinated multiple simultaneous air strikes.

"Yet the center [Taliban] continued forward relentlessly. In the midst of the chaos and the potential for impending doom, they began to tally the black clouds rising above the labyrinth. One dozen and counting—each representing a truck packed with as many as twelve men, yet the Taliban pressed forward."

That was when men from Tarin Kowt began to arrive.

In those first few minutes the Tarin Kowt townsmen were mostly curious spectators, but some came armed to help. Soon, more men carrying everything from AK-47s to bolt-action rifles that likely predated World War II showed up, and were immediately placed in a defensive line. Several ODA 574 operators watched two Afghans pull a canvas tarp off a rusty Soviet antitank weapon in the shadows between two buildings. To their amazement, it appeared to have been maintained. The Americans watched a third man carry some large rounds out of a nearby shed, load up the gun, and point it toward the labyrinth. Several townsmen arrived with RPGs just before air support reinforcements arrived. These pilots risked their lives dropping below the altitude restrictions they'd been given, risking Taliban air defense threats to strafe the enemy.

Suddenly an F-14 swooped toward the center convoy, white smoke erupting from its nose. Its six-barrel Vulcan Gatling–style cannon fired sixty rounds of 20mm ammunition per second, making a belching sound as it strafed the [Taliban] trucks and depleting in ten seconds all 676 rounds the aircraft carried. A single RPG arced upward from somewhere in the labyrinth and missed the plane by hundreds of yards, coming harmlessly back to earth in the desert to the west [of Tarin Kowt]. One by one, jets dived down over the labyrinth, firing the last of their ammunition before returning to their ships to refuel and rearm.

What happened next might have been in a war movie: "As if on cue, a second wave of fully armed aircraft checked in. Alex quickly directed them to strike the middle column. After their first run, marked by a rumble of explosions, the pilots radioed back some good news." The middle Taliban column seemed to be turning around, even as the smaller Taliban column on the eastern flank began retreating. Now Alex asked the pilots to focus on the larger western column that was still advancing and pressing on toward the edge of town, where they were met with gunfire.

But who was doing the shooting?

"The gunfire was coming from townsmen shooting at a single Taliban truck, which quickly turned and sped away even as American aircraft continued their runs, dropping bombs on the retreating trucks. The sky had gone brown, hazy from dust and smoke from the destroyed vehicles. The columns of black smoke reminded the Gulf War veterans among the ODA 574 team of the burning fields of the Kuwaiti desert."

So ended the first ODA 574 victory of the War in Afghanistan.

CHAPTER 14

Contact Across the River

THE CHOW HALL WAS FULL OF SOLDIERS FROM PRACTICALLY EVERY country in NATO that Thursday, October 29, 2009, in Herat, Western Afghanistan. Danes, Italians, and even a few Spaniards talked among themselves in their native languages as the breakfast line moved along ever so slowly—a common experience in armies across the world. The US Marine contingent—more specifically, Marine Special Operations Team 8222—had seen it all before. This was old hat to them; only the location was different: Camp Stone near Herat in Western Afghanistan. Michael Golembesky remembered that morning all too well. His book *Level Zero Heroes: The Story of US Marine Special Operations in Bala Murghab, Afghanistan* is the primary source for this chapter.

"Truth is, everyone was edgy," Golembesky recalled. "Herat was garrison hell. Clean uniforms being used as accessories abounded. The closer to the flagpole, the more the little shit matters, and Herat was our flagpole. Not only was [the] MSOC [Marine Special Operations Company] headquarters element here, but the command element from Special Operations Task Force–West (SOTF-W) had set up shop right next door, since we were only about a hundred kilometers [62 miles] from the Iranian border."

Golembesky and the marines in his company didn't think much of the Herat headquarters. They had been working around the clock to prepare for the move to a permanent headquarters some 180 kilometers northeast of Herat.

Zeroing weapons, prepping gear, modifying our [vehicles] with homemade metal side racks so we could carry more gear, had dominated the last few days. While we worked to get into combat, the headquarters culture here was cast straight from the peacetime stateside mold. Officers chastised us about the state of our uniforms and choice of footwear. Paperwork inundated us. The people here seemed out of touch with where they were and what we were supposed to be doing. And while Camp Stone was probably one of the safest places in Afghanistan, all of the personnel here drew combat pay and hazardous duty pay.

Soon they would be out of here. Golembesky was a Joint Terminal Attack Conductor (JTAC) and even had his own call sign. The next day they would leave the chair-borne Rangers behind, meet up with a convoy from the 82nd Airborne, and move out for the Bala Murghab Valley— their home away from home for the rest of this deployment.

Only the Filipino cooks handing out breakfast omelets were smiling that morning. The subject during breakfast was Rules of Engagement (ROEs). Golembesky believed that the Brits had the most aggressive approach to this war. More significantly, he wrote that "our own ROEs had undergone a radical revision now that General Stanley McChrystal had taken over as field commander (COMISAF). Where once our troops had flexibility on the battlefield, in my opinion, McChrystal's feel-good tactical directives had clipped the wings of our aggressiveness and ability to effectively kill the enemy in a timely manner."

Golembesky and his team spent hour upon hour talking through these limitations, which, in his opinion, "struck right at the heart of what Special Operations units do best. Night raids had to be specially approved at the Special Operations Task Force (SOTF) level now, which was a challenge, since that was when Special Operations units" were most effective. They couldn't bomb enemy fighters in civilian compounds or open fire unless they could see weapons in the hands of enemy fighters. The Taliban were quick studies who rapidly developed ways to capitalize on these self-imposed American restrictions. In one new approach, the Taliban would fire upon Americans, then drop the weapons and run into compounds where they were relatively safe under these new rules. Golembesky observed that the Taliban "used civilian homes as ambush positions, knowing we couldn't bring our superior firepower to bear." McChrystal's new directives were designed to better protect the civilian population, but from what? Golembesky and his crew were hearing that "the new rules made it easier for the Taliban to infiltrate communities and then terrorize the locals into collaboration."

Friday, October 30, 2009, brought a mission to Bala Murghab. The marine convoy linked up with an 82nd Airborne element for the trip. Golembesky remembered later that "As dawn broke on the eastern horizon, we inched out through the front gate and turned onto Highway 1 (Ring Road), the only paved highway in western Afghanistan. We followed it straight through the heart of downtown Herat and into the bazaar area. Already, the place teamed with people. Cooking fires burned, dead animals dangled from hooks in the tin-shack butcher shops. Men haggled over goods, others wandered around. I noticed some of the shops were built out of metal shipping containers. They'd simply cut windows and doors and open up for business."

Getting through Herat took most of the morning, or so it seemed to Golembesky.

Within minutes of leaving, the convoy kicked up a massive dust cloud. I watched it form ahead of us; then we drew closer until we were engulfed in the brown fog. The dust got into my eyes, mouth and nose; it coated my machine gun and all our gear around us. A layer of it formed and grew on the truck floor around our boots. Moving around kicked up little powdery swirls of the stuff. Hour after hour we bounced and rolled over this shitty road. Occasionally, we came to a village, each one more and more primitive and impoverished as we traveled away from Herat. Being in the back of the Ground Mobility Vehicle (GMV) was like being in a time machine . . . we felt like visitors to the Stone Age.

Along the way, a veteran who had been through this before claimed that the Spanish, who operated in Bala Murghab first, had made a deal with the Taliban. The deal was the Spaniards would be left alone so long as they didn't go more than five hundred meters north or south from the Forward Operating Base. "They could go to the Bazaar and the District Center to the east on the other side of the Murghab River, but that was about it," Golembesky recounted. The veteran claimed that the Spanish in effect had a truce with the enemy, and called it "the dirty little secret of the Afghan War."

Golembesky also learned that the US Army, which needed more boots on the ground for patrols in Afghanistan, had begun using "infantillery" units—that is, artillery battalions converted into makeshift infantry units, often composed of state National Guard outfits. They followed a steep, dangerous road over the Sabzek Pass and spent the night in what he thought was a nearly deserted town.

Golembesky described Qal-e-naw as "a city on the edge of forever, the last outpost of civilization in Badghis Province." The next morning, the seemingly deserted town "bustled with mopeds and small pickup trucks. Throngs of people spilled into the streets in the bazaar area, where goods and animals hung from racks in front of businesses [operating out of] ramshackle tin huts. The Afghans here built their dwellings with anything available, which made the city a checkerboard of brick buildings, mud huts and metal shacks."

November 1, 2009, All Saints Day, brought a firefight with the Taliban that almost got the entire convoy killed. Two rocket-propelled grenades exploded in midair just above them. Worse yet, a Taliban RPG skipped onto the road and sizzled under the fuel truck before bouncing around and exploding a few meters away. Somehow they escaped.

The next morning brought them closer to Forward Operating Base Todd. Along the way, one of the fuel trucks sank into some mud and had to be destroyed. In his memoir, *Level Zero Heroes*, Golembesky remembered staring "at the spectacle of thousands of gallons of gasoline burning in the middle of nowhere, as a $50,000 truck melted down at the same time." Later that morning they burned a second truck in similar circumstances.

As they approached an enemy-infested portion of the road to Bala Murghab, Golembesky called in air support. "The two A-10s fell out of the blue sky in a row; engines throttled all the way forward. The pilots pulled out less than two hundred feet over the road and blasted over us, their four huge turbofan engines thundering. They shot ahead of us, going perhaps 450 miles an hour, and followed the road the six more kilometers down the valley. Hoots and hollering came over our team's radio. After all the frustration of the past several days, seeing these two magnificent aircraft served as an adrenaline shot to our morale."

They were nearing the end of their journey.

"The convoy reached the end of Alkazai Valley just after sundown. We paused briefly before making the final jump to FOB Todd. We were just outside of Bala Murghab, a twenty-four-kilometer [fifteen-mile] valley that was oriented north-south and split right down the middle by the Murghab River. We regrouped the convoy near an Afghan Border Police outpost atop a massive hill to put our night-vision devices on. From there we slowly poured into the valley itself."

Soon they eased around a sharp turn in the road and somebody spotted FOB Todd, or so they said. "Through my night vision," Golembesky recalled, "I stood up in the trunk of my vehicle, looked out over the front of the convoy and saw a guard tower, walls, and Italian and American flags fluttering in the evening breeze. FOB Todd in all its glory. The guard in the tower waved us inside. Our convoy split; the 82nd Airborne went to their part of the Forward Operating Base, leaving what remained of their trucks just outside the front wall. Just before midnight, we shut our engines off and dismounted."

A few hours later, after taking their cargo and gear out of the trucks, they set up some cots in a tent. Golembesky hit the sack with his boots still on. They were through for the day—or so they thought. All too soon he heard a C-130 passing overhead—or was he dreaming?

"A rash of gunfire bloomed from somewhere nearby. I could hear the bark of AK-47s intermingled with the sharper crack of M4s [assault rifles]. A machine gun tore off a long burst in the distance." Day one at FOB Todd, and the shit was hitting the fan.

Half-dressed marines carrying gun boxes, sniper rifles, and extra magazines ran out of the tent in the midst of the gunfire. Two of them ran for an empty guard tower as Golembesky and other marines jammed themselves into an RG-33 armored vehicle that was already rolling.

"The rig began to roll. The RG-33 had only one window located in the rear door. It was thick, blast-resistant glass that had been smeared with grime and coated with Afghan moon dust, making it all but impossible to see out of it. The RG turned sharply and we leaned into each other. A few other turns and I'd lost all sense of where we were or which way we were going. The rig bounced and jerked over the hardscrabble terrain, tossing us around violently."

While it did, one of his teammates told Golembesky that two 82nd Airborne soldiers had just drowned and their team was going out as a quick reaction force (QRF). Somebody asked how the hell that happened. "The bundles from the container drop drifted out of the drop zone," Golembesky recalled. "Some landed in the water and the east side of the river. Two paratroopers went into the river and tried to secure one of the bundle chutes. One fell into the water and the other went in to grab him. They both went under with all their gear on."

All Golembesky could say was "Holy shit." They were heading straight into a fight at half-strength. A few minutes later they were in a gun battle.

"Around us, some 82nd Airborne soldiers sprinted past carrying loads of gear down to the riverbank. Some of them were in the water holding on to parachute suspension lines as they eased out into the rushing current. The opposite bank was high enough that it seemed to protect them from incoming fire, but if any of the Taliban shooting at us maneuvered closer, the men in the water would be trapped in the open."

In the midst of this, the so-called Afghan National Army troops hid behind walls and huts, but, to their credit, some would expose themselves to incoming fire long enough to shoot long bursts from the AK-47s. The ANA was spraying at whatever with no fire discipline. Several Italian armored vehicles had parked with guns manned but silent. "Bullets smacked into compound walls as the Taliban raked our positions with machine guns and AKs."

Golembesky secured a firing position behind a compound wall just before a burst of automatic fire sprayed some nearby trees. One of his team members opened up with their heavy machine gun, which diminished the incoming Taliban fire—if only for the moment. When one of his team members joined him, Golembesky asked why the Italians weren't doing anything, and learned that they could only engage if they were personally being fired on.

Within minutes half of Golembesky's teammates set up on the rooftop of a nearby hut. Although it was hard to see much, it was apparent that most the Taliban were in a village on the other side of the river. Many of them were setting up in a series of trenches and ratlines (escape routes). Some of the ANA troops, to their credit, tried to get into the action. Trouble was, they were exposing themselves to enemy fire in the open.

There was also good news: An Air Force Joint Terminal Attack Controller deployed with them had just called in a Predator missile and a pair of F-16s. The bad news was that the air force guy was not fully qualified and was serving an internship of sorts. Golembesky, a fully qualified forward observer, took over immediately.

Within minutes, "an F-16 streaked down out [of] the cloud layer, afterburners searing the sky with a cone of blue-red flame like a comet's tail. At first, it was nothing but a dot in the sky, no sound to accompany its five-hundred-mile-an-hour approach." Somehow it became a flat gray bird, with a single tail fin, pointed nose, and "a big air intake nestled under the fuselage, giving it a sleek, deadly look." The Taliban firing stopped when they could see the jet wash ruffling the tree leaves above them.

That's when the Predator drone arrived to scan the river, as the F-16s continued their mission for another forty-five minutes, even as a pair of A-10 Thunderbolts joined the fray. Following afternoon prayers, the Taliban started a brief firefight, even as the 82nd Airborne men tried to find the bodies of their two drowned buddies on the bottom of the river with grappling hooks.

Regrettably, those efforts were not successful. So after regrouping, the operation would move downstream as Golembesky and the aviation group he was directing would protect the searchers with overwatch services. The problem was, the crew, consisting of ten "non-shooters" and two Humvees, would be practically helpless if challenged. Fortunately, Golembesky convinced the mission leadership that they needed firepower. Now accompanied by elements of the 82nd Airborne and the Afghan National Army, Golembesky and the rest of the team resumed the mission. Alkazai, chock-full of Taliban the night before, was now a ghost town. The convoy broke into the open countryside to the north and located a spot some fifty meters (fifty-seven yards) from the river where they could watch the recovery operation and call in aviation help if needed, in the coming darkness.

They arrived at the observation point and positioned the vehicles about thirty meters (thirty-three yards) apart in a circle to ensure that they had 360-degree security. Golembesky flipped on his night-vision equipment and began working the computer and radio, which were vital to the operation. The Predator was still downriver, "scanning the water with its thermal sight in hopes of locating the fallen." Suddenly there was a flash on the opposite bank. "A split second later, an RPG sliced the darkness with its red-orange exhaust. The rocket whooshed overhead" and hit a hill behind them. Before anyone in Golembesky's group could react, "the trees lining the river flared with muzzle flashes." He heard someone yell, "Contact! Across the river!" Enemy AK-47 PKM Soviet machine-gun reports rattled the night air.

"They were so close it sounded like I was inside a popcorn machine loaded with ball bearings. They'd caught us in a point-blank ambush from concealed positions less than a hundred meters [109 yards] away behind compound walls."

Years later, Golembesky still remembered the desperation.

We needed all guns in this fight. I dropped to a shooter's crouch and swung my M4 [assault rifle] underneath the vehicle door. The tree line sparkled with orange flares from all the muzzle flashes. I began triggering off rounds. Movement to my right caused me to pause; I took my eye out of my weapon sight long enough to see Mark and an ANA soldier run by toward the river. The Afghan carried an RPG launcher. Mark used his NVGs [night-vision goggles] to find the trees. A few steps later, both men stopped. The ANA soldier took a stance and fired. The rocket sparked and spewed flames but did not leave the launcher. In an instant, the whole front of the weapon was sheathed in flames. The ANA dropped the weapon and began to back away. Mark grabbed him and together they ran back for the Toyota pickup.

Suddenly the heavy weapons went silent because they had jammed. While Golembesky pondered the chances of having four heavy guns all jam at once, one of the guys from the other vehicle dealt with a .50 caliber machine gun up in the vehicle turret.

"Bullets pinged off the rigs as the Taliban shooters walked full-auto fire back and forth across our position, but Pat seemed unfazed. He climbed atop the massive rig, disconnected the .50 cal from the automatic turret, and swung it manually toward the enemy. He stood high above the vehicle's roof, completely exposed to the incoming fusillade. But he never flinched. He lowered the barrel level to the tree line and uncorked a long burst. The Ma Deuce Browning M2 machine gun bucked and boomed, its muzzle belching flame."

One of the other guys reappeared, "wielding an AT4 rocket launcher that Pat had tossed down to him before he got to the M2 [machine gun]. He let it fly toward the trees. The rocket exploded with such force that the ground beneath us shook. A moment later, the enemy responded with another RPG. It landed long, exploding beyond one of our vehicles."

Now, once again, the fate of his team was in Golembesky's hands, if only for the moment.

"OLDS 4-4, OLDS 4-5, troops in contact, troops in contact," he said, as calmly as possible. "On the other side of the world, the Predator crew operating out of Hancock Field in the suburbs of Syracuse, New York, heard my distress call."

"Stand by to copy grid," he added, since the crew at Hancock Field didn't know their location yet.

He checked his map and plotted their position, but that wasn't the real problem.

"Where was the enemy?" Golembesky asked himself. Looking across the river he made his best guess all too quickly. He yelled into the radio and the Predator crew sent a drone toward the battle site.

Using the "eye in the sky" from one of the aircraft above them, he spotted four guys "between the trees and a compound wall not far from the edge of the river." Two men scampered along the back side of the nearest compound. Soon, the three turned into five, but Golembesky could not tell whether they had weapons yet. If they did, they qualified for a Predator strike under the Rules of Engagement in effect that day.

Just about then one of his buddies sailed several grenades across the river but landed long, sparing the Taliban. Golembesky turned his laptop toward the American shooter so that he could see the monitor and determine where his grenades were landing. Amazingly, Golembesky could now use a viewing device on a Predator above the battlefield to walk more grenades into the Taliban position. He passed the crew at Hancock Field in Syracuse a "9-line," consisting of all the data they needed to do a precision bomb drop.

Now multitasking the best he could, Golembesky saw a Taliban "stand up and spray a long burst of full-auto fire at us with an AK. His muzzle flash illuminated the area around him, and I could see he was using a wall for cover." Golembesky had one of his buddies launch a few 40mm grenades at this target, but the Taliban managed to crawl into a culvert for cover. He coaxed Andy, the team commander, to bring in a Hellfire missile on the five Taliban across the river, but Andy hesitated, however momentarily, with good reason. Dropping ordnance was one of the surest ways to destroy a career. One wrong number in the 9-line and innocent civilians might die.

"We would be hitting Taliban near a compound, so were skirting the edges of General McChrystal's new tactical guidance. If we screwed this up, Andy or I—or both of us—could end up in a court-martial," Golembesky recalled,

After a brief hesitation, Andy green-lighted the strike. And as he did, Golembesky could "see all five, clustered together down by the tree line, most of them using that wall for cover. If we could keep them there, the one Hellfire Predator would take them all out."

The operator yelled out missile-talk to let Golembesky know that the missile was on the way. Golembesky flicked his eyes between his wristwatch and the video feed. "The seconds ticked down. The enemy stayed hunkered down. Outside, our men kept up a steady fire. Mark was beside the Afghan National Army rig, triggering off rounds from his M4 carbine, side by side with our Afghan allies."

We just might have them, Golembesky thought to himself as he barked "Twenty seconds!" to the men around him. He noticed that "one of the fighters stood up and began walking away from the group. He reached the nearest compound and ducked inside it." Never mind—they still had four Taliban in their sites.

"Suddenly, the video feed went completely white. Outside, an orange glow and sparks tore away the blackness on the far side of the river. A moment later, the shock wave rattled through us," Golembesky recalled in his memoir. "A plume of smoke rose over the trees. The lone surviving enemy fighter slipped away, wanting no part of martyrdom that night."

Golembesky was more determined than ever to settle the Lone Taliban's hash.

"As the patrol mounted up, I put the Predator on him and followed his progress as he went from compound to compound farther east of the engagement area. At each stop, he emerged with several more individuals. Keeping them around him, he herded the people to the next compound where he gathered up several more. By the fourth compound, he had surrounded himself with at least fifteen men, women, and children."

What kind of man turns kids into human shields? Golembesky thought.

CHAPTER 15

A National Treasure

BRENT TAYLOR WAS A MULTITASKER IF EVER THERE WAS ONE. THE father of seven small children, he also served as mayor of North Ogden, Utah, a town of some 17,000 souls, when he wasn't serving in the Army National Guard. That National Guard service took Taylor to Kabul, Afghanistan, on Saturday, November 3, 2018, to train Afghan security forces in special operations. No one could have known that one of the trainees would kill Taylor and severely wound the Utah National Guard adjutant general before he himself was killed. Yet this tragedy is emblematic of the risks American military men involved in special operations take every day.

Taylor told his North Ogden constituents on Facebook Live in January 2018 that he would soon be deployed to help train Afghan commando units. His explanation of personal priorities couldn't have been more straightforward: "There are three great loyalties that have guided my life and everything in it: God, family, and country. While I am far from perfect in any of these respects," Taylor continued, "I have given my life to serve all three of these loyalties whenever and however I can. And right now there is a need for my experience and skills to serve in our nation's long-lasting war in Afghanistan."

No sooner had Donald Trump become president than he endorsed and doubled down on the special operations strategy employed by his predecessor, President Barack Obama. The first special operation of the Trump presidency launched on January 29, 2017, in Yemen, only nine days after the inauguration targeted the leader of Al-Qaeda in the Arabian Peninsula. The action resulted in fourteen Al-Qaeda deaths, but also took the life of Navy SEAL William "Ryan" Owens. The target, Qasim al-Raymi, somehow survived—at least for now—but fourteen Al-Qaeda fighters were killed, along with some twenty civilians.

US Special Operations troops have been in constant battle mode since the 9/11 attacks, operating in areas of the world one might expect, as well as others, such as West Africa, which would surprise many Americans. Most special operations missions between 9/11 and the present have related to training foreign allies. An early February 2017 analysis by *Forbes* magazine revealed that during 2016, American Special Forces deployed to 138 nations. Although not officially acknowledged, available information establishes that American special operations have been conducted or led in Somalia, Syria, and Yemen. American elite troop deployments to Africa increased 1,600 percent in the ten-year period ending in 2016. These special operations missions in the aggregate traveled to 70 percent of the countries in the world.

The *New York Times* noted in late September 2017 that some experts at the time suggested that this strategy should be reconsidered. More specifically, the *Times* noted, the concern among experts is "that these elite forces—Navy SEALS, Green Berets, Rangers, and Delta Force," as well as other units, "are stretched thin, with about 8,000 of them active on any given day in more than 80 countries." The *Times* also noted that "With Americans weary of war without end since September 11, 2001, President Obama withdrew most conventional soldiers from Iraq and Afghanistan. At the same time, he turned the Joint Special Operations Command into a dray horse. Its members are just about everywhere: Afghanistan, Iraq, Yemen, Syria, Somalia, Pakistan, you name it. Their impact can be deadly, but their footprint is lighter and less costly than that of a fully decked-out Army operation."

That said, relying on special operations comes at a cost. The *Times* recognized that even though special operations personnel "make up roughly 5 percent of the total armed forces, they have accounted for at least half of the nation's combat deaths since 2015."

Time magazine reported one such tragic incident in West Africa in a November 30, 2017, report. A joint team of twelve US Special Forces and some thirty Nigerian troops were ambushed, resulting in the death of four American soldiers. *Time* noted that "Over the past 16 years, Special Operations have become the new American way of war." Once mainly used to supplement regular forces, the elite units are now the go-to option for policymakers looking to manage a complicated world. The eleven special operations soldiers killed that year by late November 2017 died in four missions. Many Americans would be surprised to learn that during the ten-year period ending in 2016, deployments to the Middle East dropped by 35 percent.

These pressures on special operators have not been without consequences. Suicides among special operations personnel tripled in 2018, while at the same time, confirmed and suspected suicides among active-duty Marine Corps and navy personnel reached a ten-year high in 2018.

Despite these pressures, special operations professionals launched a new "secret surrogate" initiative in February 2019. The *Military Times* reported in early February 2019 that "US counterterrorism missions will soon place more emphasis on a little-known Pentagon program designed to help 'surrogate forces' rather than traditional allied units that are dependent on US training, advice and assistance."

Major General James Hecker told a congressional committee on February 6, 2019, that "This evolving counterterrorism [CT] operation construct will place even greater emphasis on successful programs . . . which provide us viable surrogate forces designed to achieve US CT objectives at relatively low cost in terms of resources and especially risk to our personnel. The small-footprint approach . . . in addition to lessening the need for large-scale US troop deployments fosters an environment where local forces take ownership of the problem."

Hecker also provided some insight into future special operations priorities, relating that "The US military needs to pull troops from places where they're focused on fighting violent extremist groups and shift them to focus on great power competition in places like the South China Sea or Eastern Europe." Hecker elaborated that distribution of forces across the counterterrorism fight will be reviewed monthly "to make sure the proper amount of pressure is applied in the right places to keep US and Western interests safe."

Retired Brigadier General Russell D. Howard described the true value of American Special Operations forces, whose deployments will no doubt increase in the future, in a statement reported by the *New York Times* in February 2017. "These guys are amazing warriors," said General Howard, "but they're more than that. They are smart, flexible, adaptable and unafraid.

"These guys are a national treasure."

Bibliography

BOOKS

Benedict, Bryce. *Jayhawkers: The Civil War Brigade of James Henry Lane*. Norman: University of Oklahoma Press, 2009.

Blehm, Eric. *The Only Thing Worth Dying For: How Eleven Green Berets Fought for a New Afghanistan*. New York: HarperCollins, 2010.

Durnford-Slater, John, DSO. *Commando: Memoirs of a Fighting Commando in World War II*. London: Greenhill Books, 2002.

Finlayson, Andrew R. *Killer Kane: A Marine Long-Range Recon Team Leader in Vietnam, 1967–1968*. Jefferson, NC: McFarland & Company, 2013.

Golembesky, Michael, and John R. Bruning. *Level Zero Heroes: The Story of US Marine Operations in Bala Murghab, Afghanistan*. New York: St. Martin's Press, 2015.

Goode, Frederick C. *No Surrender in Burma: Behind Enemy Lines, Captivity and Torture*. Barnsley, South Yorkshire: Pen & Sword, Limited, 2014.

Hogan, David W., Jr. *US Army Special Operations in World War II*. Washington, DC: Center of Military History, Department of the Army, 1992.

Holober, Frank. *Raiders of the China Coast: CIA Covert Operations During the Korean War* (Special Warfare Series). Annapolis, MD: US Naval Institute Press, 2018.

Leslie, Edward E. *The Devil Knows How to Ride: The True Story of William Clarke Quantrill and His Confederate Raiders*. New York: Random House, 1996.

McCorkle, John, and O. S. Barton. *Three Years with Quantrill: A True Story* (Western Frontier Library). Norman: University of Oklahoma Press, Revised Edition (February 15, 1998).

Moore, Steven L. *Uncommon Valor: The Recon Company that Earned Five Medals of Honor and Included America's Most Decorated Green Beret*. Annapolis, MD: Naval Institute Press, September 1, 2018.

Oller, John. *The Swamp Fox: How Francis Marion Saved the American Revolution*. Boston: Da Capo Press, 2016.

Peterson, Paul R. *Quantrill at Lawrence: The Untold Story*. Gretna, LA: Pelican Publishing Company, 2011.

Plaster, John L. *SOG: The Secret Wars of America's Commandos in Vietnam*. New York: Simon & Schuster, 1997.

Speer, John. *Life of James H. Lane, the Liberator of Kansas: With Corroborative Incidents of Pioneer History*. Whitefish, MT: Kissinger Press, LLC (July 25, 2007).

PERIODICALS

Castel, Albert. "Order No. 11 and the Civil War on the Border," *Missouri Historical Review*, vol. 57 (1963).

Harris, Charles F. "Catalyst for Terror: The Collapse of the Women's Prison in Kansas City," *Missouri Historical Review* (April 1995).